LAST CALL

Last Call

Picking Up The Sword Of The Spirit

Terry Hipp

Mill City Press

Author website:
AssaultPrevention.Info
AssaultPrevention.Org

Mill City Press, Inc.
212 3rd Avenue North, Suite 290
Minneapolis, MN 55401
612.455.2294

ISBN-13: 978-1-937600-41-9
LCCN: 2011942850

Typeset by Tim Parlin

Printed in the United States of America

Table of Contents

Introduction

For almost three years I have been conducting an unscientific, informal survey. I have been asking fellow Christians two questions.

- Do you think the world perceives Christians as being strong or weak?

The answer, without exception, has always been the same — weak.

- Why does the world think Christians are weak?

This answer varies but is usually tied to the basic tenets of Christianity. Those tenets include love, forgiveness, gentleness, meekness, kindness, generosity and the like. These traits are considered lame and a sign of weakness to many secular people when it appeared to them something much stronger was called for. The second most common answer to this question is tied to the personal failure of Christians and their leaders. These answers include the sexual sin, corruption and other actions that are considered personal failures.

Christians are Weak?

The notion that Christians are weak, in spite of all the strong promises the Bible gives the believer, is deeply disturbing, and it drives me nuts. It seems to me the world should be shaking in fear when they consider the Christian for each one stands not only with God, Jesus and the Holy Spirit, but also with all the powers of heaven at their disposal.

This book is not about judging weak Christians — "for all have sinned and fall short of the glory of God." (Romans 3:23) This book is about strength. It is a call to action to a different way of thinking and viewing the world, then interacting with it.

The Final Quest, a great little book by Rick Joyner, depicts Christians in the last days trudging along, slumped over with oppression and shame from demons riding on their back for so long they act as though it is normal — seemingly oblivious to the knowledge of Ephesians 6.

> Ephesians 6:10-18 "Finally, be strong in the Lord and in his mighty power. Put on the full armor of God so that you can take your stand against the devil's schemes. For our struggle is not against flesh and blood, but against the rulers, against the authorities, against the powers of this dark world and against the spiritual forces of evil in the heavenly realms. Therefore put on the full armor of God, so that when the day of evil comes, you may be able to stand your ground, and after you have done everything, to stand. Stand firm then, with the belt of truth buckled around your waist, with the breastplate of righteousness in place, and with your feet fitted with the readiness that comes from the gospel of peace. In addition to all this, take up the shield of faith, with which you can extinguish all the flaming arrows of the evil one. Take the helmet of salvation and the sword of the Spirit, which is the word of God. And pray in the Spirit on all occasions with all kinds of prayers and requests."

These verses indicate we are in a constant struggle.

Lt. Colonel Dave Grossman, author of On Combat, writes: "If you have no capacity for violence then you are a healthy productive citizen, a sheep. If you have a capacity for violence and no empathy for your fellow citizens, then you have defined an aggressive sociopath, a wolf. But what if you have a capacity for violence, and a deep love for your fellow citizens? What do you have then? A sheepdog, a warrior, someone who is walking the hero's path. Someone who can walk into the heart of darkness, into the universal human phobia, and walk out unscathed."

The Sheepdog is the person who naturally walks towards trouble instead of running from it. The Christian Sheepdog is one who also understands that evil on this earth is usually manifested in and through people at the prompting of Satan. This person is also savvy to the fact that evil understands only one thing — an overwhelming amount of force.

There are many well-meaning evangelical leaders who preach passivity in the face of any violence, and there are many Christians who agree with this theology. I will respectfully disagree on this point. My personal opinion, which I believe is validated by Scripture, is that the intent of verses containing instructions such as "turn the other cheek" and "put your swords away" are specifically directed toward behavior we are to emulate when being persecuted in the name of Jesus. This, of course, stands in stark contrast to the divine violence Jesus used when He dealt with Satan. It also contradicts other verses in the Bible.

There are acts committed by human beings that can only be ascribed to evil. The notion of turning the other cheek while a loved one is being beaten, raped or stabbed is not what these verses refer to. The Bible is clear that Christians should come against evil wherever they find it.

In Romans 13, it is clear that God designed a system, and people within it, to be agents of wrath bringing punishment on the wrongdoer. There is no suggestion of wrongdoing being met with passivity in these verses.

> Romans 13:1-4 "Everyone must submit himself to the governing authorities, for there is no authority except that which God has established. The authorities that exist have been established by God. Consequently, he who

> rebels against the authority is rebelling against what God has instituted, and those who do so will bring judgment on themselves. For rulers hold no terror for those who do right, but for those who do wrong. Do you want to be free from fear of the one in authority? Then do what is right and he will commend you. For he is God's servant to do you good. But if you do wrong, be afraid, for he does not bear the sword for nothing. He is God's servant, an agent of wrath to bring punishment on the wrongdoer."

Ephesians 6 tells us that we are in a war. How would passivity work as an effective tactic in a war?

> Ephesians 6:12 "For our struggle is not against flesh and blood, but against the rulers, against the authorities, against the powers of this dark world and against the spiritual forces of evil in the heavenly realms."

Someone Is Trying To Kill Me?

1 Peter 5 is like a neon sign flashing in front of our faces. Satan is trying to kill us. Passivity with Satan? Let's take this one step further. Satan does not usually appear personally to do his dirty work. He uses people to do it. As an extreme example, consider Hitler. We can probably all agree Hitler's actions were prompted by Satan, who was working evil and manifesting himself through Hitler. Passivity? I don't think so.

> 1 Peter 5:8 "Be self-controlled and alert. Your enemy the devil prowls around like a roaring lion looking for someone to devour."

- Self-controlled: Control or restraint of oneself or one's actions and feelings.

- Alert: Fully aware and attentive, wide-awake, keen; swift, agile, nimble, an attitude of vigilance, readiness or caution before an expected attack.

- Enemy: A person who feels hatred toward, fosters harmful designs against, or engages in antagonistic activities against another, an adversary or opponent. An armed foe.

- Evil: The supreme spirit of evil, a subordinate evil spirit at enmity with God, and having the power to afflict human beings with both bodily disease and spiritual corruption.

- Prowls: To rove or go about stealthily, as in search of prey, something to steal, etc.

- Roaring Lion: Characterized by noisy, disorderly behavior, boisterous and riotous. Lions are powerful animals that usually hunt in coordinated groups and stalk their chosen prey. They sneak up to the victim until they reach a distance of approximately 30 meters (98 ft) or less. The attack is short and powerful; they attempt to catch the victim with a fast rush and final leap.

- Devour: To swallow or eat up hungrily, voraciously or ravenously, to consume destructively.

John 10 is talking about Satan and referring to him as a thief, then goes on to describe his mission — to kill and destroy. Do you think when John wrote this he was just being dramatic to make a point? No. He was describing what Satan does.

John 10:10 "(Jesus said) The thief comes only to steal

> and kill and destroy; I have come that they may have life, and have it to the full."

- Thief: A person who steals something from another.
- Only: Exclusively, solely, without anything further.
- Kill: To put to death, to deprive of life, to put an end to, to extinguish, to destroy a vitally essential quality, to cause to cease operating, to turn off, to tire out completely, to exhaust.
- Destroy: To ruin completely; spoil, to tear down or break up, to demolish, to do away with, to put an end to. To kill, to subdue or defeat completely, to crush, to render useless or ineffective.

In Matthew 10, Jesus is giving the disciples their marching orders. He describes the believer as sheep in the midst of wolves. Should sheep be passive around the wolf?

> Matthew 10:16 "Behold, I send you out as sheep in the midst of wolves. Therefore be wise as serpents and harmless as doves."

Onward Christian Soldier

Most of the Christians I know believe we are living in the End Times. This is also reflected by current writing, commentary and talk coming out of the mainstream evangelical community at large.

If we review what the Bible indicates through prophecy, and specifically what Jesus said about the End Times, we would have to come to the conclusion that things will become worse, not better, as we approach the Tribulation and the end of this Age.

XIV

Many people take comfort in the belief that God will rapture Christians out of here when it gets rough. However, even respected experts from many denominations who have spent their lives studying these matters cannot agree on the timing of the rapture. And God is not telling us.

Others believe God will supernaturally protect them like He did the Israelites when God brought the plagues upon Pharaoh. This thinking is faulty to a great degree. Was David spared of Saul? Was Moses spared of griping people and trying to manage survival in a desert? Was Joseph spared prison? Were the disciples spared prison and persecution? Look at your own life as a Christian. Have you been spared every problem, heartache and challenge just because you are a Christian? God gives people strength and supernatural provision to get through things, and He does spare life. I know this. I should be dead. But He does not remove all the difficulties.

This leads me back to what Jesus said about the End Times. One of the things that need to happen is for government to practice ungodly control and direction. Some would make a strong case that there has been a slow, steady decline in government character and integrity for years. This is pre-empted by ungodly principles being played out in all types of relationships. This is happening now. Yet, most Christians sit on the sidelines and do nothing about it. If you do not have the courage, desire, passion or obedience to confront the ungodly relations around you, how do you expect to feed yourself or your family if you do not take the mark of the beast? What will you do if you find yourself in a war-zone? This may be hard to believe if you live in America. But the reality brought to us by the financial crises should have taught us things can change overnight. Have you thought about how you will handle the betrayal you might experience at the hands of friends and family? How about your own children rebelling against you and having you put to death?

Most Christians have not given this any thought. Therein lays the problem, and the motivation to write this book. Most Christians agree we are in the End Times and logically agree things will get progressively worse, yet have given no thought as to how they will deal with them. In fact, when I look at the petty, backbiting differences between Christians and I compare that pettiness to how the Body of Christ is supposed to function, I can make a strong case for the Church living through some tough stuff.

Why? Because you and I may disagree, even argue, about theological differences that might mean a lot to us but little to God. However, if you and I are stuck on an elevator or trapped in a burning building, I doubt we will be arguing theology. We will quickly agree to pray together and work together to get out. This type of pressure for survival is a great equalizer. I see no reason God would not use it to unite the Body. The alternative is that the Holy Spirit moves so powerfully that we all just wake up one day and get along. It's possible but unlikely.

"But wait!" you say. "Why can't I just die if things get ugly and go to heaven?" After all, the Bible also says we are supposed to fear nothing and have no anxiety about anything, and assures us that nothing can separate us from the love of God. All these things are true. You can do nothing, suffer and die, and reap rewards in heaven based on your relationship with Jesus. But if God created and wired you to be a Christian Sheepdog, this will never happen. You will fight for the privilege to stay alive in an effort to bring others to the kingdom of God through your influence, prayers and actions.

Jude is a Call to Action

I do not think it was an accident that the book of Jude comes right before the book of Revelation in the Bible. Jude is a call to action, and as you may notice, it comes right before a graphic description of the end of this Age and the triumphant return of Jesus.

XVI

Jude was the brother of Jesus. In his opening greeting, he acknowledges that he was eager to write about salvation but felt compelled to write and urge us to contend for the faith. What does this mean? Jude was driven to encourage all believers to forcefully struggle and fight for the faith — that being the truth of the Bible and salvation.

> Jude 1:22-23 "Be merciful to those who doubt; snatch others from the fire and save them; to others show mercy, mixed with fear – hating even the clothing stained by corrupted flesh."

When we investigate the original Greek definitions of these words, this verse could be paraphrased as follows.

> ***Reach out and act immediately with deep-seated emotion to those who doubt; quickly yank and seize others from dangerous situations and do so immediately, continuously and in an unending fashion. Show compassion, kindness, forgiveness and clemency to those who are in distress and offenders who are within your power, mixed with a strong dose of knowing you are dealing with something that is life threatening – having a radical, violent aversion to sinful attitudes and behavior that have the potential to permeate and penetrate people's lives.***

Within most of us there is a hard-wired instinct to fight for our own survival and for those we love. Throughout history rugged defenders have gone to war, built walls, battled hand-to-hand and endured incredible circumstances to protect nations from harm. Likewise, individuals have fought for their families and loved ones with total abandonment, amazing courage and incredible commitment. Our survival instinct is strong. We defend things that are most precious to us. It is how God created us.

XVII

The Essence of Evil

Biblical prophecy is coming to pass before our eyes. Although it may not be the primary threat to the American Church, radical Islamic Jihad is dead set against Israel, the Jewish people, Christians and Democracy. There are too many corrupt, inept or ineffective politicians who are serving their own self-interests instead of truly serving those who elected them. Criminals show little remorse for the victims they prey upon. The common man or woman will lie to their friends, cheat on their taxes, steal from their employers, beat their significant others, neglect their children, or commit adultery all while rationalizing their behavior. And most Christians just lean against the wall, watching it all unfold.

These desires are evil in nature. Evil is promoted by Satan. Evil does not respond to the basic tenants of Christianity: love, forgiveness, mercy, grace, generosity and kindness. Rather, evil takes advantage of these things. Evil will manipulate these things for its own self-serving purposes. Evil understands only one thing — an overwhelming amount of power. This is a spiritual and physical principle. Those of you who have ever tried to give direction or negotiate with a person influenced by evil should understand this clearly.

Jesus dealt with evil spirits by divine violence. He never negotiated or offered mercy. Nor did He have lengthy discussions with them. He commanded them. There is evil violence in this world which is manifested through people. There is divine violence available to the Christian to deal with it. Do you know the difference? This book is dedicated to those who do and hopefully serves as an education for those who do not.

The Book of Jude

Jude, a servant of Jesus Christ and a brother of James, To those who have been called, who are loved in God the Father and kept

XVIII

for Jesus Christ: Mercy, peace and love be yours in abundance. Dear friends, although I was very eager to write to you about the salvation we share, I felt compelled to write and urge you to contend for the faith that was once for all entrusted to God's holy people. For certain individuals whose condemnation was written about long ago have secretly slipped in among you. They are ungodly people, who pervert the grace of our God into a license for immorality and deny Jesus Christ our only Sovereign and Lord. Though you already know all this, I want to remind you that the Lord at one time delivered his people out of Egypt, but later destroyed those who did not believe. And the angels who did not keep their positions of authority but abandoned their proper dwelling—these he has kept in darkness, bound with everlasting chains for judgment on the great Day. In a similar way, Sodom and Gomorrah and the surrounding towns gave themselves up to sexual immorality and perversion. They serve as an example of those who suffer the punishment of eternal fire. In the very same way, on the strength of their dreams these ungodly people pollute their own bodies, reject authority and heap abuse on celestial beings. But even the archangel Michael, when he was disputing with the devil about the body of Moses, did not himself dare to condemn him for slander but said, "The Lord rebuke you!" Yet these people slander whatever they do not understand, and the very things they do understand by instinct—as irrational animals do—will destroy them. Woe to them! They have taken the way of Cain; they have rushed for profit into Balaam's error; they have been destroyed in Korah's rebellion. These people are blemishes at your love feasts, eating with you without the slightest qualm—shepherds who feed only themselves. They are clouds without rain, blown along by the wind; autumn trees, without fruit and uprooted—twice dead. They are wild waves of the sea, foaming up their shame; wandering stars, for whom blackest darkness has been reserved forever. Enoch, the seventh from Adam, prophesied about them: "See, the Lord is coming with thousands upon thousands of his holy ones to judge everyone, and to convict all of them of all the ungodly acts they have committed in their ungodliness, and of all the defiant words ungodly sinners have spoken against him." These people are grumblers and faultfinders; they follow their own evil desires; they boast about themselves and flatter others for their own advantage. But, dear friends, remember what the apostles of our Lord Jesus Christ foretold. They said to you, "In the last times there will be scoffers who will follow their own ungodly desires." These are the people who divide you, who follow mere natural instincts and do not have the Spirit. But you, dear friends, by building yourselves up in your most holy faith and praying in the Holy Spirit, keep yourselves in God's love as you wait for the mercy of our Lord Jesus Christ to bring you to eternal life. Be merciful to those who doubt; save others by snatching them from the fire; to others show mercy, mixed with fear—hating even the clothing stained by corrupted flesh. To him who is able to keep you from stumbling and to present you before his glorious presence without fault and with great joy— to the only God our Savior be glory, majesty, power and authority, through Jesus Christ our Lord, before all ages, now and forevermore! Amen.

Author Note

There are details about the End Times that are mentioned but have not been elaborated upon in this book such as the one world order, the mark of the beast or projections regarding the economy. I have excluded lengthy explanations, personal revelations regarding scripture or great justification for my opinions. I think the Bible is able to speak for itself and does so quite plainly. I am compelled to reach out to brothers and sisters in the Lord and ask them to wake up and unite. I pray that secular people read this book, and it causes them to wonder — to wonder enough to drive them to God with questions and to Jesus for the ultimate, eternal resolution of their souls.

Acknowledgments

> 1 Corinthians 12:12 "The body is a unit, though it is made up of many parts; and though all its parts are many, they form one body. So it is with Christ."

I believe this verse. In the same respect, I believe God used many influences to shape and mold me bringing me constantly closer to that which he intended when He breathed me into creation.

I could write a book that does nothing but acknowledge the people, circumstances, events, verses, revelation, prayers and churches that God has used to shape me. If I do try to mention everyone who has had a significant impact on my life, I know I will miss someone. Some of you may know who you are but many do not. To all of you, I am deeply grateful.

I have been blessed with a family that, although as dysfunctional as any good American Christian family, has always been supportive.

I would like to:

Thank God for His enduring love, grace and mercy.

Thank Jesus for his selfless example of living, the promise of His life and the power of His blood.

Thank the Holy Spirit for bringing to the forefront of my mind, soul and spirit that which I should be thinking about and doing next.

Thank my parents, Grant & Helen, for the foundation they laid within me. Through them I learned perseverance, strength and the love of God.

Thank my siblings, Jim, Gary & Cyndi, for the love, counsel

and refuge they have provided.

Thank my children, Jenessa & Zechariah, for giving me the incredible experience of parenting, enriching my life and gracefully challenging me in ways they could never imagine.

Thank my wife, Dayna, for her uncompromising support and love. There are no adequate words to describe her. She is simply amazing. This book would not have been written without her, nor would Assault Prevention be in existence. For many years she has been the financial backbone that kept us going. There are few mates I know, if any, that would willingly support this type of grand experiment with God which was to simply get on my knees and ask Him to lead me wherever He wanted to serve His kingdom the best I could with whatever time He had left for me on earth. This meant I had to be willing to sacrifice anything and everything professionally and personally, and simply walk through doors He opened. It also meant Dayna sacrificed many of her own desires. On several occasions when I was ready to walk away from all of this, she reminded me of my commitment and encouraged me to move forward.

I never looked for a job. I simply walked through doors God opened. This has been one incredible journey. I would like to share some of it with you and what God has impressed upon me through it.

Author Notes

- Thanks to Char Torkelson for making editorial suggestions to the manuscript, and for her passion in teaching others about writing.

- Thanks to Susan Lund for being a vessel God used many years ago to artistically express the vision of a spiritual warrior; which became the cover art for this book.

- Thanks to Brenda Elliott for designing the front and back cover of the book.

- All scripture references are New International Version unless otherwise noted.

- The vast majority of quotes were taken from Thinkexist.com and cross-referenced unless otherwise noted.

- There are no footnotes or endnotes. There is no bibliography. If you are reading the eBook version there are hyperlinks to sources that are cited. If you are reading a print copy of this book there is ample information within the material cited to discoverable sources.

- I have cited a number of statistics in this book. Statistics change frequently and I am sure that some of the statistics will have changed between the time this book was written and the time it gets into the readers hands. I encourage the reader to "look through" the statistics to the underlying points or principles that those statistics are representing.

SECTION ONE:
AUTHORITY

CHAPTER 1
RELATIONAL AUTHORITY

"Government is instituted for the common good; for the protection, safety, prosperity, and happiness of the people; and not for profit, honor, or private interest of any one man, family, or class of men; therefore, the people alone have an incontestable, unalienable, and indefensible right to institute government; and to reform, alter, or totally change the same, when their protection, safety, prosperity, and happiness require it."

John Adams

"The Lord is my light and my salvation; whom shall I fear? The Lord is the strength of my life; of whom shall I be afraid? When the wicked came against me to eat up my flesh, my enemies and foes, they stumbled and fell. Though an army should encamp against me, my heart shall not fear; though war should rise against me, in this I will be confident." Psalm 27:1

Lessons Learned

"You have made your bed, Mr. Hipp, and now you will have to sleep in it." I am sitting across the desk from my program director. I do not know how to interpret this comment except as a threat of some type.

I am working at a juvenile correctional facility in 1977. It is considered a secure facility in the sense that the juveniles who are sentenced to programs here are held accountable for their behavior and tightly supervised, although plenty of them seem to escape into the surrounding woods, much to the chagrin of the middle-upper class neighborhoods that are just beyond those woods. There are multiple programs here. There are programs for felony-level offenders in which residents who are adjudicated as juvenile delinquents might be residing for more than a year. There is a sex-offender program for males. There is a female offender program.

This place was a sit-com waiting for a producer to discover it. Although the majority of the work, programming, rehabilitation and activities were professional and effective, there were some strange things going on as well. Like the program that went camping for a weekend. The staff decided to leave all the youth alone at the campsite while they went into town to drink. Or the staff member who decided to come out of the closet in what would have been considered a group therapy session for the youth – not for him. Or the staff member who thought it might be therapeutic to have all the kids in his program run naked across the institution grounds.

There was also the tragic. A guy I worked with eventually ended up working in the female offender program, where it was alleged he was recruiting these girls for prostitution upon their release. Eventually, there was an investigation and this man shot himself in the head. It was all kept very quiet.

Working in a correctional facility will change you. The crimes some of these kids commit are almost unbelievable in the depth of their viciousness. And often, the prior victimization of these same kids was just as gruesome. What I might consider normal, these kids seemingly had no ability to wrap their heads around. With these kids, there was always an edgy aura of potential violence breaking out, and it did with some frequency.

There was a short-term, boot-camp style program for "first-time" offenders. This program was a 3-6 week intensive work program. Residents addressed staff as "Mr." or "Ms." or "Sir". Essentially, the residents were assigned useful physical labor all day, such as dismantling condemned property or cutting up diseased trees for firewood. In the evenings, they had one hour of free-time and about 90 minutes of tutoring so they could either keep up or catch-up with their schooling. They cleaned their rooms and cleaned assigned areas in their cottage. The staff inspected these areas with the "white-glove" treatment. These kids were graded several times a day on a score sheet. Categories ranged from "room cleaning" to "attitude" to "work habits". By receiving good scores, the youth could earn "good time", thereby reducing their sentence by up to a week or two. There was very high accountability.

This program, which I was assigned to, was designed to be a deterrent to young men entering the criminal justice system. Typically, kids sentenced to this program were guilty of property crimes and minor personal offenses, although as time went on, the program received a lot of youth that were committing violent crimes and considered "inappropriate commitments" to those of us who worked there. The program's original design perfectly accomplished its mission to discourage early entry delinquents from delving deeper into the criminal justice system. The program worked so well that the Juvenile Court figured it would work for more dangerous offenders if it worked for less sophisticated offenders. This would have been fine except for the fact that we were putting hammers, saws, axes, picks and other weapons in these offenders' hands for 8-10 hours a day and trotting off to remote worksites with a ratio of 1 staff to 12 offenders. More about that later.

The director of this program appeared to be biased in his view of minorities. There is no way to gently spin his racial views, despite the fact that this man claimed to be a Christian and had discussions with me regarding his faith and relationship with the Lord. He shared his views with me regarding his perception of the offenders coming through this program, and a theme quickly developed. Native-American youth were lazy, and African-American kids showed little respect. The Hispanics worked hard but were not very bright. I knew this guy was way over the top when he explained to me one day in his office that the African-American "plan" was to populate the US through procreation to the point that they were the majority.

I was 21 years old, attending college, newly married, and working part-time at this correctional facility. I was told I was the youngest staff person they had ever hired. I was closer in age to these offenders than I was to most of the other staff, since offenders ages ranged from 13-18. My program director was handpicked to run this program. No great surprise as he was a straightforward, no-nonsense, ex-Green Beret. He was given authority to personally select his staff. Lucky me.

Staff members were encouraged to review the court file of each youth committed to the program and to leave our personal views via notes regarding each youth as they worked their way through the program. Presumably, these were to be used for a summary report regarding the youth's participation and success in the program. This report was submitted to the court and became part of the juvenile's court record. All the staff in my program had access to the final court report for review. I began to notice another disturbing pattern. It seemed that a great percentage of the minority youth who entered this program ended up exiting the program with a negative report.

I spoke to some of my colleagues about this along with a few staff members I had gotten to know from other programs. None of them were surprised by my observations. My own colleagues agreed. None of them had any useful advice, and it was clear to me they were either intimidated personally by the program director or were more concerned about their own job security. They were fearful, which in turn pushed their own self interests above character and integrity — the same virtues that the criminal justice system was supposed to uphold. I knew about this stuff. I was a criminal justice major.

Had I been more mature in my understanding of the politics of the criminal justice system, or my developing spirituality, I might have sat down with this program director and had a discussion with him about my observations. What did I know? I wasn't even out of college. Instead, I wrote my concerns down and submitted them to the Director of Community Corrections — the person charged with overseeing all the correctional facilities, correctional programs and probation/parole in this large metropolitan county.

I was not completely naïve. I knew there would be consequences. The experience of working in this facility was an eye-opening education and a wake-up call. It is where I watched good and evil go head-to-head in battle from a lot of different directions.

"You have made your bed, Mr. Hipp, and now you will have to sleep in it." Obviously, someone has spoken to him about my letter to the Director. I felt like throwing up. I also felt like going over the top of his desk and tossing him up against the wall. I looked back at him and our eyes locked. "Yes, I have, and yes, I will." I got up and walked out of his office, knowing I was screwed.

It turned out to be a bluff. Nothing changed except that we were not having private, friendly conversations in his office anymore, and I was being congratulated by those staff who knew what I had done. Life went on.

Lesson learned: Sometimes the bully just needs to be stood up to, confronted and challenged. Most of their strength lies in the perception others have of their power, and often that perception of power is just a facade. Stand up to the bully. Just like I had done before growing up.

Fast forward. Soon thereafter, I accepted a job offer in law enforcement. My concerns were investigated, and the program director was transferred out of this facility to another program where his responsibilities were such that his racial views had little, if any, influence.

Years later this man tried to block my re-appointment to the same correctional facility after I left law enforcement and returned to corrections. He was not successful. An advocate emerged. It was someone who was equal in power and supervisory status to my former boss. This advocate re-appointed me to a position at the same correctional facility while my former program director was on vacation. The unexpected advocate told me he respected my confrontation of the bully years before, and that my actions eventually led to a systematic change in the way these court reports were written, reviewed and submitted to the Court.

In fact, another staff member who overheard a conversation between my advocate and former boss upon his return from vacation, reported the conversation went something like this:

> Former Boss: So, what is the status on the hiring process?
> Advocate: I reinstated Hipp.
> Former Boss: You did what?!!!

Lesson learned: People don't like the truth when it reflects poorly on them. They do not like to be held accountable. They often lash out when confronted with their own weaknesses, ungodly attitudes or sin. Doing the right thing often carries a price. When you confront evil, you will get burned, threatened or even seriously hurt sometimes. God, however, will prevail. He often uses other people to do it.

Irony: The program director was the enemy. He claimed to be a Christian. My upbringing and understanding of the Bible taught me all people are equal in the eyes of God, and we are to love our neighbors as ourselves — one of the greatest commandments. His racial views were not consistent with any part of Christianity. Conversely, the advocate was a guy whose faith I knew nothing about. He just liked me and respected me.

I learned to carry another lesson the rest of my life, which was consistent with my upbringing and scripture. Don't judge the person – judge the behavior. Hate the sin – love the sinner.

Reward & Punishment

God's laws are eternal. He created not only spiritual law but the natural ones as well. What happens if you put your hand into a fire? You burn your hand. This is a natural law. So too there are spiritual laws in which actions lead to outcomes. Natural laws may pass away. Spiritual laws and principles are eternal. Amongst the spiritual laws is the principle of gifts and rewards coming from God and punishment as well.

> 2 John 1:8 "Watch out that you do not lose what we have worked for, but that you may be rewarded fully."
>
> Proverbs 11:31 "If the righteous receive their due on earth, how much more the ungodly and the sinner!"
>
> James 1:16-17 "Don't be deceived, my dear brothers and sisters. Every good and perfect gift is from above, coming down from the Father of the heavenly lights, who does not change like shifting shadows."
>
> Ephesians 5:3-8 "But among you there must not be even a hint of sexual immorality, or of any kind of impurity, or of greed, because these are improper for God's holy people. Nor should there be obscenity, foolish talk or coarse joking, which are out of place, but rather thanksgiving. For

> this you can be sure: No immoral, impure or greedy person – such a man is an idolater – has any inheritance in the kingdom of Christ and of God. Let no one deceive you with empty words, for because of such things God's wrath comes on those who are disobedient. Therefore do not be partners with them. For you were once darkness, but now you are light in the Lord. Live as children of light."

There are different degrees of reward, some of which are based on showing honor to others. There is much justification in the Bible regarding honor being related to reward.

Honor

> Mark 6:2-6 "When the Sabbath came, he began to teach in the synagogue, and many who heard him were amazed. "Where did this man get these things?" they asked. "What's this wisdom that has been given him? What are these remarkable miracles he is performing? Isn't this the carpenter? Isn't this Mary's son and the brother of James, Joseph, Judas and Simon? Aren't his sisters here with us?" And they took offense at him. Jesus said to them, "Only in their own towns, among their relatives and in their own homes are prophets without honor." He could not do any miracles there, except lay his hands on a few sick people and heal them. He was amazed at their lack of faith."

Jesus' own hometown people could not believe Him. They did not honor Him, and they lacked faith. They took offense at Him. The result was little healing in his hometown. There is a direct correlation between the flow of spiritual power and honor, faith — even offense.

> Isaiah 29:13 "The Lord says: 'These people come near

to me with their mouth and honor me with their lips, but their hearts are far from me. Their worship of me is based on merely human rules they have been taught.'"

1 Samuel 2:30 "Therefore the LORD, the God of Israel, declares: 'I promised that the members of your family would minister before me forever.' But now the LORD declares: 'Far be it from me! Those who honor me I will honor, but those who despise me will be disdained.'"

Matthew 10:40-42 "Anyone who welcomes you welcomes me, and anyone who welcomes me welcomes the one who sent me. Whoever welcomes someone known to be a prophet will receive a prophet's reward, and whoever welcomes someone known to be righteous will receive a righteous person's reward. And if anyone gives even a cup of cold water to one of these little ones who is known to be my disciple, truly I tell you, that person will certainly be rewarded."

Honor is defined as "high regard or respect". There are behaviors that are generally associated with showing high regard and respect to someone in a position in which honor would be due. It should be clear there is a direct relationship between honor and reward.

Who do we need to honor?

Authority

Romans 13:1-2 "Let everyone be subject to the governing authorities, for there is no authority except that which God has established. The authorities that exist have been established by God. Consequently, whoever rebels against the authority is rebelling against what

God has instituted, and those who do so will bring judgment on themselves."

Romans 13:6-7 "This is also why you pay taxes, for the authorities are God's servants, who give their full time to governing. Give to everyone what you owe: If you owe taxes, pay taxes; if revenue, then revenue; if respect, then respect; if honor, then honor."

There are divisions of authority.

I Timothy 6:1-2 "All who are under the yoke of slavery should consider their masters worthy of full respect, so that God's name and our teaching may not be slandered. Those who have believing masters are not to show less respect for them because they are brothers. Instead, they are to serve them even better, because those who benefit from their service are believers, and dear to them. These are the things you are to teach and urge on."

Ephesians 6:1-3 "Children, obey your parents in the Lord, for this is right. 'Honor your mother and father' - which is the first commandment with a promise – 'that it may go well with you and that you may enjoy long life on the earth.'"

Ephesians 6:5-8 "Slaves, obey your earthly masters with respect and fear, and with sincerity of the heart, just as you would obey Christ. Obey them not only to win their favor when their eye is on you, but like slaves of Christ, doing the will of the God from your heart. Serve wholeheartedly, as if you were serving the Lord, not men, because you know that the Lord will reward

> everyone for whatever good he does, whether he is slave or free."

Note: the Greek word for "slave" is "doulos". It has a fairly nasty definition. A slave's sole purpose was to fulfill the wishes of their owner. A servant had no destiny of their own. The slave is engulfed in the will of the owner.

Segue: What is the deal with slavery, and why didn't the early church condemn it?

> Philemon "Paul, a prisoner of Christ Jesus, and Timothy our brother, To Philemon our dear friend and fellow worker, to Apphia our sister, to Archippus our fellow soldier and to the church that meets in your home: Grace to you and peace from God our Father and the Lord Jesus Christ. I always thank my God as I remember you in my prayers, because I hear about your faith in the Lord Jesus and your love for all the saints. I pray that you may be active in sharing your faith, so that you will have a full understanding of every good thing we have in Christ. Your love has given me great joy and encouragement, because you, brother, have refreshed the hearts of the saints. Therefore, although in Christ I could be bold and order you to do what you ought to do, yet I appeal to you on the basis of love. I then, as Paul—an old man and now also a prisoner of Christ Jesus— I appeal to you for my son Onesimus, who became my son while I was in chains. Formerly he was useless to you, but now he has become useful both to you and to me. I am sending him—who is my very heart—back to you. I would have liked to keep him with me so that he could take your place in helping me while I am in chains for the gospel. But I did not want to do anything without your consent, so that any favor you do will be

> spontaneous and not forced. Perhaps the reason he was separated from you for a little while was that you might have him back for good— no longer as a slave, but better than a slave, as a dear brother. He is very dear to me but even dearer to you, both as a man and as a brother in the Lord. So if you consider me a partner, welcome him as you would welcome me. If he has done you any wrong or owes you anything, charge it to me. I, Paul, am writing this with my own hand. I will pay it back—not to mention that you owe me your very self. I do wish, brother, that I may have some benefit from you in the Lord; refresh my heart in Christ. Confident of your obedience, I write to you, knowing that you will do even more than I ask. And one thing more: Prepare a guest room for me, because I hope to be restored to you in answer to your prayers. Epaphras, my fellow prisoner in Christ Jesus, sends you greetings. And so do Mark, Aristarchus, Demas and Luke, my fellow workers. The grace of the Lord Jesus Christ be with your spirit."

We take this field trip into the issue of slavery for those that may be reading this and cannot fathom the thought of a loving God condoning slavery. Please remember that God did not institute slavery; man did through his free will. God clearly recognizes what man has instituted as evidenced by some of the verses presented above, and provides instruction through the author as to what the relationship between slave and master should be.

Although the traditional notion of slaves is a thing of the past in many countries, it is present all over the world in the form of sex slaves, forced labor, arranged marriages and people as inherited property. There are plenty of people who view their relationship to their employer, bank or credit card company as a form of slavery.

We do not find direct condemnation of slavery in the Bible.

Slavery in biblical times was more a reflection of social status than racial status, and racial slavery is clearly condemned in the Bible. There is plenty of instruction as to how it should be dealt with. Paul is writing his friend and brother in the Lord, Philemon, probably from prison. Philemon owned a slave, Onesimus, who had stolen from Philemon and run away to Rome. There, he becomes a believer through Paul's influence. It is clear that Onesimus and Paul have developed a tight relationship as Paul affectionately refers to Onesimus as "my son" and describes him as being "very dear to me".

Paul makes a plea to Philemon that puts the relationship in Christ above theft, slavery and ownership. Roman law and Mosaic Law gave Philemon the right to punish Onesimus. Paul encourages Philemon to rise above it.

Can you imagine what the world might look like if employers and financial institutions followed these instructions? With Christ-like values at the center of personal and business relationships there would be no slavery.

Eventually, every "master" will be held accountable to God for their actions.

More Authority

> 1 Peter 2:13-23 "Submit yourselves for the Lord's sake to every authority instituted among men: whether to the king, as the supreme authority, or to governors, who are sent by him to punish those who do wrong and to commend those who do right. For it is God's will that by doing good you should silence the ignorant talk of foolish men. Live as free men, but do not use your freedom as a cover-up for evil; live as servants of God. Show proper respect to everyone: Love the brotherhood of believers, fear God, honor the king. Slaves, submit yourselves to

> your masters with all respect, not only to those who are good and considerate, but also to those who are harsh. For it is commendable if a man bears up under the pain of unjust suffering because he is conscious of God. But how is it to your credit if you receive a beating for doing wrong and endure it? But if you suffer for doing good and you endure it, this is commendable before God. To this you were called, because Christ suffered for you, leaving you an example, that you should follow in his steps. 'He committed no sin, and no deceit was found in his mouth.' When they hurled their insults at him, he did not retaliate; when he suffered, he made no threats. Instead, he entrusted himself to him who judges justly."

Peter was directing believers to submit to civil authorities in the days of Nero, who was a cruel ruler. Peter was not telling people to compromise their principles in Christ, as evidenced by Peter telling the high priest in front of the Sanhedrin, "We must obey God rather than men!"

> Ephesians 5:22-27 "Wives, submit to your husbands as to the Lord. For the husband is the head of the wife as Christ is the head of the church, his body, of which he is the Savior. Now as the church submits to Christ, so also wives should submit to their husbands in everything. Husbands, love your wives, just as Christ loved the church and gave himself up for her to make her holy, cleansing her by the washing with water through the word, and to present her to himself as a radiant church, without stain or blemish, but holy and blameless."

Christ died for the church. Husband, what lengths of sacrifice will you go to for your wife? Additionally, we live in a time in which the idea of a wife submitting to her husband is for many, a repulsive, oppressive and old-fashioned idea. This is not rocket science. Someone has to be the ultimate decision-maker in any relationship. If the husband is sacrificing as Christ did for the church in his relationship with his wife, he has respectfully solicited input from her and considers it valuable in regards to her view on any matter. I once heard a speaker describe the core emotional needs of a marriage like this: Women desire sincere interest and attention. Men need a cheerleader.

The Creation of Judges

In Exodus, a system of judges (authority) was created and inspired by God through Jethro, which would settle disputes.

> Exodus 18:13-26 "The next day Moses took his seat to serve as judge for the people, and they stood around him from morning till evening. When his father-in-law saw all that Moses was doing for the people, he said, 'What is this you are doing for the people? Why do you alone sit as judge, while all these people stand around you from morning till evening?' Moses answered him, 'Because the people come to me to seek God's will. Whenever they have a dispute, it is brought to me, and I decide between the parties and inform them of God's decrees and laws.' Moses' father-in-law replied, "What you are doing is not good. You and these people who come to you will only wear yourselves out. The work is too heavy for you; you cannot handle it alone. Listen now to me and I will give you some advice, and may God be with you. You must be the people's representative before God and bring their disputes to him. Teach them the decrees and laws, and show them the way to live and the duties they are to perform. But select capable men from all the people—men who fear God,

> trustworthy men who hate dishonest gain—and appoint them as officials over thousands, hundreds, fifties and tens. Have them serve as judges for the people at all times, but have them bring every difficult case to you; the simple cases they can decide themselves. That will make your load lighter, because they will share it with you. If you do this and God so commands, you will be able to stand the strain, and all these people will go home satisfied." Moses listened to his father-in-law and did everything he said. He chose capable men from all Israel and made them leaders of the people, officials over thousands, hundreds, fifties and tens. They served as judges for the people at all times. The difficult cases they brought to Moses, but the simple ones they decided themselves."

The Word of God makes clear it is He who created governments, authority, and division of authorities. We need to respect that which God has created.

Individual Reflection or Group Discussion

1. What authority are you directly under at work?

2. What authority are you directly under at home?

3. What authority are you directly under at church, (if you attend one)?

4. Are there other organizations or relationships in which you are under authority?

5. Are you in authoritative relationships over others?

Chapter 2
Respecting the Office

"The most fatal blow to progress is slavery of the intellect. The most sacred right of humanity is the right to think, and next to the right to think is the right to express that without fear."

Helen H. Gardner

"Now I urge you, brethren, note those who cause divisions and offenses, contrary to the doctrine which you have learned, and avoid them. For those who are such do not serve our Lord Jesus Christ, but their own belly, and by smooth words and flattering speech deceive the hearts of the simple." Romans 16:17

Lessons Learned

I have worked with a number of churches over the last decade, primarily in a consulting and teaching role with regard to church security, safety and executive protection. In this capacity I have developed wonderful relationships with brothers and sisters in the Lord, and have seen the great work of God being carried out. Like anything else in life, churches are not perfect. Some people refer to churches as hospitals for the spiritually sick.

In my role as a consultant I require "inside" information to be effective. As such, I have personal knowledge of situations in which a Christian supervisor is providing direction or displaying behavior that contradicts scripture, is damaging to the people involved, or borders on spiritual abuse.

In one church there were several people affected by the sinful behavior of a ministry supervisor who was also a department administrator. Several of the people affected had already spoken to this offender about the behavior. The supervisor seemed to acknowledge their concerns but continued the behavior. The behavior was a form of idolatry, as defined by an individual who gives their complete devotion to something other than God. This supervisor was obsessed with a worldly fringe subject that had little to do with the ministries he supervised, and the obsession with it had grown to the point where he had little credibility which had reduced his effectiveness as a leader.

A number of the affected people had (privately) expressed their concerns to a pastor of this church who supervised the offender over the course of a number of years. However, nothing about this man's behavior seemed to change. The people affected attempted to arrange for a group meeting with this same pastor. The pastor refused to meet with them as a group. Instead, he met with them individually with the offender sitting in the room. The pastor told several of these people that they might consider leaving that particular ministry. The pastor made it clear that the chain of authority and "respecting the office" must be adhered to. Several others who met with the pastor reported fascination with the pastor's support for the supervisor whose offending behavior was clearly unscriptural. Collectively, they felt the whole matter had been "brushed under the carpet". All who met with this pastor were given a CD from him. I was given a copy. The main message of the CD was that the "sheep" are not to create division amongst the body of Christ.

This was remarkable. Rather than tackling the tough stuff of leadership, which would have been to determine the facts and deal with the sinful behavior along with the effects it was having on the ministry, this pastor chose to suggest to some they leave the ministry and chastise the concerned parties through a CD that focused on unity in the body. It seemed to be a clever way of restraining and containing those who were questioning this supervisor's leadership abilities. This was manipulative at a minimum.

Lesson Learned: Churches are not perfect. The people who work in churches are not perfect and do not necessarily reach for excellence nor do they always handle circumstances appropriately by following scriptural directives. Of course, nothing is perfect but we should strive for progress which was absent here.

Who is in the Office?

Many Christian leaders use the verses presented in the previous chapter to encourage and instruct believers to "respect the office". When applied properly, "respecting the office" is a vital part of God's game plan for orderly living. It is Good Orderly Direction.

Although the verses presented are very clear in their intent, they can also be used within the Body of Christ in an abusive manner. If you have worked or walked for any length of time amongst the Body of Christ, you are well aware of individuals who twist, pervert or take out of context the Word of God with the purpose of manipulation, preservation of power or rationalizing their own ignorance and behavior. Whatever the root, it is not of Christ. Usually this is observed and experienced in personal relationships but can become a serious crisis when used by people in positions of authority. Jesus certainly didn't behave in this manner.

Fear of the Lord is beneficial for living, but using scripture as a sledge hammer is a direct affront to God. He never forces His way into our lives and neither should any person in authority lead by dictatorship.

There is a difference between the offices which represent God's structural authority and the person sitting in the office. The office is instituted by God, but the power it wields is often misused by the person sitting in it.

> Ephesians 6:9 "And masters, treat your slaves in the same way. Do not threaten them, since you know that he who is both their Master and yours in heaven, and there is no favoritism with him."

The "same way" refers to the preceding verses in Ephesians 6:5-8. If this verse is to be taken literally, it would read like this:

> *Masters, obey your earthly slaves with respect and fear, and with sincerity of the heart, just as you would obey Christ. Obey them not only to win their favor when their eye is on you, but like slaves of Christ, doing the will of the God from your heart. Serve (your slaves) wholeheartedly, as if you were serving the Lord, not men, because you know that the Lord will reward everyone for whatever good he does, whether he is slave or free.*

The strong directive is a servant leadership approach to exercising authority if you are a "master".

This leads us to several natural questions:

If God created these levels of authority, why is there unjust, incompetent and harsh authority?

What is the Christian to do when under the authority of a Christian or secular leader who is abusive or whose supervision runs contrary to scriptural principles and truths?

First of all, there are many people in positions of authority that are not walking in their calling, anointing or gifting. How did they get there? They were hired, promoted or appointed by man. Since the fall of Adam and Eve man by nature is sinful, selfish and far from perfect. Therefore many of these positions of authority are not filled by perfect men. Some positions have been filled without any consideration as to whether someone actually possessed the talent to perform in it admirably.

Marcus Buckingham and Curt Coffman co-authored a book in

1999 entitled First, Break All The Rules. In it, they assert that talent is not the same a skill or knowledge, and that talent cannot be taught. It is hard-wired into us. They claim we all have a "filter" that directs us to pay attention to some things and ignore others. This "filter" creates talents at an early age. These things cannot be taught. You either have it or you do not.

One of the things they discovered while writing the book was that much of corporate America hires people based on the notion that they can be taught skills and knowledge for a job, which is true to some degree. However, the person placed in a position with the requisite talent for that position is a much better performer and much more satisfied than the person placed in a position based on other factors.

How many people in authority have been placed there with considerable time committed to discovering whether they have the talent to serve in that position?

God gave man free will, and He usually does not bend it. However, He will often create incredible circumstances to change it, in order for His sovereign will to be accomplished.

The Israelites

> Exodus 1:8-11 "Then a new king, who did not know about Joseph, came to power in Egypt. 'Look,' he said to his people, 'the Israelites have become much too numerous for us. Come, we must deal shrewdly with them or they will become even more numerous and, if war breaks out, will join our enemies, fight against us and leave the country.' So they put slave masters over them to oppress them with forced labor, and they built Pithom and Rameses as store cities for Pharaoh. But the more they were oppressed, the more they multiplied and spread; so the Egyptians came to dread the Israelites and worked them ruthlessly."

Notice that God did not spare the Israelites of captivity just because they were His people. Even in their deliverance they faced a long journey to the Promised Land. Also note God gave Pharaoh a chance to do the right thing. That is because God is righteous and just. He sent Moses and Aaron to Pharaoh several times. They asked Pharaoh to let the Israelites go. Pharaoh refused and put even more pressure on the Israelites.

> Exodus 7:3-5 "'But I will harden Pharaoh's heart, and though I multiply my miraculous signs and wonders in Egypt, he will not listen to you. Then I will lay my hand on Egypt and with mighty acts of judgment I will bring out my divisions, my people the Israelites. And the Egyptians will know that I am the Lord when I stretch out my hand against Egypt and bring the Israelites out of it.'"

God accomplished this by turning all the water in Egypt to blood. He created a plague of frogs, a plague of gnats, a plague of flies, and a plague that killed all the livestock and put boils on men's and animals bodies. Next, an incredible hailstorm was followed by a plague of locusts. Pharaoh would not relent or repent. God sent a plague of darkness, then a plague that killed every firstborn male in Egypt including livestock. Pharaoh finally released the Israelites. In every instance of God's terrible power, He spared the Israelites from the consequences. "But on that day I will deal differently with the land of Goshen, where my people live…"

There are many great examples of God's workings in relation to oppressive authority in our lives.

The Apostles Persecuted

> Acts 5:17-42 "Then the high priest and all his associates, who were members of the party of the Sadducees, were

filled with jealousy. They arrested the apostles and put them in the public jail. During the night an angel of the Lord opened the doors of the jail and brought them out. 'Go, stand in the temple courts,' he said, "and tell the people the full message of this new life." At daybreak they entered the temple courts, as they had been told, and began to teach the people. When the high priest and his associates arrived, they called together the Sanhedrin – the full assembly of the elders of Israel – and sent to the jail for the apostles. But on arriving at the jail, the officers did not find them there. So they went back and reported, "We found the jail securely locked, with the guards standing at the doors; but when we opened them, we found no one inside." On hearing this report, the captain of the temple guard and the chief priests were puzzled, wondering what would come of this. Then someone came and said, "Look! The men you put in jail are standing in the temple courts teaching the people." At that, the captain went with his officers and brought the apostles. They did not use force, because they feared that the people would stone them. Having brought the apostles, they made them appear before the Sanhedrin to be questioned by the high priest. "We gave you strict orders not to teach in this name (Jesus)," he said. 'Yet you have filled Jerusalem with your teaching and are determined to make us guilty of this man's blood.' Peter and the other apostles replied: 'We must obey God rather than men! The God of our fathers raised Jesus from the dead – whom you had killed by hanging him on a tree. God exalted him to his own right hand as Prince and Savior that he might give repentance and forgiveness of sins to Israel. We are witnesses of these things, and so is the Holy Spirit, whom God has given to those who obey him.' When they heard

> this, they were furious and wanted to put them to death. But a Pharisee named Gamaliel, a teacher of the law, who was honored by all the people, stood up in the Sanhedrin and ordered that the men be put outside for a little while. Then he addressed them: 'Men of Israel, consider carefully what you intend to do to these men. Some time ago, Theudas appeared, claiming to be somebody, and about four hundred men rallied to him. He was killed, all his followers were dispersed, and it all came to nothing. After him, Judas the Galilean appeared in the days of the census and led a band of people in revolt. He too was killed, and all his followers were scattered. Therefore, in the present case I advise you: Leave these men alone! Let them go! For if their purpose or activity is of human origin, it will fail. But if it is from God, you will not be able to stop these men; you will only find yourselves fighting against God.' His speech persuaded them. They called the apostles and had them flogged. Then they ordered them not to speak in the name of Jesus, and let them go. The apostles left the Sanhedrin, rejoicing because they had been counted worthy of suffering disgrace for the Name. Day after day, in the temple courts and from house to house, they never stopped teaching and proclaiming the good news that Jesus is the Christ."

God was establishing His early church through the apostles. His sovereign will and the establishment of His church was not about to be obstructed by man. God moved through Gamaliel, who was not a believer, to influence the Sanhedrin, which resulted in the apostle's release.

- We are expected to honor and submit to authority instituted by God.

- God does not always remove the trouble that comes from ungodly authority. You will not escape trouble in this world. As a Christian, you are guaranteed trouble coming from Satan. Satan often uses authoritative figures to create trouble. Why wouldn't he? He knows scripture better than most Christians. He is very well aware of these verses admonishing and directing Christians to honor and obey authority. Satan is the author of confusion and his primary playground is your mind. If he can guilt you into obedience through the use of these verses, even if it is ungodly obedience, he will.

- God always provides resolution and very often provides protection.

- The believer can rest assured in a sincere relationship with God and Jesus that His sovereign will in their lives will not be thwarted by man or women.

What about when we make stupid or sinful decisions that get us into trouble?

> Romans 8:28 "And we know that in all things God works for the good of those who love him, who have been called according to his purpose."

God can use even our mistakes and sin to shape our lives and move us toward our purposes in Him.

Harsh Authority

Not all authority is godly, as evidenced by the apostle's experience with the Sanhedrin. Some authority is harsh, unjust or incompetent. Some is ungodly. Some is both.

Christians are not doormats and punching bags for the world. If you are oppressed under harsh authority you can always leave and move on. Jesus told His disciples in Matthew 10, "If anyone will not welcome you or listen to your words, shake the dust off your feet when you leave that home or town." Although He was speaking to his disciples in direct relation to them spreading the gospel, I think it has implications for us when dealing with harsh authority as well. You can always just walk away.

However, there are benefits of submitting to harsh authority which need to be considered.

> James 1:2-8 "Consider it pure joy, my brothers, whenever you face trials of many kinds, because you know that the testing of your faith develops perseverance. Perseverance must finish its work so that you may be mature and complete, not lacking anything. If any of you lacks wisdom, he should ask God, who gives generously to all without finding fault, and it will be given to him. But when he asks, he must believe and not doubt, because he who doubts is like a wave of the sea, blown and tossed by the wind. That man should not think he will receive anything from the Lord; he is a double-minded man, unstable in all he does."

There is suffering we will experience in this world. Christ suffered. We will suffer. We can grow in suffering. I hear my wife frequently tell others, "It is not about the problem. It is about how you deal with the problem and what you do with it". Amen!

For the most part, I attempt to approach life with the view that God is always moving me towards becoming more like Him. He does this in many ways, and I fully recognize that His ways are higher than mine. I have built a paradigm that views life as "chapters" or "courses" — each one successive to the last and building upon each other. When I face uncomfortable and difficult circumstances, the first thing I try to do is to figure out what God is attempting to do through it. Usually this means looking at myself first. God may be confronting a personal problem, exposing sin, or growing and stretching me through uncomfortable circumstances, which might include putting me under unjust, harsh, or incompetent authority.

> Ephesians 2:10 "For we are God's workmanship, created in Christ Jesus to do good works, which God prepared in advance for us to do."

> Ephesians 4:11-16 "It was he who gave some to be apostles, some to be prophets, some to be evangelists, and some to be pastors and teachers, to prepare God's people for works of service, so that the body of Christ may be built up until we all reach unity in the faith and in the knowledge of the Son of God and become mature, attaining to the whole measure of fullness of Christ. Then we will no longer be infants, tossed back and forth by the waves, and blown here and there by every wind of teaching and by the cunning and craftiness of men in their deceitful scheming. Instead, speaking the truth in love, we will in all things grow up into him who is the Head, that is, Christ. From him the whole body, joined and held together by every supporting ligament, grows and builds up in love, as each part does its work."

> James 4:8 "Come near to God and he will come near to you."

I know that God had a specific purpose in mind when he breathed me into existence. I have a very clear view of what that is because I have taken the time with God to figure it out. Although not the focus of this book, I believe there are few Christians willing to devote the time to do this. I strongly encourage you to do so. Find your natural skills, spiritual gifts, personality type, working style and God's specific purpose for you. Why is it important? Because when you do find yourself in difficult circumstances or under difficult authority, it helps focus on what God's purpose might be in it.

He is always moving me toward that which He intended for me. He loves me so much and so deeply desires me to fulfill that purpose, that He will provide correction and punishment if that is what is required. I can also veer off course through my own free will. In either case, His intent is to move me toward wholeness in Him and complete His purpose in me.

Therefore, I must consider His purposes in difficult times, including being placed under harsh authority. The bottom line is that I need to finish each "course" well. If I fail, God loves me enough that He will find a similar course to put me through until I pass the course. That is how much God loves me. He will not give up on me. He will continue to provide progressive opportunities, trials, circumstances and blessings in moving me towards Him and that purpose He has for me.

Do you know a brother or sister who seems to struggle with the same issues over and over? They are not passing the course, and it is difficult to watch. God will not give up on them until they "get it" and pass the course. Sadly, some will be stuck in elementary school most of their lives.

This should be your first consideration when finding yourself under harsh, unjust or incompetent authority. Man, by nature, is self absorbed, self centered and defensive, making it difficult to look in the mirror. However, that should be your first course of action.

> 1 Peter 3:9-17 "Do not repay evil with evil or insult with insult, but with blessing, because to this you were called so that you may inherit a blessing. For, 'Whoever would love life and see good days must keep his

> tongue from evil and his lips from deceitful speech. He must turn from evil and do good; he must seek peace and pursue it. For the eyes of the Lord are on the righteous and his ears are attentive to their prayer, but the face of the Lord is against those who do evil.' Who is going to harm you if you are eager to do good? But even if you should suffer for what is right, you are blessed. "Do not fear what they fear; do not be frightened." But in your hearts set apart Christ as Lord. Always be prepared to give an answer to everyone who asks you to give the reason for the hope that you have. But do this with gentleness and respect, keeping a clear conscious, so that those who speak maliciously against your good behavior in Christ may be ashamed of their slander. It is better, if it is God's will, to suffer for doing good than for doing evil."

If it is God's will? Why would it be God's will that you are in a situation that is subjecting you to harsh, unjust or incompetent authority? The previous verses answer those questions. The answer has to do with His purpose for your life. God may have chosen you and placed you under uncomfortable authority to demonstrate the heart of Jesus to that authority.

Most people are not led to Christ because one day they feel an urge to pick up a Bible and read it. Most people come to Christ by observing your behavior, your attitude and what comes out of your mouth — the words you speak. God may have placed you there to plant seeds of Godly influence.

Conversely, God may have placed you under harsh, unjust or incompetent authority in order to break it, teach it, influence it or shake it up. There are many biblical examples of God choosing specific individuals to do just that. When I read some of the exchanges Jesus had with the religious leaders of his day, I am inspired by his sharp wit and directness. He called them hypocrites. He took their rules and rationale and turned it upside down with truth, then tossed it back at them.

> Matthew 12:34 "You brood of vipers, how can you who are evil say anything good? For out of the overflow of the heart the mouth speaks."

> Matthew 23:1-33 "Then Jesus said to the crowds and to his disciples: 'The teachers of the law and the Pharisees sit in Moses' seat. So you must obey them and do everything they tell you. But do not do what they do, for they do not practice what they preach. They tie up heavy loads and put them on men's shoulders, but they themselves are not willing to lift a finger to move them. Everything they do is done for men to see: They make their phylacteries wide and the tassels on their garments long; they love the place of honor at banquets and the most important seats in the synagogues; they love to be greeted in the marketplaces and to have men call them 'Rabbi.' But you are not to be called 'Rabbi,' for you have only one Master and you are all brothers. And do not call anyone on earth 'father,' for you have one Father, and he is in heaven. Nor are you to be called 'teacher,' for you have one Teacher, the Christ. The greatest among you will be your servant. For whoever exalts himself will be humbled, and whoever humbles himself will be exalted. Woe to you, teachers of the law and Pharisees, you hypocrites! You shut the kingdom of heaven in men's faces. You yourselves do not enter, nor will you let those enter who are trying to. Woe to you, teachers of the law and Pharisees, you hypocrites! You travel over land and sea to win a single convert, and when he becomes one, you

make him twice as much a son of hell as you are. Woe to you, blind guides! You say, 'If anyone swears by the temple, it means nothing; but if anyone swears by the gold of the temple, he is bound by his oath.' You blind fools! Which is greater: the gold, or the temple that makes the gold sacred? You also say, 'If anyone swears by the altar, it means nothing; but if anyone swears by the gift on it, he is bound by his oath.' You blind men! Which is greater: the gift, or the altar that makes the gift sacred? Therefore, he who swears by the altar swears by it and by everything on it. And he who swears by the temple swears by it and by the one who dwells in it. And he who swears by heaven swears by God's throne and by the one who sits on it. "Woe to you, teachers of the law and Pharisees, you hypocrites! You give a tenth of your spices—mint, dill and cummin. But you have neglected the more important matters of the law—justice, mercy and faithfulness. You should have practiced the latter, without neglecting the former. You blind guides! You strain out a gnat but swallow a camel. "Woe to you, teachers of the law and Pharisees, you hypocrites! You clean the outside of the cup and dish, but inside they are full of greed and self-indulgence. Blind Pharisee! First clean the inside of the cup and dish, and then the outside also will be clean. "Woe to you, teachers of the law and Pharisees, you hypocrites! You are like whitewashed tombs, which look beautiful on the outside but on the inside are full of dead men's bones and everything unclean. In the same way, on the outside you appear to people as righteous but on the inside you are full of hypocrisy and wickedness. Woe to you, teachers of the law and Pharisees, you hypocrites! You build tombs for the prophets and decorate the graves of the righteous. And you say, 'If we

> had lived in the days of our forefathers, we would not have taken part with them in shedding the blood of the prophets.' So you testify against yourselves that you are the descendants of those who murdered the prophets. Fill up, then, the measure of the sin of your forefathers! You snakes! You brood of vipers! How will you escape being condemned to hell?'"

Jonah was sent to Nineveh. Paul was sent to Rome. David had to deal with Saul. Moses wanted nothing to do with leading the Israelites. The list goes on and on. God often sends those He trusts into uncomfortable situations.

The tricky part is determining why you are there, and that is something only God can answer. There is no magic or spiritual formula to apply in these situations. The best preparation beforehand is to be connected intimately to God. If you do this, you will hear God's voice and perceive His direction.

Submitting the situation to God through prayer allows Him to move within His perfect will to resolve it. Once you do determine God's will, you must walk it out faithfully. He will honor and bless your obedience.

Is there ever a time we should confront ungodly authority?

Individual Reflection or Group Discussion

1. Go back and review the list you made from the discussion questions in Chapter 1.

2. For each authoritative relationship, based on what you have read so far, define each relationship as basically Godly or ungodly.

3. Explain your rationale for assigning each relationship as Godly or ungodly.

4. For those ungodly relationships, try to imagine what possible reasons God might have you in them.

Chapter 3
Confronting Ungodly Authority

"You can only protect your liberties in this world by protecting the other man's freedom. You can only be free if I am free."

Clarence S. Darrow

"If your brother sins against you, go show him his fault, just between the two of you. If he listens to you, you have won your brother over. But if he will not listen, take one or two others along, so that 'every matter may be established by the testimony of two or three witnesses.' If he refuses to listen to them, tell it to the church; and if he refuses to listen even to the church, treat him as you would a pagan or tax collector." Matthew 18:15-17

Lessons Learned

In my role as a church consultant, I may have intermittent or long and deep involvement in a church. It all depends on their needs. In this capacity I have met and observed different leaders with different styles of leadership.

As an outside observer, I am personally fascinated when there is difficulty in authoritative church relationships and very few of the individuals caught up in these situations follow the simple and clear instructions from the mouth of Jesus.

In one situation, I was asked by several leaders of a ministry to counsel those concerning problems they were having with the supervisor of their ministry. I directed them to Matthew 18:15-17. They did not follow these instructions from Jesus. I was curious, so I asked why. Those who had come to me for advice told me that they could not confront the offender because their church instructed them to "respect the office", and the offender was their supervisor. By confronting him they felt they would not be respecting the office. This, of course, is a perversion of what Jesus made perfectly clear — step by step.

Eventually, due to my own intense curiosity, I had a brief discussion with one of the leaders of the affected group. It went something like this:

Me: So, let me see if I understand this correctly. You all agree this supervisor has misused scripture in an attempt to manipulate you, and is spreading the fruit of fear by virtue of his direction?

Him: Yes.

Me: And you will not go to the offender directly, either one-on-one or as a small group, and confront the offender on this behavior because to do so would be violating your mandate to "respect the office"?

Him: Yes.

Me: Would you agree that Satan is having a good time with at least a part of this supervisor's life and mind, using it to spread fear, and to drip poison into this ministry?

Him: Yes.

Me: Is it also true that you and the other leaders will not get together privately to pray about the matter because you fear the backlash if this supervisor discovers you had gotten together without his knowledge to ask God what should be done about the situation?

Him: Yes.

Me: And you will not take these concerns, as a group, to an authority over this supervisor?

Him: No. What should we do?

Me: Step down as a leader or quit. You do not have the courage to do what Jesus instructed.

Lesson learned: To do nothing, changes nothing.

Jesus is talking about Christian relationships. However, consider using the same general approach in secular and business relationships. Obviously, in a secular relationship you will probably not be praying with the other party or quoting Bible verses. But you can still speak the truth in love. You can still point out the oppressive, sinful or ungodly behavior in secular terms.

> 1 Corinthians 5:11 "But now I am writing you that you must not associate with anyone who calls himself a brother but is sexually immoral or greedy, an idolater or slanderer, a drunkard or a swindler. With such a man do not even eat."

In the story shared above, several of the affected people asked me to speak directly to this supervisor's pastor. I refused. It was not my role to do so. I was an advisor and consultant to this church and this issue went well beyond what I had been recruited to do. I did, however, tell them I would ask God to prompt this pastor to come to me if God so desired. Within two weeks this pastor asked for a meeting with me.

The meeting was interesting. After establishing the facts and coming to agreement on what the affected individual's perceptions were, I began to ask some difficult questions — all along the lines of what you have read thus far in this book. The pastor was struggling with the answers. At one point he simply threw his hands up and told me I was making him uncomfortable because I sounded like an attorney. I asked him if any of the senior staff in this church could provide the answers to my questions.

He informed me that all the staff was simply following the senior pastor's directives.

This pastor had no ability to address the circumstances through the scriptures cited thus far, as would be applied to this particular situation. This was sad.

The Heat of Ungodly Authority

> Daniel 3 "King Nebuchadnezzar made an image of gold, ninety feet high and nine feet wide, and set it up on the plain of Dura in the province of Babylon. He then summoned the satraps, prefects, governors, advisers, treasurers, judges, magistrates and all the other provincial officials to come to the dedication of the image he had set up. So the satraps, prefects, governors, advisers, treasurers, judges, magistrates and all the other provincial officials assembled for the dedication of the image that King Nebuchadnezzar had set up, and they stood before it. Then the herald loudly proclaimed, 'This is what you are commanded to do, O peoples, nations and men of every language: As soon as you hear the sound of the horn, flute, zither, lyre, harp, pipes and all kinds of music, you must fall down and worship the image of gold that King Nebuchadnezzar has set up. Whoever does not fall down and worship will immediately be thrown into a blazing furnace.' Therefore, as soon as they heard the sound of the horn, flute, zither, lyre, harp and all kinds of music, all the peoples, nations and men of every language fell down and worshiped the image of gold that King Nebuchadnezzar had set up. At this time some astrologers came forward and denounced the Jews. They said to King Nebuchadnezzar, 'O king, live forever! You have issued a decree, O king, that ev-

eryone who hears the sound of the horn, flute, zither, lyre, harp, pipes and all kinds of music must fall down and worship the image of gold, and that whoever does not fall down and worship will be thrown into a blazing furnace. But there are some Jews whom you have set over the affairs of the province of Babylon—Shadrach, Meshach and Abednego—who pay no attention to you, O king. They neither serve your gods nor worship the image of gold you have set up.' Furious with rage, Nebuchadnezzar summoned Shadrach, Meshach and Abednego. So these men were brought before the king, and Nebuchadnezzar said to them, 'Is it true, Shadrach, Meshach and Abednego, that you do not serve my gods or worship the image of gold I have set up? Now when you hear the sound of the horn, flute, zither, lyre, harp, pipes and all kinds of music, if you are ready to fall down and worship the image I made, very good. But if you do not worship it, you will be thrown immediately into a blazing furnace. Then what god will be able to rescue you from my hand?' Shadrach, Meshach and Abednego replied to the king, 'O Nebuchadnezzar, we do not need to defend ourselves before you in this matter. If we are thrown into the blazing furnace, the God we serve is able to save us from it, and he will rescue us from your hand, O king. But even if he does not, we want you to know, O king, that we will not serve your gods or worship the image of gold you have set up.' Then Nebuchadnezzar was furious with Shadrach, Meshach and Abednego, and his attitude toward them changed. He ordered the furnace heated seven times hotter than usual and commanded some of the strongest soldiers in his army to tie up Shadrach, Meshach and Abednego and throw them into the blazing furnace. So these men, wearing their robes, trousers, turbans and other clothes, were bound and thrown into the blazing furnace. The king's command was so urgent and the furnace so hot that the flames of the fire killed the soldiers who took up Shadrach, Meshach and Abednego, and these three men, firmly tied, fell into the blazing furnace. Then King Nebuchadnezzar leaped to his feet in amazement and asked his advisers, "Weren't there three men that we tied up and threw into the fire?" They replied, 'Certainly, O king." He said, "Look! I see four men walking around in the fire, unbound and unharmed, and the fourth looks like a son of the gods.' Nebuchadnezzar then approached the opening of the blazing furnace and shouted, 'Shadrach, Meshach and Abednego, servants of the Most High God, come out! Come here!' So Shadrach, Meshach and Abednego came out of the fire, and the satraps, prefects, governors and royal advisers crowded around them. They saw that the fire had not harmed their bodies, nor was a hair of their heads singed; their robes were not scorched, and there was no smell of fire on them. Then Nebuchadnezzar said, 'Praise be to the God of Shadrach, Meshach and Abednego, who has sent his angel and rescued his servants! They trusted in him and defied the king's command and were willing to give up their lives rather than serve or worship any god except their own God. Therefore I decree that the people of any nation or language who say anything against the God of Shadrach, Meshach and Abednego be cut into pieces and their houses be turned into piles of rubble, for no other god can save in this way.' Then the king promoted Shadrach, Meshach and Abednego in the province of Babylon."

Shadrach, Meshach & Abednego did not compromise their God-given principles or beliefs. But even in disagreement and their refusal to cooperate with ungodly authority, they were respectful. God honored their disobedience, because it was in perfect alignment with His word: "Thou shall have no other gods before me. You shall not make for yourself an idol in the form of anything in heaven above or in the waters below. You shall not bow down to them or worship them; for I, the Lord your God, am a jealous God."

We do not obey ungodly authority when it contradicts the Word of God. We do not obey authority which is telling us to do something that is contrary to Scripture.

There is a difference between obedience and submission. Submission involves your attitude. Obedience involves your actions. The Bible teaches unconditional submission (attitude) but not unconditional obedience (actions).

There is a simple test to determine your actions. It was a phrase that was a popular part of evangelical culture a number of years ago: What would Jesus do?

Look at the story of David and King Saul. For a while, David was Saul's "golden boy". The people of Saul's kingdom began to talk about the skill David had in battle and began to compare him to King Saul. Eventually, Saul became jealous of all the praise David was getting. Ultimately, this jealousy drove Saul to madness. He was obsessed with killing David.

> 1 Samuel 24 "After Saul returned from pursuing the Philistines, he was told, 'David is in the Desert of En Gedi.' So Saul took three thousand chosen men from all Israel and set out to look for David and his men near the Crags of the Wild Goats. He came to the sheep pens along the way; a cave was there, and Saul went in to relieve himself. David and his men were far back in the

cave. The men said, 'This is the day the LORD spoke of when he said to you, 'I will give your enemy into your hands for you to deal with as you wish.' Then David crept up unnoticed and cut off a corner of Saul's robe. Afterward, David was conscience-stricken for having cut off a corner of his robe. He said to his men, 'The LORD forbid that I should do such a thing to my master, the LORD's anointed, or lift my hand against him; for he is the anointed of the LORD.' With these words David rebuked his men and did not allow them to attack Saul. And Saul left the cave and went his way. Then David went out of the cave and called out to Saul, 'My lord the king!' When Saul looked behind him, David bowed down and prostrated himself with his face to the ground. He said to Saul, 'Why do you listen when men say, 'David is bent on harming you'? This day you have seen with your own eyes how the LORD delivered you into my hands in the cave. Some urged me to kill you, but I spared you; I said, 'I will not lift my hand against my master, because he is the LORD's anointed.' See, my father, look at this piece of your robe in my hand! I cut off the corner of your robe but did not kill you. Now understand and recognize that I am not guilty of wrongdoing or rebellion. I have not wronged you, but you are hunting me down to take my life. May the LORD judge between you and me. And may the LORD avenge the wrongs you have done to me, but my hand will not touch you. As the old saying goes, 'From evildoers come evil deeds,' so my hand will not touch you. Against whom has the king of Israel come out? Whom are you pursuing? A dead dog? A flea? May the LORD be our judge and decide between us. May he consider my cause and uphold it; may he vindicate me by deliv-

> ering me from your hand.' When David finished saying this, Saul asked, 'Is that your voice, David my son?' And he wept aloud. 'You are more righteous than I,' he said. 'You have treated me well, but I have treated you badly. You have just now told me of the good you did to me; the LORD delivered me into your hands, but you did not kill me. When a man finds his enemy, does he let him get away unharmed? May the LORD reward you well for the way you treated me today. I know that you will surely be king and that the kingdom of Israel will be established in your hands. Now swear to me by the LORD that you will not cut off my descendants or wipe out my name from my father's family.' So David gave his oath to Saul. Then Saul returned home, but David and his men went up to the stronghold."

God did deliver King Saul to David. David submitted (attitude) as evidenced by his refusal to harm or kill Saul. However, had David obeyed Saul he would have been dead. He did confront Saul with the truth, and he did let God take revenge.

One of the things we miss out on when we take circumstances into our own hands is we never get to see what God would have done had we waited. And this is where it gets tricky. Should you keep your mouth shut, pray and wait? Or should you speak? Should you take action?

> Romans 12:9–21 "Love must be sincere. Hate what is evil; cling to what is good. Be devoted to one another in brotherly love. Honor one another above yourselves. Never be lacking in zeal, but keep your spiritual fervor, serving the Lord. Be joyful in hope, patient in affliction, faithful in prayer. Share with God's people who are in need. Practice hospitality. Bless those who persecute you; bless and do not curse. Rejoice with those who rejoice; mourn with

> those who mourn. Live in harmony with one another. Do not be proud, but be willing to associate with people of low position. Do not be conceited. Do not repay anyone evil for evil. Be careful to do what is right in the eyes of everybody. If it is possible, as far as it depends on you, live at peace with everyone. Do not take revenge, my friends, but leave room for God's wrath, for it is written: "It is mine to avenge; I will repay," says the Lord. On the contrary: "If your enemy is hungry, feed him; if he is thirsty, give him something to drink. In doing this, you will heap burning coals on his head." Do not be overcome by evil, but overcome evil with good."

You do not have to get even or take revenge. God is fully capable of doing that on your behalf. Do not confuse the instructions above, which are about love - with obedience to ungodly authority. They are completely different principles. Demonstrating love does not include participating in ungodly behavior.

Confrontation

So how do we confront illegal, immoral, sinful and oppressive supervision and authority?

- You can submit to it.
- You can report it if it is illegal.
- You can walk away from the circumstances.
- You can pray about it and wait to see what God does.
- You should refuse to participate with your actions but honor the authority with your attitude.
- You can demonstrate love if you are given the op-

portunity.

- You can confront it head on if that is God's will.

Galatians 6:1 "Brothers, if someone is caught in a sin, you who are spiritual should restore him gently."

To follow these instructions, you would have to be familiar enough with scripture to recognize sin. Next, you would go to this brother and begin to "restore him gently". This would require going to the offender and having a prayerful, loving, compassionate and firm discussion regarding their sin. If you wonder what you should say, just put yourself in their shoes and imagine if it was you, and how you would like to be approached.

Colossians 3:13 "Bear with each other and forgive whatever grievances you may have against one another. Forgive as the Lord forgave you."

Forgiveness is not an option. It is a necessity.

Matthew 6:14-15 "For if you forgive men when they sin against you, your Heavenly Father will also forgive you. But if you do not forgive men their sins, your Father will not forgive your sins."

Forgiveness is not something you "will" yourself into or out of. It is the simple act of recognizing that you harbor offense against someone and taking that to the cross. There is much we do not understand about the way God works, or the spiritual mysteries that go on between our minds, souls, spirits and the Trinity. This is one of them. Your responsibility is to recognize it and ask Jesus to do the work of forgiveness within you. He will.

I Timothy 5:19-21 "Do not entertain an accusation against an elder unless it is brought by two or three wit-

> nesses. Those who sin are to be rebuked publicly, so that the others may take warning. I charge you, in the sight of God and Christ Jesus and the elect angels, to keep these instructions without partiality, and to do nothing out of favoritism."

The word elder in this context is generally agreed to be the official or ordained members of the local church. Do you think Timothy was trying to be dramatic when he wrote, "in the sight of God and Christ Jesus and the elect angels"? I don't. I think he used these words to emphasize the importance of these instructions.

Unequally Yoked

> 2 Corinthians 6:14-16 "Do not be yoked together with unbelievers. For what do righteousness and wickedness have in common? Or what fellowship can light have with darkness? What harmony is there between Christ and Belial? What does a believer have in common with an unbeliever? What agreement is there between the temple of God and idols? For we are the temple of the living God. As God has said: 'I will live with them and walk among them, and I will be their God and they will be my people.'"

The "yoke" is the Greek word *zugos.* This describes an actual yoke, which is a wooden yoke that joins two animals together so they could combine their strength to pull a load that would have probably been too difficult for one animal to pull. Their combined strength made the task possible, and much easier. Belial is a name that Paul used for Satan.

My perception is that in the mainstream evangelical world, the focus of this verse has always been used in the context of marriage. At the risk of being controversial, I disagree, although I recognize it can be applied to the marriage relationship.

Both Paul and Jesus make significant references to the marriage relationship and behavior in it. This is unmistakable and unarguable. They had no problem addressing the marriage relationship directly. So, if these verses are specifically about marriage, why didn't Paul just include them in 1 Corinthians 7:12, where he addresses marriages between a believer and non-believer? Or why didn't Jesus talk about it when he talked about marriage in Mark 10? These are not the only places marriage is referred to directly in the Bible.

Additionally, most people do not get married with the primary motivation being to lighten their load through a yoke, even though that may be a benefit of marriage. Most marriages occur under the banner of love.

I am not advocating marriage between believers and unbelievers, but Paul clearly recognized that it happens. If you are a Christian, the wisdom and benefits of marrying someone like-spirited should be obvious, as should the potential pitfalls of marrying someone who is not.

Life isn't perfect. Christians do not make perfect choices. People come to Christ after they get married. God's ways are higher than our ability to understand them. God does not fit into a box. My own former prayer partner, whom I have tremendous respect for, married her unbelieving husband at the prompting of God.

This verse is clearly addressing relationships in which you, as a Christian, would be pressured to sacrifice your principles in Christ. Does that apply to marriage? Of course it does. Is it exclusive to marriage? Of course, it is not. Does it apply to other relationships, including work, secular and authoritative relationships? Of course, it does.

By their nature, our relationships with government and within our careers bring us into unequally yoked relationships. In these types of relationships, we are working together to accomplish a task in which the lone individual would not be able to accomplish on their own. Although Paul's instructions are clear, how do you apply this towards practical living? If you have a mortgage and other bills to pay, and work for a secular company, are you supposed to leave and go find a Christian employer because you do not want to be unequally yoked?

Jesus addressed this when he gave the disciples their marching orders:

> Matthew 10:16 "I am sending you out like sheep amongst wolves. Therefore be as shrewd as snakes and as innocent as doves."

Looking at the Greek roots of this verse, we could transpose it to: *"Therefore be prudent, careful, wise, cunning, discerning, thoughtful and intelligent as snakes (or serpents) and free from evil, guile, wrongdoing or malicious intention, as doves."*

This requires a balance between wisdom, the secular, Satan's nature, and the appropriate strategies to effectively deal with them that gives the world no cause to point the finger at you.

I believe we are all representatives of Christ in whatever place He has us working, walking and living. As He sent his disciples into a dangerous world to spread the gospel and establish God's church, Jesus knew the mission was going to be full of danger, opposition and problems. He knew Satan was loose. He knew exactly what power Satan has on earth. This was His advice to these men. Is the advice any less prudent if we apply it to our secular relationships?

Accountability

Every leader and every person I have ever met has a blind side. There is a blemish or spot in their life that seems abundantly clear to many people around them, but they do not see it. When Israel had no king, there was chaos because everyone did as they saw fit. There was no accountability. We all need accountability, but none of us really want it. Accountability is not a one-way street that runs downhill. The verses in this chapter allow for, even encourage and provide for, accountability to run back uphill as well.

I have plenty of my own flaws. I have studied them for years, and people tell me about them frequently. I have developed several relationships with men whom I ask to hold me accountable. One of my former professional partners in training and fugitive apprehension now protects a VIP. This is his full-time job. When our schedules agree, we make a concerted effort to meet. We actually go over a checklist and ask each other direct questions. We know each other's sins, weaknesses and strengths intimately. There is no judgment when one of us fails. There is prayerful and compassionate discussion always pointing toward the direction of restoration. My wife holds me accountable, and I have given her permission, even encouraged her to do so. I don't always like it. But it is good for me. She has given me permission to do the same.

If you do not have a relationship like this, go find one. The Bible uses a significant amount of space giving behavioral instruction in particular regard to authority and what to do when authority becomes oppressive, sinful, harsh or ungodly. There needs to be some accountability in regards to confronting what needs to be confronted. Look at this as preventative medicine. You may not like it, but it will keep you well.

Within the context of ungodly supervision or authority in our lives, there are times we need to provide some type of accountability to that authority. It is okay to question authority. It is okay to question what they do and say. If you don't do it, who will? You may have been sent into that relationship to do just that. You may, and should, judge the fruit that the authority is producing.

Being Judgmental

1 Corinthians 5:9-12 instructs us not to judge those outside the church, yet in the preceding verses we are required to exercise judgment to discern the immoral, the greedy, the swindler and

the idolater. There is a misconception amongst many Christians regarding the action of judging others. We all make judgments every day. If you did not, you would be dead. We judge people and circumstances constantly in search of appropriate responses. Can you imagine what type of chaos would exist if police and military personnel never made any judgments? How about prosecutors never exercising judgment in a country where our statutes specifically requires intent as a critical factor in determining whether the law was violated?

Criminals use con games all the time to get close to victims. In these types of situations we are always trying to judge motive and intentions. In fact, God has hard-wired all of us with intuition, which is a survival signal – telling you something is wrong. Intuition triggers judgment. Additionally, discernment, the ability to discern between good and evil, is a gift of the Spirit. Discernment requires judgment.

Intent, or motive, helps us differentiate behavior. There is a great difference between me driving down the street and hitting someone who jumps out in front of my car suddenly (an accident) and stalking someone I don't like for six months and purposely running over them with my car (premeditated murder).

The Greek root of the word "judge" and "judgment" is "krino", which means to make a decision on the basis of information. Without citing all the Biblical references here warning us not to judge others, a study of the subject reveals most of these admonitions are in regards to a person's relationship to God and their eternal status. Some may argue with this, but the core message of this chapter, backed by scripture, is that we do make judgments about behavior and then act on them accordingly either through submission, a refusal to participate or accountability.

Summary

Why do so many Christians lack the courage to do the tough

stuff of Christianity? We all love to do the cuddly, gentle, loving fruits of the Spirit thing. Do you think the Biblical instructions of dealing with ungodly relationships are any less important to the body of Christ or the Church?

From Entrepreneurial Faith: Launching Bold Initiatives to Expand God's Kingdom by Walt Kallestad, Kirbyjon Caldwell & Paul Sorensen:

"In the church, it is tough, because we don't want to hurt anybody. We've bought into a myth. We have concluded that because God made everyone wonderful, we have to let people lead music, for instance, who have no talent and little musical ability. In truth, we allow this to continue because we don't want to enter the difficult area of evaluation, which might lead to disappointment but in the long term leads to people being placed where their gifts can be exercised more fully. Evaluation can help identify a person who is talented, but perhaps not in the position where he or she is currently serving. Evaluating your staff allows you to make some moves that will put everyone in positions where God can use their strengths to the best advantage."

The authors are addressing church leaders and exhorting them to have the courage to be honest within their evaluation of people they work with. We would all be far better off if we did the same thing with all of our relationships by honestly and courageously evaluating them and then taking Biblical, corrective action.

How Does All of This Affect Me?

If indeed we are living in the last days of this age, we know that things are going to get progressively worse as we move toward the return of Jesus. Those things will be brought forth by Satan, through people. If no one confronts those who Satan is using to carry these things out, fewer souls will enter the Kingdom of God. It is that simple, and it is that complex.

Individual Reflection or Group Discussion

1. Please review your answer to #4 from the Individual Reflection or Group Discussion at the end of Chapter 2.

2. For any ungodly relationship you have identified in which confrontation is a possibility, discuss or sketch out a plan of how confrontation will be best accomplished.

3. This plan does not need to be acted upon unless you determine that it is appropriate. However, there will be great value that comes from thinking this through or discussing it in a small group.

SECTION TWO:

THE END OF THIS AGE

Chapter 4
Signs of the End

"Don't wake me for the end of the world unless it has very good special effects."

Roger Zelazny

"Blessed is the one who reads the words of this prophecy, and blessed are those who hear it and take to heart what is written in it, because the time is near." Revelation 1:3

Lessons Learned

I am picking myself up off of the floor of a bedroom due to the fact that a man who is growling like an animal and has been levitating off of his bed has just thrown me like a rag doll across the room and into a wall. I jump back on him, looking him straight in the face. His eyes look crazy. There is a low, guttural and unearthly sound coming from his throat. Even though he is a good sized individual, it seems as though he has inhuman strength. I am face to face with a demon and literally wrestling with evil.

It is not uncommon for law enforcement officers from different agencies and even different jurisdictions to back each other up. I did that one night as I heard a dispatcher send several police officers to a residence due to some type of disturbance. Domestic disturbances are dangerous because they are usually charged with high emotions, which cause people to think and act irrationally.

- On average, one law enforcement officer is killed in the line of duty somewhere in the United States every 53 hours. Since the first known line-of-duty death in 1792, nearly 19,000 U.S. law enforcement officers have made the ultimate sacrifice. In the last decade, there has been an average of 163 deaths, 58,659 assaults and 16,188 injuries per year to law enforcement officers.

Arriving at the same time as the two dispatched police officers, I am comforted by the fact that I know them both. They are both very large men and guys I would want to have with me in a violent situation. One of them is a police chaplain. We are met by a woman at the front door who indicated her husband was in the bedroom at the end of a long hallway, and he was acting strange.

Us: What do you mean by acting strange?

Her: He is down there growling like an animal.

Us: Has he taken any drugs?

Her: Not that I know of.

Us: Has he been drinking?

Her: Not that I know of.

Us: Does he have a history of taking drugs or drinking?

Her: Not that I know of.

Us: Does he have any mental health issues?

Her: Apparently. Can't you hear him?

I walk to the hallway. I hear some noise and what sounds like an animal growling coming from the other end of the hallway.

Us: Does he own any weapons?

Her: No.

Us: Are there any weapons in the bedroom?

Her: Not that I know of.

We proceed down the hallway towards the bedroom and the animal noises just as another officer arrives and joins us. I notice as we slowly ease down the hallway that it seems to be getting colder. I brush this off as an adrenaline reaction knowing that strange things can happen between my brain and body when it prepares for a confrontation.

As we come around the corner of the hallway and stand in front of the door to the bedroom, we are somewhat taken back by what we see. There on the bed is a middle-aged man wearing only his underwear. He is on the bed, looking at us and growling, propped up on his hands and knees. One of the officers began to talk to him and ask him what was going on. The man's growling simply intensified in tone and volume. He then began to levitate off the bed. There was an instantaneous reaction from all of the officers, including myself, which was to attempt to restrain this man. To do so, we had to enter the bedroom which felt like a refrigerator in comparison to the rest of the residence.

The man in his underwear proceeded to toss four officers around the room for the next minute or so as if it was sport. No easy feat, considering that the three other officers were all over 6 feet tall and weighed over 200 pounds. The chaplain alone must have weighed at least 250 pounds.

In situations like these, time always slows down. It feels much longer than it really is. After what felt like way too long, we finally got this man into handcuffs. Emergency Medical Services were called and the paramedics transported the growling man in his underwear to the hospital after we handcuffed him to the gurney. Once at the hospital, he was injected with some type of sedative that essentially put him to sleep. I went to the hospital to retrieve the handcuffs. The officers involved held an informal debriefing after I left the hospital. We compared notes. Everyone agreed the temperature seemed to drop as we got closer to the bedroom. There were no rational reasons we could find for this man's behavior. Trust me; we tried to justify his behavior. The chaplain, of course, knew exactly what was going on. He explained in no uncertain terms that this man was possessed by a demon. Word of this incident spread quickly through the law enforcement agencies in that area and local church services were filled with police officers for the next several weeks.

Oddly enough, the growling man in his underwear appeared the next day at our department offices to apologize for his behavior the night before.

His explanation: "I don't know what got into me".

No joke.

Lesson learned: Evil is real. Demons are real. Evil can manifest itself through human beings with unearthly strength and violent, irrational behavior. In this case, it had to be physically overwhelmed.

What's the Point?

Did you know that the Bible dedicates almost 40% of its content to prophecy? There are 150 chapters that talk of or mention what is commonly referred to as the End Times. This is more than any other single genre or subject in the Bible. In fact, the Bible talks more about End Times prophecy than it does all of the teachings of Jesus combined. God must have considered it important.

The prophecies found in the Bible have all come to pass, and those that have not surely will. There is no other document on earth that has the Bible's 100% track record. This alone should be reason enough to pay attention to it.

There are a number of secular and Christian theologians, seminarians and scholars who have dedicated great portions of their lifetimes studying prophecy and the End Times. I am not part of that crowd, but I have read a significant amount of their material. Most agree on the major issues and events, and many differ on the finer points, the chronological order and the timing of these events.

The study of the End Times can be very confusing, particularly for the average person who does not have the time or natural inclination to study these passages in depth. Many of the verses are filled with imagery and historical references that might easily overwhelm the layman. It is my hope to present some key principles about the End Times in a simple, straightforward manner so that the reader might gain some insight and knowledge into how these End Time prophecies fit into your everyday life.

There are several ways to study End Time Prophecy. One is chronologically. The other is parenthetically. The latter gives the reader perspective while the former provides a timeline. I encourage you to conduct your own independent study of the End Times. There are a great number of books, studies and DVDs that are available on the subject. There will be more specific detail in the next several chapters.

In the meantime, here is what I believe to be a reasonable chronological timeline based on my studies. It may or may not be entirely accurate, but it really doesn't matter. What is important is for you to consider how you are going to react to these events and how you plan on dealing with them. You will not escape any of them unless you are already dead by the time they come to pass.

- First, Israel becomes a nation.

- That kicks off the Beginning of Birth Pangs.

- This is followed by a 3.5 year period of Increased Labor Pangs.

- The next 3.5 years are marked by Hard Labor Pangs which include the Great Tribulation. During this time, the earth will experience the 7 Seals, then the 7 Trumpets, with the Rapture of the Saints coming near the 7th Trumpet. Thereafter, the 7 Bowls of Wrath are poured out. Armageddon will also take place during this time.

- This is followed by Jesus' triumphant return to Jerusalem.

- Next is the Millennium for 1,000 years.

- At the end of the Millennium, the earth will be cleansed.

- This is followed by Eternity.

Those of us who are still living will experience unprecedented violence and upheaval that the earth has never seen. The wars that this world has experienced will seem like pop-gun affairs compared to what is coming. The social upheaval and personal oppression we will experience will outweigh anything we have seen in the past.

The standard reaction most Christians have to these coming events is to minimize them, deny them, dismiss them or denounce them due to the Rapture. Let's briefly examine what each of these periods has to offer so you can decide if you are adequately prepared.

Individual Reflection or Group Discussion

1. Do you believe the Bible is the inspired Word of God?

2. Do you think the prophecy in the Bible is creative imagery or an account of things that are actually going to take place?

3. Do you think you will be around to experience the End Time events?

4. If you are, do you believe God will protect you from End Times events either through the Rapture or some other supernatural method?

Note: Everyone has an opinion. Opinions that have no basis or foundation carry little weight. Satan's primary weapon is deception and He is a master with it. His primary battleground is your head — your mind. When you answer these questions, please consider the basis on which you answer them.

Chapter 5
The Kickoff

"Demons were riding on Christians, but not in them, as was the case with non-Christians. It was clear all the believers had to do was stop agreeing with the demons riding on them to be free of them. The demons weakened quickly once they were questioned about their "root" mission. The demons power was rooted almost entirely in the power of deception. Captive Christians were wounded and guarded by demons of fear. These prisoners still had their swords and shields, but did not use them. Many were kept captive by only a few demons of fear. These Christians marched along submissively, although they could have easily freed themselves and probably done great damage to the entire horde of demons."

Notes from The Final Quest by Rick Joyner

"'No weapon formed against you shall prosper, and every tongue which rises against you in judgment you shall condemn. This is the heritage of the servants of the Lord, and their righteousness is from me,' says the Lord." Isaiah 54:17

Lesson Learned

I am standing in the middle of an ad-hoc church located in a deserted rural area. It appears to be an old barn which has been converted into a house of worship — to Satan. There are red pentagrams painted on the walls. There is a table filled with candles near a makeshift pulpit at the front of the room. A small stage has been built behind it with a ram's head hanging on the wall. There are children's clothes strewn everywhere. Outside there are several cow carcasses littering the landscape. There is what appears to be blood or red paint on the floor. Suddenly, from behind me a shot rings out, and I dive behind the pulpit.

Several days before I found myself diving for cover, my undersheriff, who was not known to be a particularly religious or spiritual man, had asked me to meet with him. I had a good relationship with this man. I respected him. I remember one of the first times I received a citizen's complaint over my actions in the field, this undersheriff had reached out to me and told me: "Terry, if you are not receiving complaints from the public, you probably are not doing your job. After all, we are not out there to entertain people. You will be upsetting as many people as you are helping."

I met with him in his office. The conversation went something like this:

Undersheriff: Terry, do you believe in Satan?

Me: Yes, I do.

Undersheriff: Do you know people worship him?

Me: I have read accounts of such activity as well as a biography from an alleged Satanist.

Undersheriff: Do you know people are involved in the occult?

Me: Yes

Undersheriff: Do you know there are witches and others who are involved in covens?

Me: This is getting creepy. What is your point?

Undersheriff: I have word from an informant that in the next week there will be some type of outdoor event that is to take place at (given location), and I want you to conduct surveillance and report back to me. The intelligence information I have received is that people from surrounding states will be attending this event, and it is mostly witches that will be attending.

Me: OK.

So for the next week, every evening I would drive out to this remote location looking for any signs of activity. On the third night, we hit the jackpot. Together with my partner and night-vision equipment, we observed approximately 100 people dancing and moving around a huge fire they had built. Leaving the SUV far behind, we snuck up to their vehicles on foot under the cover of darkness. We looked at the license plates and observed vehicles from a number of different states.

There wasn't much else we could do as I had not been directed to take any further action outside of confirming this event was taking place.

Lesson learned: There are people who worship the dark side and prefer the cover of darkness and secrecy to do it.

The next day I reported this to the undersheriff who gave me another assignment. He asked me to drive to another remote location that he had been given by a confidential informant who had advised him there was satanic worship taking place, and the worshippers were conducting sacrificial rituals.

The day after that meeting, I took a fellow deputy and good friend with me that was tough as nails. He was an ex-Ranger who had served two tours in Vietnam and was someone I would want standing next to me in a dark alley. Although I worked the "power-shift", which was 5pm-2am, I needed to explore this area during the day for obvious reasons; we needed to be able to see as much as possible.

The dirt road we turned onto from the paved county road quickly became a rough and rocky weed-grown mess several miles into our adventure. It seemed like we were going nowhere, which did not much matter to me because it was a beautiful summer morning. Just about the time we started talking about turning around and going back, my buddy noticed a structure in the far distance. We were already about 5 miles from the closest paved road.

As we drove toward the structure we noticed clothing and animal carcasses strewn on the sides of this old road. There were just a few items to begin with, but they increased in number the closer we got to this structure, which now looked to be an old barn. Finally, ahead of us several hundred yards away was the building. There was one problem, which was the rickety old bridge in front of us that spanned a washed-out dry creek bed — about 25 yards in length. There was no way I was taking the vehicle over this little bridge. We parked and walked the rest of the way.

I noticed in the dry creek bed a great number of garments, carcasses and animal skulls. I jumped in to examine them. The carcasses and skulls appeared to be from cows. The clothing, however, was exclusively children's clothing, and some of the items had what appeared to be red paint on them. This quickened my pulse as we approached the old barn. I stepped in not knowing what to expect. As I walked around and took pictures, I could hear the other deputy beginning to curse Satan and taunt him with Bible verses. We briefly discussed the fact that we could both feel and sense an uncomfortable presence there. This place was creepy. It was creepy to the point where I started talking to God out loud. I just wanted to get some pictures and get out of there. My friend had other ideas.

He decided he was going to desecrate this place of worship by tearing the place up a bit, then firing off a few rounds into the wall near the pentagrams — all the while quoting scripture. After picking myself up from behind the pulpit, I went over and insisted he put his gun away before he killed me. I had no idea that he had any strong religious convictions. We finally left, and none too soon for me.

I had the pictures developed and turned them over to my undersheriff, asking him if he would like me to return to the barn and burn it down. He politely thanked me for going out there, took the pictures, and instructed me to leave it alone. That is the last time he ever talked to me about the occult.

Lesson learned: There was a whole other world I knew very little about.

After these experiences I began to study several sources in an effort to understand the depth and realities of the occult in regards to how it would affect me at my job, as that is how I originally experienced this type of evil. People tell me today that in my major metropolitan area there are 448 cult groups and over 20,000 witches. If this is a close representation to what is happening in other urban areas, we have a serious problem which requires immediate and dramatic action.

As we move toward the end of this age, we should expect activity like this will increase.

Israel Becomes a Nation & Kicks off the Birth Pangs

The great majority of eschatologists agree that Israel re-establishing itself as a nation in 1948 had historical and prophetic relevance. After 2000 years of being scattered across the world, Israel became a nation once again in 1948. This is a major fulfillment of Old Testament prophecy and a primary sign that the end of this age was here.

> Deuteronomy 28:64 "Then the LORD will scatter you among all nations, from one end of the earth to the other. There you will worship other gods—gods of wood and stone, which neither you nor your fathers have known."

> Deuteronomy 30:3 "Then the LORD your God will restore your fortunes and have compassion on you and gather you again from all the nations where he scattered you."

> Ezekiel 36:24 "For I will take you out of the nations; I will gather you from all the countries and bring you back into your own land."

Ezekiel 37:21 "...and say to them. 'This is what the Sovereign LORD says: I will take the Israelites out of the nations where they have gone. I will gather them from all around and bring them back into their own land.'"

Ezekiel 36:8-12 "But you, O mountains of Israel, will produce branches and fruit for my people Israel, for they will soon come home. I am concerned for you and will look on you with favor; you will be plowed and sown, and I will multiply the number of people upon you, even the whole house of Israel. The towns will be inhabited and the ruins rebuilt. I will increase the number of men and animals upon you, and they will be fruitful and become numerous. I will settle people on you as in the past and will make you prosper more than before. Then you will know that I am the LORD. I will cause people, my people Israel, to walk upon you. They will possess you, and you will be their inheritance; you will never again deprive them of their children."

Isaiah 11:11-12 "In that day the Lord will reach out his hand a second time to reclaim the remnant that is left of his people from Assyria, from Lower Egypt, from Upper Egypt, from Cush, from Elam, from Babylonia, from Hamath and from the islands of the sea. He will raise a banner for the nations and gather the exiles of Israel; he will assemble the scattered people of Judah from the four quarters of the earth."

Isaiah 43:5-6 "Do not be afraid, for I am with you; I will bring your children from the east and gather you from the west. I will say to the north, 'Give them up!' and to the south, 'Do not hold them back.' Bring my sons from afar and my daughters from the ends of the earth."

Jeremiah 29:14 "I will be found by you, declares the LORD, and will bring you back from captivity. I will gather you from all the nations and places where I have banished you, declares the LORD, and will bring you back to the place from which I carried you into exile."

Jeremiah 30:3 "The days are coming, declares the LORD, when I will bring my people Israel and Judah back from captivity and restore them to the land I gave their forefathers to possess, says the LORD."

Amos 9:14-15 "I will bring back my exiled people Israel; they will rebuild the ruined cities and live in them. They will plant vineyards and drink their wine; they will make gardens and eat their fruit. I will plant Israel in their own land, never again to be uprooted from the land I have given them, says the LORD your God."

Let's see what Jesus had to say about those of us that have watched this come to pass.

Matthew 24:34 "I tell you the truth, this generation will certainly not pass away until all these things have happened."

All what things?

Individual Reflection or Group Discussion

Many people have had spectacular and supernatural experiences. For those who have, there are rare opportunities to talk about them in a safe and non-judgmental environment. Many people who have had supernatural experiences are reluctant to share these stories out of fear others will think they are crazy or that they should be locked up.

If you believe the Bible, you can expect there will be an increase in supernatural activities as we approach the end of this age.

1. Do you believe Satan exists?

2. Do you believe there are demons?

3. Do you think there are people who knowingly worship Satan?

4. Do you think there are witches and other people who are involved in occult activities?

5. Have you ever had any personal experiences in which you were quite sure Satan or his demons were present?

Chapter 6
The Beginning of the Birth Pangs

"Fear is the father of courage and the mother of safety."
Henry H. Tweedy

"I sought the Lord, and he answered me, and delivered me from all my fears." Psalm 34:4

Lesson Learned

It is 1977. I am newly married. I am the youngest person ever hired by this correctional facility. I am assigned to work with first-offenders in a boot-camp style program, which involves taking juvenile delinquents out in the community and cutting wood all day long followed by a highly structured program in the evening. I am new at this and have much to learn. The court–ordered youth do not want to be there. Many come from dysfunctional families in which there is very little accountability. Some of them are just plain old mean. They are not used to having other people tell them what to do.

The work breaks and meals during the day are at specifically scheduled times even down to the second. I am alone with 10 of these kids in a remote area long before cell phones existed. I have a radio in my van that connects me to the correctional facility. Sometimes it works. On this day a kid on my crew decided he was taking breaks when he wanted to. I directed him to continue to work, and he became angry. He cursed me, taunted me and threatened me. The rest of the group looked at me to see what I was going to do. I pulled this kid off to the side and out of view of the others. He had an axe in his hands. He turned toward me, stared at me and continued cursing me. I thought: "This is crazy. They have weapons, and I have nothing. Now what am I supposed to do?" Although I possessed the skills to deal with an armed assailant, I had no idea what the rules were for using force on these kids. I am looking into the eyes of hatred trying to figure out if this kid is going to swing the axe. I am filled with fear.

This kid finally calmed down after about five minutes of talking and went back to work. Later that day, I spoke to one of my mentors and a colleague about this situation. He was a tough ex-cop who always had a cigarette or a cup of coffee in his hand, and he had the demeanor of a drill sergeant. Heeding his advice, the next day I pulled this kid off into some woods away from the rest of the crew. I handed him an axe and then we had a brief exchange.

Him: What do you want me to do with this?

Me: Take your best shot.

Him: Huh?

Me: Take your best shot. It's just me and you. But here's the deal. As soon as I see that axe move, I am going to do to you what I should have done yesterday.

Him: What's that?

Me: You are about to find out.

Him: You're crazy. I'm going back to work.

Me: Yes, you are, and if you ever pull that crap again with me, you and I are going to be standing back here alone with a different outcome. Do you understand?

Him: Yes.

Me: Excuse me?

Him: Yes, sir.

Lesson learned: I was not prepared to deal with a situation like this so I did not know what to do. No one had told me or prepared me or trained me. There are some people who are so filled with rage, for whatever reason, they have little ability to control themselves. Anything that stands in the way of their liking pushes that rage button and off they go. Rage can be diminished through verbal de-escalation and can be controlled through the perception of superior power.

What Did Jesus Say About the End of this Age?

Let's look at what the Bible says about birth pangs, because in the best case scenario, this is what most Christians are going to have to figure out how to live through. The worst case is that Christians will be here through much of the Great Tribulation. The beginning of birth pangs will include, among other things: False Christs, War, Ethnic Conflict, Economic Warfare, Famine, Pestilence, & Earthquakes.

> Matthew 24 "Jesus left the temple and was walking away when his disciples came up to him to call his attention to its buildings. 'Do you see all these things?' he asked. 'I tell you the truth, not one stone here will be left on another; every one will be thrown down." As Jesus was sitting on the Mount of Olives, the disciples came to him privately. 'Tell us,' they said, "when will this happen, and what will be the sign of your coming and of the end of the age?" Jesus answered: 'Watch out that no one deceives you. For many will come in my name, claiming, 'I am the Christ,' and will deceive many. You will hear of wars and rumors of wars, but see to it that you are not alarmed. Such things must happen, but the end is still to come. Nation will rise against nation, and

kingdom against kingdom. There will be famines and earthquakes in various places. All these are the beginning of birth pains. 'Then you will be handed over to be persecuted and put to death, and you will be hated by all nations because of me. At that time many will turn away from the faith and will betray and hate each other, and many false prophets will appear and deceive many people. Because of the increase of wickedness, the love of most will grow cold, but he who stands firm to the end will be saved. And this gospel of the kingdom will be preached in the whole world as a testimony to all nations, and then the end will come. 'So when you see standing in the holy place 'the abomination that causes desolation,' spoken of through the prophet Daniel—let the reader understand— then let those who are in Judea flee to the mountains. Let no one on the roof of his house go down to take anything out of the house. Let no one in the field go back to get his cloak. How dreadful it will be in those days for pregnant women and nursing mothers! Pray that your flight will not take place in winter or on the Sabbath. For then there will be great distress, unequaled from the beginning of the world until now—and never to be equaled again. If those days had not been cut short, no one would survive, but for the sake of the elect those days will be shortened. At that time if anyone says to you, 'Look, here is the Christ!' or, 'There he is!' do not believe it. For false Christs and false prophets will appear and perform great signs and miracles to deceive even the elect—if that were possible. See, I have told you ahead of time. 'So if anyone tells you, 'There he is, out in the desert,' do not go out; or, 'Here he is, in the inner rooms,' do not believe it. For as lightning that comes from the east is visible even in the west, so will be the coming of the Son of Man. Wherever there is a carcass, there the vultures will gather. 'Immediately after the distress of those days 'the sun will be darkened, and the moon will not give its light; the stars will fall from the sky, and the heavenly bodies will be shaken.' 'At that time the sign of the Son of Man will appear in the sky, and all the nations of the earth will mourn. They will see the Son of Man coming on the clouds of the sky, with power and great glory. And he will send his angels with a loud trumpet call, and they will gather his elect from the four winds, from one end of the heavens to the other. 'Now learn this lesson from the fig tree: As soon as its twigs get tender and its leaves come out, you know that summer is near. Even so, when you see all these things, you know that it is near, right at the door. I tell you the truth, this generation will certainly not pass away until all these things have happened. Heaven and earth will pass away, but my words will never pass away. 'No one knows about that day or hour, not even the angels in heaven, nor the Son, but only the Father. As it was in the days of Noah, so it will be at the coming of the Son of Man. For in the days before the flood, people were eating and drinking, marrying and giving in marriage, up to the day Noah entered the ark; and they knew nothing about what would happen until the flood came and took them all away. That is how it will be at the coming of the Son of Man. Two men will be in the field; one will be taken and the other left. Two women will be grinding with a hand mill; one will be taken and the other left. 'Therefore keep watch, because you do not know on what day your Lord will come. But understand this: If the owner of the house had known at what time of night the thief was coming, he would have kept watch and would not have let his house be broken into. So you also must be ready, because the Son of Man will come at an hour when you do not expect him. 'Who then is the faithful and wise servant, whom the master has put in charge of the servants in his household to give them their food at the proper time? It will be good for that servant whose master finds him doing so when he returns. I tell you the truth, he will put him in charge of all his possessions. But suppose that servant is wicked and says to himself, 'My master is staying away a long time,' and he then begins to beat his fellow servants and to eat and drink with drunkards. The master of that servant will come on a day when he does not expect him and at an hour he is not aware of. He will cut him to pieces and assign him a place with the hypocrites, where there will be weeping and gnashing of teeth."

Mark 13 and Luke 21 also report this same exchange.

Mark 13 "As he was leaving the temple, one of his disciples said to him, 'Look, Teacher! What massive stones! What magnificent buildings!' 'Do you see all these great buildings?' replied Jesus. 'Not one stone here will be left on another; everyone will be thrown down.' As Jesus was sitting on the Mount of Olives opposite the temple, Peter, James, John and Andrew asked him privately, 'Tell us, when will these things happen? And what will be the sign that they are all about to be fulfilled?' Jesus said to them: 'Watch out that no one deceives you. Many will come in my name, claiming, 'I am he,' and will deceive many. When you hear of wars and rumors of wars, do not be alarmed. Such things must happen, but the end is still to come. Nation will rise against nation, and kingdom against kingdom. There will be earthquakes in various places, and famines. These are the beginning of birth pains. 'You must be on your guard. You will be handed over to the local councils and flogged in the synagogues. On account of me you will stand before governors and kings as witnesses to them. And the gospel must first be preached to all nations. Whenever you are arrested and brought to trial, do not worry beforehand about what to say. Just say whatever is given you at the time, for it is not you speaking, but the Holy Spirit. "Brother will betray brother to death, and a father his child. Children will rebel against their parents and have them put to death. All men will hate you because of me, but he who stands firm to the end will be saved. "When you see 'the abomination that causes desolation' standing where it does not belong—let the reader understand—then let those who are in Judea flee to the mountains. Let no one on the roof of his house go down or enter the house to take anything out. Let no one in the field go back to get his cloak. How dreadful it will be in those days for pregnant women and nursing mothers! Pray that this will not take place in winter, because those will be days of distress unequaled from the beginning, when God created the world, until now—and never to be equaled again. If the Lord had not cut short those days, no one would survive. But for the sake of the elect, whom he has chosen, he has shortened them. At that time if anyone says to you, 'Look, here is the Christ!' or, 'Look, there he is!' do not believe it. For false Christs and false prophets will appear and perform signs and miracles to deceive the elect—if that were possible. So be on your guard; I have told you everything ahead of time. 'But in those days, following that distress, 'the sun will be darkened, and the moon will not give its light;

the stars will fall from the sky, and the heavenly bodies will be shaken.' 'At that time men will see the Son of Man coming in clouds with great power and glory. And he will send his angels and gather his elect from the four winds, from the ends of the earth to the ends of the heavens. 'Now learn this lesson from the fig tree: As soon as its twigs get tender and its leaves come out, you know that summer is near. Even so, when you see these things happening, you know that it is near, right at the door. I tell you the truth, this generation will certainly not pass away until all these things have happened. Heaven and earth will pass away, but my words will never pass away. 'No one knows about that day or hour, not even the angels in heaven, nor the Son, but only the Father. Be on guard! Be alert! You do not know when that time will come. It's like a man going away: He leaves his house and puts his servants in charge, each with his assigned task, and tells the one at the door to keep watch. 'Therefore keep watch because you do not know when the owner of the house will come back—whether in the evening, or at midnight, or when the rooster crows, or at dawn. If he comes suddenly, do not let him find you sleeping. What I say to you, I say to everyone: 'Watch!' "

Luke 21: 5-36 "Some of his disciples were remarking about how the temple was adorned with beautiful stones and with gifts dedicated to God. But Jesus said, 'As for what you see here, the time will come when not one stone will be left on another; every one of them will be thrown down.' 'Teacher,' they asked, 'when will these things happen? And what will be the sign that they are about to take place?" He replied: 'Watch out that you are not deceived. For many will come in my name, claiming, 'I am he,' and, 'The time is near.' Do not follow them. When you hear of wars and revolutions, do not be frightened. These things must happen first, but the end will not come right away.' Then he said to them: 'Nation will rise against nation, and kingdom against kingdom. There will be great earthquakes, famines and pestilences in various places, and fearful events and great signs from heaven. 'But before all this, they will lay hands on you and persecute you. They will deliver you to synagogues and prisons, and you will be brought before kings and governors, and all on account of my name. This will result in your being witnesses to them. But make up your mind not to worry beforehand how you will defend yourselves. For I will give you words and wisdom that none of your adversaries will be able to resist or contradict. You will be betrayed even by parents, brothers, relatives and friends, and they will put some of you to death. All men will hate you because of me. But not a hair of your head will perish. By standing firm you will gain life. 'When you see Jerusalem being surrounded by armies, you will know that its desolation is near. Then let those who are in Judea flee to the mountains, let those in the city get out, and let those in the country not enter the city. For this is the time of punishment in fulfillment of all that has been written. How dreadful it will be in those days for pregnant women and nursing mothers! There will be great distress in the land and wrath against this people. They will fall by the sword and will be taken as prisoners to all the nations. Jerusalem will be trampled on by the Gentiles until the times of the Gentiles are fulfilled. 'There will be signs in the sun, moon and stars. On the earth, nations will be in anguish and perplexity at the roaring and tossing of the sea. Men will faint from terror, apprehensive of what is coming on the world, for the heavenly bodies will be shaken. At that time they will see the Son of Man coming in a cloud with power and great glory. When these things begin to take place, stand up and lift up your heads, because your redemption is drawing near.' He told them this parable: 'Look at the fig tree and all the trees. When they sprout leaves, you can see for yourselves and know that summer is near. Even so, when you see these things happening, you know that the kingdom of God is near. I tell you the truth, this generation will certainly not pass away until all these things have happened. Heaven and earth will pass away, but my words will never pass away. Be careful, or your hearts will be weighed down with dissipation, drunkenness and the anxieties of life, and that day will close on you unexpectedly like a trap. For it will come upon all those who live on the face of the whole earth. Be always on the watch, and pray that you may be able to escape all that is about to happen, and that you may be able to stand before the Son of Man.'"

The List

By examining the three reports of this exchange between Jesus and his inner circle, we can create a list of the things Jesus talked about coming to pass:

- Every stone of the temple will be thrown down. In this particular verse, most theologians believe Jesus was talking about the temple. The temple was destroyed by the Romans in 70 AD. In fact, some reports indicate the temple burned with such intensity that metal was melted.

- These events will come upon those who live on the face of the whole earth.

- There will be great deceit. Many will come claiming, "I am Christ". There will be false prophets who will perform great signs and miracles to deceive the elect. Since prophecy virtually guarantees an increase in false prophets, would you know how to spot one? What does a false prophet look like?

- Wars and rumors of wars. There were 16 million deaths as a result of WWI. There are 60 million deaths attributed to WWII. There has been mass slaughter of millions through ethnic cleansing.

- Nation will rise against nation. Kingdom will rise against kingdom.

- Brother will betray brother to death.

- A father will betray his child.

- Children will rebel against their parents and have them put to death.

- You will be betrayed by friends and relatives.

- Famines.

- Earthquakes. One report I read indicated there are more than 50 earthquakes a day. It seems like on any given day you can turn on the television and hear about floods, tornadoes, earthquakes or some other horrific natural occurrence causing death.

- You will be handed over to be persecuted and put to death. You will stand before governors and kings as witnesses. Over 3 million people have been martyred since Stephen. There will be an increase.

- You will be hated by all nations.

- Many will turn from the faith and will betray and hate each other. All men will hate you.

- There will be an increase in wickedness.

- The love of most will grow cold.

- There will be great distress.

- Men will faint in terror.

- At some point, the sun and moon will not give light, the stars will fall and heavenly bodies will be shaken. Nations will be in anguish and perplexity at the roaring and tossing of the sea.

- It will be like in the days of Noah. People will be eating, drinking and marrying. Think about that. It was bad enough in Noah's day that God decided He needed to start over.

Corroborating Evidence

2 Timothy 3:1-9 "But mark this: There will be terrible times in the last days. People will be lovers of themselves, lovers of money, boastful, proud, abusive, disobedient to their parents, ungrateful, unholy, without love, unforgiving, slanderous, without self-control, brutal, not lovers of the good, treacherous, rash, conceited,

lovers of pleasure rather than lovers of God— having a form of godliness but denying its power. Have nothing to do with them. They are the kind who worm their way into homes and gain control over weak-willed women, who are loaded down with sins and are swayed by all kinds of evil desires, always learning but never able to acknowledge the truth. Just as Jannes and Jambres opposed Moses, so also these men oppose the truth—men of depraved minds, who, as far as the faith is concerned, are rejected. But they will not get very far because, as in the case of those men, their folly will be clear to everyone."

Example in Matthew 15:1-9 "Then some Pharisees and teachers of the law came to Jesus from Jerusalem and asked, "Why do your disciples break the tradition of the elders? They don't wash their hands before they eat!" Jesus replied, "And why do you break the command of God for the sake of your tradition? For God said, 'Honor your father and mother' and 'Anyone who curses his father or mother must be put to death.' But you say that if a man says to his father or mother, 'Whatever help you might otherwise have received from me is a gift devoted to God,' he is not to 'honor his father' with it. Thus you nullify the word of God for the sake of your tradition. You hypocrites! Isaiah was right when he prophesied about you: "'These people honor me with their lips, but their hearts are far from me. They worship me in vain; their teachings are but rules taught by men.'"

2 Thessalonians 2:1-4 "Concerning the coming of our Lord Jesus Christ and our being gathered to him, we ask you, brothers, not to become easily unsettled or

alarmed by some prophecy, report or letter supposed to have come from us, saying that the day of the Lord has already come. Don't let anyone deceive you in any way, for (that day will not come) until the rebellion occurs and the man of lawlessness is revealed, the man doomed to destruction. He will oppose and will exalt himself over everything that is called God or is worshiped, so that he sets himself up in God's temple, proclaiming himself to be God."

1 Timothy 4 "The Spirit clearly says that in later times some will abandon the faith and follow deceiving spirits and things taught by demons. Such teachings come through hypocritical liars, whose consciences have been seared as with a hot iron. They forbid people to marry and order them to abstain from certain foods, which God created to be received with thanksgiving by those who believe and who know the truth. For everything God created is good, and nothing is to be rejected if it is received with thanksgiving, because it is consecrated by the word of God and prayer. If you point these things out to the brothers, you will be a good minister of Christ Jesus, brought up in the truths of the faith and of the good teaching that you have followed. Have nothing to do with godless myths and old wives' tales; rather, train yourself to be godly. For physical training is of some value, but godliness has value for all things, holding promise for both the present life and the life to come. This is a trustworthy saying that deserves full acceptance (and for this we labor and strive), that we have put our hope in the living God, who is the Savior of all men, and especially of those who believe. Command and teach these things. Don't let anyone look down on you because you

are young, but set an example for the believers in speech, in life, in love, in faith and in purity. Until I come, devote yourself to the public reading of Scripture, to preaching and to teaching. Do not neglect your gift, which was given you through a prophetic message when the body of elders laid their hands on you. Be diligent in these matters; give yourself wholly to them, so that everyone may see your progress. Watch your life and doctrine closely. Persevere in them, because if you do, you will save both yourself and your hearers."

2 Timothy 4:3-4 "For the time will come when men will not put up with sound doctrine. Instead, to suit their own desires, they will gather around them a great number of teachers to say what their itching ears want to hear. They will turn their ears away from the truth and turn aside to myths."

2 Timothy 3:10-15 "You, however, know all about my teaching, my way of life, my purpose, faith, patience, love, endurance, persecutions, sufferings—what kinds of things happened to me in Antioch, Iconium and Lystra, the persecutions I endured. Yet the Lord rescued me from all of them. In fact, everyone who wants to live a godly life in Christ Jesus will be persecuted, while evil men and impostors will go from bad to worse, deceiving and being deceived. But as for you, continue in what you have learned and have become convinced of, because you know those from whom you learned it, and how from infancy you have known the holy Scriptures, which are able to make you wise for salvation through faith in Christ Jesus."

2 Peter 3:3-4 "First of all, you must understand that in the last days scoffers will come, scoffing and following their own evil desires. They will say, 'Where is this 'coming' he promised? Ever since our fathers died, everything goes on as it has since the beginning of creation.'"

Isaiah 5:20 "Woe to those who call evil good and good evil, who put darkness for light and light for darkness, who put bitter for sweet and sweet for bitter."

The Days of Noah

Genesis 6 "When men began to increase in number on the earth and daughters were born to them, the sons of God saw that the daughters of men were beautiful, and they married any of them they chose. Then the LORD said, 'My Spirit will not contend with man forever, for he is mortal; his days will be a hundred and twenty years.' The Nephilim were on the earth in those days—and also afterward—when the sons of God went to the daughters of men and had children by them. They were the heroes of old, men of renown. The LORD saw how great man's wickedness on the earth had become, and that every inclination of the thoughts of his heart was only evil all the time. The LORD was grieved that he had made man on the earth, and his heart was filled with pain. So the LORD said, "I will wipe mankind, whom I have created, from the face of the earth—men and animals, and creatures that move along the ground, and birds of the air—for I am grieved that I have made them." But Noah found favor in the eyes of the LORD. This is the account of Noah. Noah was a righteous man, blameless among the people of his time, and he walked with God. Noah had three sons: Shem, Ham and Japheth. Now the earth was corrupt in God's sight and was full of violence. God saw how corrupt the earth had become, for all the people on earth had corrupted their ways. So God said to Noah, 'I am going to put an end to all people, for the earth is filled with violence because of them. I am surely going to destroy both them and the earth. So make yourself an ark of cypress wood; make rooms in it and coat it with pitch inside and out. This is how you are to build it: The ark is to be 450 feet long, 75 feet wide and 45 feet high. Make a roof for it and finish the ark to within 18 inches of the top. Put a door in the side of the ark and make lower, middle and upper decks. I am going to bring floodwaters on the earth to destroy all life under the heavens, every creature that has the breath of life in it. Everything on earth will perish. But I will establish my covenant with you, and you will enter the ark—you and your sons and your wife and your sons' wives with you. You are to bring into the ark two of all living creatures, male and female, to keep them alive with you. Two of every kind of bird, of every kind of animal and of every kind of creature that moves along the ground will come to you to be kept alive. You are to take every kind of food that is to be eaten and store it away as food for you and for them.' Noah did everything just as God commanded him."

The Critical Question

What are your plans for surviving all these things?

Go back and read that list again, and think about each and every one of the things on that list. Visualize yourself in the midst of that circumstance, situation or environment. What are you going to do? Do you have any idea how you will deal with each one of these issues? Have you given it any thought? Have you considered or accomplished any planning?

Jesus, while disclosing these things to the disciples, also said, "Pray that you may be able to escape all that is about to happen, and that you may be able to stand before the Son of Man."

Jesus' recommendation to pray that we might be able to escape these things would indicate things are going to be really horrible, also evidenced by the description that "there will be great distress, unequaled from the beginning of the world until now—and never to be equaled again." But, it also suggests these things are escapable.

There is a school of thought that places Christians in a protected "place" during these horrific events. That belief is based on the protection God gave the Israelites during the plagues He visited on Pharaoh and some verses in Revelation 12 which indicate protection from Satan. In fact, Jesus himself said, "But not a hair on your head will perish".

There is equal evidence that Christians will have to figure out a way to live through these things with the supernatural protection, wisdom, strength and common sense that God gave the people in Nehemiah, who worked diligently yet possessed weapons and employed strategies to defend against the enemy.

David was not spared of the trouble Saul gave him, but he survived Saul. Daniel faced the lion's den and survived. Moses faced opposition but was a great leader. The fiery furnace was prepared for Shadrach, Meshach, and Abednego. They killed Christ.

One strategy of dealing with these things is to simply take the hit, face the consequences and die. After all, as a Christian you are going to heaven to be with Jesus. Why suffer when heaven awaits you? You can do nothing, die and reap rewards in heaven based on your relationship with Jesus.

But if God created and wired you to be a Christian Shepherd, this will never happen. You will fight for the privilege to stay alive in an effort to bring others to the Kingdom of God through your influence, prayers and actions. You will rise to the call of Jude.

God did not wire everyone to be passive and complacent. In fact, I think we need to recognize that God hard wired people with intuition which is a God-given survival signal. He also gave us a strong instinct for survival – also known as the Fight or Flight Syndrome. Most people, when faced with death, fight for survival.

When I read all of the examples I have provided thus far and consider Hebrews 11 in its entirety, I believe there is a very strong Biblical case that if you have not died already you may have to figure out a way to live through it until Jesus comes to take you home.

Individual Reflection or Group Discussion

1. If you are alive when these things begin to come to pass, how do you plan on dealing with them?

2. Will God rapture you out of here before it gets too bad?

3. Will God protect you as He did the Israelites?

4. Will you have to figure out a way to survive it and live through it, combining your faith with His supernatural provision?

Chapter 7
The Increased and Hard Labor Pangs

"There are all kinds of devices intended for the protection and preservation of countries: Defensive barriers, forts, trenches, and the like. But prudent minds have as a natural gift one safeguard which is the common possession of all, and this applies especially to the dealings of democracies. What is the safeguard? Skepticism. This you must preserve. This you must retain. If you can keep this, you need fear no harm."

Demosthenes

"You who live in the shelter of the Most High, who abide in the shadow of the Almighty, will say to the Lord, 'My refuge and my fortress; my God in whom I trust.' You will not fear the terror of the night, or the arrow that flies by day, or the pestilence that stalks in darkness, or the destruction that wastes at noonday. Because you have made the Lord your refuge, the Most High your dwelling place, no evil shall befall you, no scourge come near your tent. For he will command his angels concerning you to guard you in all your ways. On their hands they will bear you up, so that you will not dash your foot against a stone." Psalm 91:1-2, 5-6, & 9-12

Lesson Learned

An armory has been broken into in another part of the state. A number of M-16 rifles were stolen with a large amount of ammunition. Several weeks later a group of people appear in my jurisdiction and are reportedly looking to sell some weapons. An officer who is an employee of the department I work for is also moonlighting as a bouncer at a local bar. While working at the bar, he makes a connection with one of the members of this group.

This officer asked me and another officer to come to a meeting he would arrange with this group in an effort to buy some of these weapons. There were unsubstantiated rumors on the street that M-16 rifles might be part of the weapons included in this sale. Thinking there might be a tie-in to the armory burglary, we were eager to proceed. The plan was for one of us to act as an interested buyer and the other to be hidden within the room the meeting was to take place, which was the restaurant that was attached to this bar. The restaurant, which only operated during daytime hours, would be closed while we met. I was the officer that would be in uniform. If a sale was consummated, I was to spring from my hiding place and arrest everyone.

The meeting was arranged at the bar/restaurant. The restaurant was separated from the bar by a wall and a door. The meeting would take place in the closed restaurant. I was given a very specific time to arrive through a back door to meet with the bouncer who had arranged this sting. The officer posing as the interested buyer would come in through the front door of the bar which was open for business. This plainclothes undercover officer would then join the others who were also meeting in the bar. They would all then move to the closed restaurant for the actual sale of the weapons.

On the arranged date I arrived on time, went through the back door and began to look for a place to hide. I was told I would be given at least 30 minutes lead time before the meeting took place in order to find a hiding spot and get comfortable. The back door of the restaurant had been left open for me. The restaurant was dark. I had only been there for a few minutes when suddenly the whole group came through the adjoining door to the bar. I immediately froze in the shadows of the restaurant not wanting to reveal myself in uniform. I slid under a table and began to slowly crawl towards the back of the restaurant. I got myself into a location where I could see this group of people who were now sitting at a table. Our officer/bouncer was there, but my partner who was posing as the interested buyer was not. Although these types of undercover operations never quite go as planned, something about this was wrong.

Why would this officer/bouncer ask me to show up in uniform, give me the wrong time, or walk into the restaurant with these guys so early? Where was our undercover "buyer"? I had heard rumor about this officer/bouncer's behavior. There were local criminal elements that questioned his behavior and found it not to be congruent with that of an officer of the law. But that kind of talk can easily come and go in the world of cops.

I edged close enough to hear the group talking about selling some weapons when suddenly the officer/bouncer got up and headed for a wall flipping on the lights! So here I am, in uniform, amongst a group of criminals allegedly selling stolen automatic weapons with a questionable officer who gave me faulty information who has suddenly turned all the lights on. I am grossly outnumbered. I cannot call for back-up for fear they will hear me. I am convinced I am being set up. I quickly look for anyplace in the restaurant I can crawl to that has shadows that will conceal me. I managed to work my way to a closet which had a staircase that lead up into the attic of the building. I spent the next two hours up there praying and trying to figure out how I was going to get out of this. My radio had no signal. The voices below finally subsided, and I left.

The next day, this discussion took place:

Officer/bouncer: What happened to you last night?

Me: I was there just as we had arranged.

Officer/bouncer: I didn't see you.

Me: Why would you have? I was hiding. What happened to our undercover officer? Why didn't you bring him into the restaurant with the rest of the group?

Officer/bouncer: He never showed up.

I knew that was not true since the "buyer" officer and I had met in the parking lot of this establishment ahead of time for a quick briefing. I had watched him walk into the bar.

Lesson learned: Betrayal is a horrible thing to experience. Things are not always what they appear to be on the surface. Be careful where you put your trust.

> John 2:23-25 "Now while he was in Jerusalem at the Passover Festival, many people saw the signs he was performing and believed in his name. But Jesus would not entrust himself to them, for he knew all people. He did not need any testimony about mankind, for he knew what was in each person."

Even Jesus was careful about who he trusted. He knew that some of those proclaiming His name would later support his crucifixion. Jesus knew the truth of an Old Testament verse.

> Jeremiah 17:9 "The heart is deceitful above all things and beyond cure. Who can understand it?"

The Increased Labor Pangs

Let's look at what the Bible says about Birth Pangs, because in the best case scenario, this is what most Christians are going to have to figure out how to live through. The worst case is that Christians will be here through much of the Great Tribulation. Birth Pangs will not be stopped. They will increase in frequency and intensity until all of these things come to pass. A seven year period of Increased and Hard Labor Pangs can be broken down into 3.5 year periods. The first three and a half years of Increased Labor Pangs will include Counterfeit Worldwide Peace & Safety, The Great Falling Away and The Great Harvest.

Counterfeit Worldwide Peace & Safety

> 1 Thessalonians 5:1-3 "Now, brothers and sisters, about times and dates we do not need to write to you, for you know very well that the day of the Lord will come like a thief in the night. While people are saying, 'Peace and safety,' destruction will come on them suddenly, as labor pains on a pregnant woman, and they will not escape."
>
> Matthew 24:37-39 "As it was in the days of Noah, so it will be at the coming of the Son of Man. For in the days before the flood, people were eating and drinking, marrying and giving in marriage, up to the day Noah entered the ark; and they knew nothing about what would happen until the flood came and took them all away. That is how it will be at the coming of the Son of Man."

The Great Falling Away

> 2 Thessalonians 2:3 "Don't let anyone deceive you in any way, for that day will not come until the rebellion occurs and the man of lawlessness is revealed, the man doomed to destruction."
>
> Matthew 24:10-12 "At that time many will turn away from the faith and will betray and hate each other, and many false prophets will appear and deceive many

people. Because of the increase of wickedness, the love of most will grow cold."

The Great Harvest

Matthew 24:14 "And this gospel of the kingdom will be preached in the whole world as a testimony to all nations, and then the end will come."

Revelation 7:9 "After this I looked, and there before me was a great multitude that no one could count, from every nation, tribe, people and language, standing before the throne and before the Lamb. They were wearing white robes and were holding palm branches in their hands."

Revelation 14:15 "Then another angel came out of the temple and called in a loud voice to him who was sitting on the cloud, 'Take your sickle and reap, because the time to reap has come, for the harvest of the earth is ripe.'"

Key events occurring during the Increased Labor Pangs include:

- The Antichrist coming forth with deceitful diplomacy: Daniel 8:23 & 25, Daniel 9:27, Daniel 11:21 & 34
- The Evil 10-Nation Federation: Revelation 17:3 & 12
- The False Prophet rising up: Revelation 13:11-18
- The Middle East and Israel having a false peace: Daniel 9:27
- The city of Babylon being re-established: Revelation 17 & 18
- The Jerusalem Temple being rebuilt: Revelation

11:1 & 2

But wait! There's more! You may not be out of here yet!

The Middle of the 7 Year Period

Key Events related to the middle of this seven year period include:

- The Antichrist demanding worship: Daniel 9:27, Matthew 24:15, Second Thessalonians 2:2-4 & Revelation 13:11-18

- The Two Witnesses coming forth: Revelation 11:3-6 & Malachi 4:5

- The 144,000 Israelites being sealed: Revelation 7:1-8

- Michael standing up against Satan: Revelation 12:7-12 & Daniel 12:1

- All Nations gathered against Jerusalem: Zechariah 12:3 & Zechariah 14:2

- An increased martyrdom among Christians: Revelation 6:11, Revelation13:7, Revelation16:6, Revelation 17:6 & Revelation18:24

- Israel's strength being shattered: Daniel 12:7

But wait! There's more! You may not be out of here yet!

The Hard Labor Pangs

During the Great Tribulation, the restraint of the Holy Spirit, which has been active, is removed. Without this restraint, the world will experience a time of previously inconceivable lawlessness and unrighteousness.

Three and a half years of Hard Labor Pangs include the Great Tribulation, the Armageddon Campaign, the Seven Seals of Revelation 6 and the Seven Trumpets of Revelation 8 & 9.

Revelation describes the Seven Seals

1st Seal: The Antichrist's conquest of political and economic aggression.

> Revelation 13:16-18 "He also forced everyone, small and great, rich and poor, free and slave, to receive a mark on his right hand or on his forehead, so that no one could buy or sell unless he had the mark, which is the name of the beast or the number of his name. This calls for wisdom. If anyone has insight, let him calculate the number of the beast, for it is man's number. His number is 666."

> Revelation 14:9-11 "A third angel followed them and said in a loud voice: 'If anyone worships the beast and his image and receives his mark on the forehead or on the hand, he, too, will drink of the wine of God's fury, which has been poured full strength into the cup of his wrath. He will be tormented with burning sulfur in the presence of the holy angels and of the Lamb. And the smoke of their torment rises forever and ever. There is no rest day or night for those who worship the beast and his image, or for anyone who receives the mark of his name.'"

2nd Seal: Military conflict, world war and violence among men.

3rd Seal: Economic crisis and famine.

4th Seal: 25% of the earth's population dies by sword, famine, plague and wild beasts of the earth.

5th Seal: The Martyrs ask the Lord for judgment and justice regarding their own deaths and are told more of their brothers that are still alive will be martyred first as they were.

6th Seal: Great earthquake, the sun turns black, the moon turns red and stars fall to the earth.

> Revelation 7:13-17 "Then one of the elders asked me, 'These in white robes—who are they, and where did they come from?' I answered, 'Sir, you know.' And he said, "These are they who have come out of the great tribulation; they have washed their robes and made them white in the blood of the Lamb. Therefore, 'they are before the throne of God and serve him day and night in his temple; and he who sits on the throne will spread his tent over them. Never again will they hunger; never again will they thirst. The sun will not beat upon them, nor any scorching heat. For the Lamb at the center of the throne will be their shepherd; he will lead them to springs of living water. And God will wipe away every tear from their eyes.'"

Implicit in this exchange between John and an elder is that suffering took place and believers were in danger, under threat, hungry, thirsty, in scorching heat, and crying.

This Seal specifically refers to a 144,000 that are sealed from the Tribe of Israel. To have the seal is to belong to God. There is some difference of opinion as to whether this passage is to be taken literally or figuratively. Figuratively, the 144,000 is a symbol of the Church. If you are a Christian, this is you.

7th Seal: Releases the Seven Trumpets

But wait! There's more! You may not be out of here yet!

Revelation describes the Seven Trumpets

1st Trumpet: Hail and fire mixed with blood which burns up a third of the world's plant life.

2nd Trumpet: Something described similar to a meteor hits the oceans causing the destruction of one third of all sea life, ships and the sea itself.

3rd Trumpet: Similar to the 2nd Trumpet, this affects one third of the rivers and springs, and people die as a result.

4th Trumpet: One third of the moon and stars and sun are affected to the point that one third of the day and night is without light.

5th Trumpet: Locusts are given the power of scorpions to torture but not kill those who do not have the seal of God on their foreheads. The agony is so great the victims of these locusts will seek death. The physical description of these locusts is right out of a sci-fi horror movie.

6th Trumpet: An army of two hundred million mounted troops are released and use fire, smoke and sulfur to kill one third of all mankind.

Between the 6th and 7th Trumpets, living Christians are sealed and appear with God. John saw "a great multitude no one could count, from every nation, tribe, people and language" standing before the throne of God worshiping. They are in white robes. John is told, "These are they who have come out of the great tribulation."

> Revelation 9:20-21 "The rest of mankind that were not killed by these plagues still did not repent of the work of their hands; they did not stop worshiping demons, and idols of gold, silver, bronze, stone and wood—idols that cannot see or hear or walk. Nor did they repent of their murders, their magic arts, their sexual immorality or their thefts."

7th Trumpet: Releases the Seven Angels with Seven Plagues, or Bowls of Wrath. It also signifies the beginning of the 2nd Coming.

Now, as a Christian, you are more than likely out of here!

As the 2nd Coming procession begins, first in the air, then across the land and finally into Jerusalem and the Mount of Olives there will be three types of people on earth. The Redeemed are raptured. The Reprobates who took the mark of the Beast will soon be judged and killed. The Resistors are those who refused to worship the Antichrist.

The Rapture of the Saints

The Rapture of the Saints (Christian believers) is strongly indicated at the 7th Trumpet, as presented above. The bottom line is that it must occur before, or as, the 2nd Coming Procession begins.

> 1 Corinthians 15:51-53 "Listen, I tell you a mystery: We will not all sleep, but we will all be changed— in a flash, in the twinkling of an eye, at the last trumpet. For the trumpet will sound, the dead will be raised imperishable, and we will be changed. For the perishable must clothe itself with the imperishable, and the mortal with immortality."

> 1 Thessalonians 4:13-18 "Brothers, we do not want you to be ignorant about those who fall asleep, or to grieve like the rest of men, who have no hope. We believe that Jesus died and rose again and so we believe that God will bring with Jesus those who have fallen asleep in him. According to the Lord's own word, we tell you that we who are still alive, who are left till the coming of the Lord, will certainly not precede those who have fallen asleep. For the Lord himself will come down from heaven, with a loud command, with the voice of the archangel and with the trumpet call of God, and the dead in Christ will rise first. After that, we who are still alive and are left will be caught up together with them in the clouds to meet the Lord in the air. And so we will be with the Lord forever. Therefore encourage each other with these words."

Many good people disagree on the timing of this event. Most serious scholars agree it must occur before the Second Coming of Christ.

The 7 Bowls of Wrath

The 7 Bowls of wrath (or plagues) are unleashed on the Antichrist Empire. Jesus returns to Jerusalem and the Great Harvest continues.

Revelation describes the Seven Bowls:

1st Bowl: Ugly and painful sores break out on those with the mark of the beast.

2nd Bowl: The sea becomes like blood and everything living thing in it dies.

3rd Bowl: The rivers and springs follow suit.

4th Bowl: The sun heats up to the point of scorching people.

5th Bowl: There is great darkness and some type of intensification of the sores.

6th Bowl: The Euphrates River dries up, and the armies are gathered for the battle of Armageddon.

7th Bowl: An earthquake beyond what history has ever experienced. Hundred pound hailstones fall from the sky.

Individual Reflection or Group Discussion

The eschatology experts cannot agree on what role the United States plays in the End Times and the Bible certainly does not make it clear. Some experts believe the US is the Beast. Others believe the Beast to be a revived Roman Empire. Wouldn't it be nice if the United States was a safe haven for Christians from around the world?

Regardless of when these things take place, please consider several questions:

1. What role do you think the United States will play in End Time prophecy?

2. Regardless of when the Rapture takes place, on a continuum headed towards the Second Coming, things will generally get worse. What things do you see happening throughout the world today that indicates things are getting worse?

3. There is reference that those who have the seal of God on their foreheads will be protected as evidenced at the 5th Trumpet found in Revelation 9:1-11. In fact, the ensuing five months will be so bad for those who do not have the seal of God that they will seek death but not be able to find it. Do you believe that Christians will be spared of all the woes that are coming? To what degree?

Chapter 8
The Promises

"The People are the ultimate guardians of their own liberty."

Thomas Jefferson

"God is our refuge and strength, an ever-present help in trouble. Therefore we will not fear, though the earth give way and the mountains fall into the heart of the sea, though its waters roar and foam and the mountains quake with their surging." Psalm 46:1-3

Lessons Learned

It is a cold September late in the evening, and I am in a patrol car. The radio comes alive with a call from my dispatcher who assigns me a hot call. I flip on the lights and siren and speed off into the night. Someone is in trouble and needs help. I am speeding to the location on a deserted interstate traveling close to 100 miles per hour. I come to a bridge and the headlights reveal a white frost in front of me. This bridge has a curve in it. As soon as I begin to turn the wheel I start to lose control of the vehicle. It fishtails one direction and then another. I know I am losing control and have an immediate adrenaline rush. I yell, "Jesus, help me!" The vehicle suddenly straightens out as if the road is dry. I get off the bridge and am stunned. I thank Jesus for saving me.

Lesson learned: God is listening, and He honors what his children ask of Him.

The Hopeful Promises of Jesus' Discourse

If we go back and look at the three chapters of the Bible where Jesus is talking to His inner circle about the End Times, there is tremendous hope and some great advice He gives. Let's examine those things.

- The gospel will be preached throughout the whole world.

Revelation 14:6-7 "Then I saw another angel flying in midair, and he had the eternal gospel to proclaim to those who live on the earth—to every nation, tribe, language and people. He said in a loud voice, 'Fear God and give him glory, because the hour of his judgment has come. Worship him who made the heavens, the earth, the sea and the springs of water.'"

Joel 2:28 "And afterward, I will pour out my Spirit on all people. Your sons and daughters will prophesy, your old men will dream dreams, your young men will see visions."

- Jesus shortens these days for the elect. If he didn't shorten them, no one would survive.

Who are the Elect?

"If those days had not been cut short, no one would survive, but for the sake of the elect those days will be shortened."

"For false Christs and false prophets will appear and perform great signs and miracles to deceive even the elect—if that were possible."

"And he will send his angels with a loud trumpet call, and

they will gather his elect from the four winds, from one end of the heavens to the other."

If you look at the mentions of the term "elect" in the Bible, you will find that none of them refer to Israel or the Jewish people. All mentions refer to Believers or Jesus himself.

- Jesus will appear on the clouds of the sky with power and great glory. Can you imagine what this will look like after the world has been cast into darkness for a period of time?

- He will send his angels with a loud trumpet call, and they will gather his elect from the four winds from one end of the heavens to the other.

- Jesus promises if we are arrested and persecuted that all we have to do is rely on the Holy Spirit who will give us the right words to respond with and that no person will be able to refute, resist or contradict.

- Those that stand firm will be saved.

- Heaven and earth will pass away, but Jesus' words will never pass away.

- Not a hair on your head will perish.

The Advice Jesus Gives in His Discourse

- Stand firm.

- Do not be deceived by false prophets or a false Christ. Don't let anyone deceive you. Do not follow them.

- Those in Judea should flee to the mountains. If you

are in the city – get out. Take nothing with you. Leave immediately. Pray that your flight will not take place in winter or on the Sabbath.

- When you see these things take place, you will know the time of Jesus return is very near.

- Be vigilant, stand guard, be ready and stay alert. You will not know what day the Lord will come. Do not let Jesus find you "sleeping".

- If you are arrested for your faith, do not be worried about what to say.

- Do not be alarmed by wars, rumors of wars and revolutions.

- These days will be unparallel to anything this world has ever seen.

- Watch!

Matthew 16:1-4 "The Pharisees and Sadducees came to Jesus and tested him by asking him to show them a sign from heaven. He replied, "When evening comes, you say, 'It will be fair weather, for the sky is red,' and in the morning, 'Today it will be stormy, for the sky is red and overcast.' You know how to interpret the appearance of the sky, but you cannot interpret the signs of the times. A wicked and adulterous generation looks for a miraculous sign, but none will be given it except the sign of Jonah.' Jesus then left them and went away."

- Pray that you might be able to escape all of this. Implicit in this suggestion is the notion that you may be able to escape all that is about to happen.

- When these things begin to take place, stand up and lift up your heads, because your redemption is drawing near.

Acts 3:19-21 "Repent, then, and turn to God, so that your sins may be wiped out, that times of refreshing may come from the Lord, and that he may send the Christ, who has been appointed for you—even Jesus. He must remain in heaven until the time comes for God to restore everything, as he promised long ago through his holy prophets."

Luke 21:34 "Be careful, or your hearts will be weighed down with carousing, drunkenness and the anxieties of life, and that day will close on you suddenly like a trap."

Individual Reflection or Group Discussion

The focus of this book is not to explain or describe all the details that surround the End Times. Nor is it to convince you that these things are going to take place. You may choose to believe these things are going to take place or ignore them. Most Christians believe we are living in the End Times, and chronologically, we are experiencing the Birth Pangs Jesus spoke of.

The world will not escape any of the things you have just read about. Prophecy will come to pass. There is nothing that is going to thwart God's sovereignty or the coming of these things. No one seems to agree on the timing of the rapture, except that it is sometime before the Second Coming of Christ. There is strong evidence that it occurs at the Seventh Trumpet. If this is the case, there are a significant number of ugly things that Christians are going to have to live through. However, very few Christians have given this any thought. Will they have access to the supernatural power and wisdom of God? Yes, they will. From the mouth of Jesus come clear instructions about how to live through it.

Consider practical things you can do based on the advice Jesus gives.

Example: Jesus said if you are in the city – get out. Take nothing with you. Leave immediately. Pray that your flight will not take place in winter or on the Sabbath.

This makes sense for several reasons. In the event of mass civil disobedience, riots, war or other types of disturbances – it makes sense to leave mass populated areas. Urban areas are the most logical places for the enemy because they provide the biggest bang for the buck.

Also, if you believe that your own government at some point will come against you, urban areas will be the easiest for them to control large numbers of people. This could be a legitimate fear based on the fact that evil most often manifests itself through people. It is hard to imagine that free people will submit to many of the things described in the End Times outside of some type of mass government coercion.

There are approximately 2.2 million active duty and reserve people in the US Military. There are approximately 700,000 sworn law enforcement officers in the United States. Add some administrative people and you have a total of approximately 3 million people that the US government can utilize to enforce orders given the general population or to control their movements.

If what Jesus said has a possibility of manifesting itself through any type of massive government effort, an escape plan out of the city along less-traveled routes into a rural area would be prudent along with some thought as to where you might stay. Why? Rural areas will be of less concern for quite some time in such a scenario. Formulating an emergency travel plan costs you nothing except time.

Write down three practical things you can do based on the advice Jesus gives.

Chapter 9
The Master List

For your convenience, here is a master list of the things that will come to pass. As you read through it please consider what your plans are for dealing with them. Ultimately, all Christians will share eternity together in a new heaven on a new earth.

- Great deceit. Many will come claiming, "I am Christ". There will be false prophets who will perform great signs and miracles to deceive the elect.
- Wars and rumors of wars.
- Nation will rise against nation. Kingdom will rise against kingdom.
- Brother will betray brother to death.
- A Father will betray his child.
- Children will rebel against their parents and have them put to death.
- You will be betrayed by friends and relatives.
- Famines.
- Earthquakes.

- You will be handed over to be persecuted and put to death.

- You will stand before governors and kings as witnesses.

- You will be hated by all nations.

- Many will turn from the faith and will betray and hate each other. All men will hate you.

- There will be an increase in wickedness.

- The love of most will grow cold.

- There will be great distress.

- Men will faint in terror.

- The sun and moon will not give light, the stars will fall and heavenly bodies will be shaken. Nations will be in anguish and perplexity at the roaring and tossing of the sea.

- It will be like in the days of Noah.

- Counterfeit Worldwide Peace & Safety.

- The Great Falling Away.

- The Great Harvest.

- The Antichrist coming forth with deceitful diplomacy.

- The Evil 10-Nation Federation.

- The False Prophet rising up.
- The Middle East and Israel having a false peace.
- The city of Babylon being re-established.
- The Jerusalem Temple being rebuilt.
- The Antichrist demanding worship.
- The Two Witnesses coming forth.
- The 144,000 Israelites being sealed.
- Michael standing up against Satan.
- All Nations gathered against Jerusalem.
- An increased martyrdom among Christians.
- Israel's strength being shattered.
- A time of previously inconceivable lawlessness and unrighteousness.

1st Seal: The Antichrist's conquest of political and economic aggression.

2nd Seal: Military conflict, world war and violence among men.

3rd Seal: Economic crisis and famine.

4th Seal: 25% of the earth's population dies by sword, famine, plague and wild beasts of the earth.

5th Seal: The Martyrs ask the Lord for judgment and justice regarding their own deaths and are told more of their brothers that are still alive will be martyred first, as they were.

6th Seal: Great earthquake, the sun turns black, the moon turns red and stars fall to the earth.

7th Seal: Releases the Seven Trumpets

1st Trumpet: Hail and fire mixed with blood which burns up a third of the world's plant life.

2nd Trumpet: Something described similar to a meteor hits the oceans causing the destruction of one third of all sea life, ships and the sea itself.

3rd Trumpet: Similar to the 2nd Trumpet, this affects one third of the rivers and springs, and people die as a result.

4th Trumpet: One third of the moon and stars and sun are affected to the point that one third of the day and night is without light.

5th Trumpet: Locusts are given the power of scorpions to torture, but not kill those who do not have the seal of God on their foreheads. The agony is so great the victims of these locusts will seek death.

6th Trumpet: An army of two hundred million mounted troops are released and use fire, smoke and sulfur to kill one third of all mankind.

Between the 6th and 7th Trumpets living Christians are sealed and appear with God. The Rapture has taken place.

If you have not been saved and redeemed, you will further experience these things.

7th Trumpet: Releases the Seven Angels with Seven Plagues, or Bowls of Wrath. It also signifies the beginning of the 2nd Coming.

1st Bowl: Ugly and painful sores break out on those with the mark of the beast.

2nd Bowl: The Sea becomes like blood and everything living thing in it dies.

3rd Bowl: The rivers and springs follow suit.

4th Bowl: The sun heats up to the point of scorching people.

5th Bowl: There is great darkness and some type of intensification of the sores.

6th Bowl: The Euphrates River dries up and the armies are gathered for the battle of Armageddon.

7th Bowl: An earthquake beyond what history has ever experienced. Hundred pound hailstones fall from the sky.

SECTION 3

RIGHTEOUS ANGER

Chapter 10
The Anger of God

"The People must fight for their laws as for their walls."
Heraclitus

"When I called, you answered me; you made me bold and stouthearted." Psalm 138:3

Lessons Learned

There was an alleged private casino I kept hearing about through various sources in my jurisdiction. I always wondered if it really existed. Gambling was illegal, and there were no casinos operating within the state at that time. Finally, I was given a location of this alleged casino by an informant. It was located in a rural area. For the next several months, my partner and I conducted surveillance on this location and recorded the vehicle license plates that were present. We also kept track of which nights seemed to be the most active. Upon checking the license plates registrations, we discovered ranking officials from local government, school district officials, prominent business owners and people from Illinois among those people frequenting this house.

Most of the activity seemed to take place after dark and into the early hours of the morning. Because the location was in a remote rural area with several dogs roaming around, it was impossible to sneak a peek through the windows to see what was going on. We needed some type of confirmation that gambling was actually taking place. We devised a plan.

We had a uniformed officer go to this residence during the day and knock on the front door. He was pretending to be looking for someone that he had civil papers to serve upon. It was just a ruse. We were hoping that if someone answered the door, our officer might get a glimpse of some gambling paraphernalia in the house, which was also illegal, and would corroborate the information we already had. This would justify a search warrant. We were lucky because the officer observed several classic gaming tables just inside the front door when the occupant answered his knock.

Knowing the people who were frequenting this casino, we were very selective in who we shared this information with. We obtained a search warrant which was signed by a judge who we felt was trustworthy. We hand-picked the officers who would be involved in serving the search warrant. We purposefully served this search warrant on a night that we knew the casino would be busy. We gathered and briefed the other officers and headed out to the casino. Upon our arrival, the first thing I noticed was that there were only a few cars there. I began to consider calling the whole thing off and waiting for another night when there was more activity and more prominent attendees.

As we crept up toward the residence in our vehicles, one of the officers driving another car suddenly turned his emergency lights on tipping off everyone in the residence we were there. I had no choice now but to serve this search warrant, and quickly. I thought it was odd for this officer to turn on his emergency lights under these circumstances.

We discovered and confiscated all the gaming paraphernalia and tables along with the money on the table. There were three people playing poker along with the "proprietor" of the casino who must have weighed in at about 300 pounds. He was not happy and generally complained while we confiscated evidence and took inventory of those items we seized. We identified the people playing poker and sent them home as they were not of any significance to us — at least not compared to the people we knew had been playing there.

I was the last officer to leave the house that night. As I walked toward the door, the "proprietor" stopped me and told me, "You think gambling is such a big deal, just remember every time you and your family put your head on your pillows at night you are gambling." I interpreted this as a threat. In what seemed to be an almost immediate involuntary reaction, I found myself with one hand on this man's throat and had him sandwiched up against a wall. My other hand now had my handgun in it, and it was placed directly under his chin. My response: "You can threaten me all you want, but don't you ever threaten my family!" I then went on to inform him that if anything happened to a family member of mine, his life would become a living nightmare. I gave him a long list of how this would be accomplished followed by a reminder that it is not really that hard to pick someone off from a distance with a decent rifle and scope. I released my grip and left.

Obviously, there were some things that did not add up. Where were all the people we had discovered over all those months? Why weren't they present on what had become the busiest night of the week for this casino? Why did the officer turn on his emergency lights? Why did the proprietor feel the need to threaten me? The next few weeks got very interesting. The top law enforcement official in my department called me into his office along with my partner, which was a very rare event. We were admonished for busting this casino — albeit gently. This man was well aware that we were two of his more aggressive officers. This meeting made me even more curious as to what was going on.

Over the next two weeks, I found several threatening notes on the windshield of my car at my house. They ceased immediately after I told several of my informants that the "proprietor" of the casino had given me the names of people who regularly played at the casino. I began to dig deeper and ended up in a meeting with an FBI agent. He revealed there were rumors that our jurisdiction was actually a "playground" for part of the Chicago crime underworld. When things would heat up for some of these individuals in Chicago and they needed to disappear for a while, they would come to our jurisdiction to cool off. They would be involved in a variety of activities including the casino. This agent also informed me who was allegedly coordinating these activities — a local businessman. The FBI had been unable to substantiate anything.

Over the course of the next year, I had several officers outside of my jurisdiction approach me at professional conferences asking me questions about this local businessman. This lead to several clandestine meetings in which a very small group of officers from different jurisdictions began to share information about this businessman and investigate leads. We began to suspect he might have relationships that went directly to state government. Ultimately I shared this information with the FBI agent I had spoken to. He forthrightly suggested that if this man was involved in criminal activities that involved criminal underworld elements, he was skilled enough to cover it up. The agent went on to inform me if this businessman was able to accomplish all of this because of the relationships he had with officials in government, it would be very difficult to uncover. This agent had not been able to uncover any direct evidence – even though there was plenty of circumstantial evidence and plenty of rumors.

The FBI agent was not willing to go out on a limb. He wanted a solid case. The agent eventually made a case against the businessman but not for any of the activities suggested here. My recollection is that it was a tax case.

As the years slid by, I was told that I was the only officer still alive of that little group of officers that met secretly throughout the state. They all died. One in a house fire, another in a car accident and several of them committed suicide. The FBI agent was transferred to another jurisdiction.

Lessons learned: Evil is no respecter of persons and will take whoever it can get. Most people are willing to go to great lengths to protect their loved ones. Anger can be a natural, intense, emotional reaction toward that which we know is not right. Anger is a great tool that needs to be channeled appropriately to accomplish the best outcomes.

What is Righteous Anger?

It is an intense desire to see a person, circumstance, or situation be the way God sees it and wants it.

God made us in His image.

As Christians we are to emulate the nature of God and Jesus.

Let's examine what makes them angry:

God's Anger

> Genesis 19:24-25 "Then the LORD rained down burning sulfur on Sodom and Gomorrah—from the LORD out of the heavens. Thus he overthrew those cities and the entire plain, destroying all those living in the cities—and also the vegetation in the land."

Sodom and Gomorrah are destroyed for their perversion and sin.

> Exodus 4:10-15 "Moses said to the LORD, 'Pardon your servant, Lord. I have never been eloquent, neither in the past nor since you have spoken to your servant. I am slow of speech and tongue.' The LORD said to him, 'Who gave human beings their mouths? Who makes them deaf or mute? Who gives them sight or makes them blind? Is it not I, the LORD? Now go; I will help

> you speak and will teach you what to say.' But Moses said, 'Pardon your servant, Lord. Please send someone else.' Then the LORD's anger burned against Moses and he said, 'What about your brother, Aaron the Levite? I know he can speak well. He is already on his way to meet you, and he will be glad to see you. You shall speak to him and put words in his mouth; I will help both of you speak and will teach you what to do. He will speak to the people for you, and it will be as if he were your mouth and as if you were God to him.'"

God is angry Moses will not do what God is asking him to do.

> Exodus 22:22-24 "Do not take advantage of the widow or the fatherless. If you do and they cry out to me, I will certainly hear their cry. My anger will be aroused, and I will kill you with the sword; your wives will become widows and your children fatherless."

> Numbers 22:20-23 "That night God came to Balaam and said, 'Since these men have come to summon you, go with them, but do only what I tell you.' Balaam got up in the morning, saddled his donkey and went with the Moabite officials. But God was very angry when he went, and the angel of the LORD stood in the road to oppose him. Balaam was riding on his donkey, and his two servants were with him. When the donkey saw the angel of the LORD standing in the road with a drawn sword in his hand, it turned off the road into a field. Balaam beat it to get it back on the road."

There are several possible explanations here. The first is that Balaam went with his own purpose in mind and not that of God's. The second is that Balaam was pretending to be a prophet and to be able to hear God but really could not. He could not see the angel that was right in front of his face.

> 2 Samuel 6:6-7 "When they came to the threshing floor of Nakon, Uzzah reached out and took hold of the ark of God, because the oxen stumbled. The LORD's anger burned against Uzzah because of his irreverent act; therefore God struck him down, and he died there beside the ark of God."

The explanation for this is historically and culturally detailed. The bottom line is that the ark was not to be transported in the manner it was when this happened. They are God's rules and laws. There are consequences for breaking them.

> Psalm 30:5 "For his anger lasts only a moment, but his favor lasts a lifetime; weeping may stay for the night, but rejoicing comes in the morning."

David is describing God's nature.

> Psalm 74:1-2 "O God, why have you rejected us forever? Why does your anger smolder against the sheep of your pasture? Remember the nation you purchased long ago, the people of your inheritance, whom you redeemed - Mount Zion, where you dwelt."

The Psalms are written with great emotion by its authors. Often, people cried out in anger for God's vengeance due to the inability or unwillingness to take revenge themselves.

> Romans 1:18 "The wrath of God is being revealed from heaven against all the godlessness and wickedness of people, who suppress the truth by their wickedness."

> Exodus 32:7-14 "Then the LORD said to Moses, 'Go

> down, because your people, whom you brought up out of Egypt, have become corrupt. They have been quick to turn away from what I commanded them and have made themselves an idol cast in the shape of a calf. They have bowed down to it and sacrificed to it and have said, 'These are your gods, Israel, who brought you up out of Egypt.' "I have seen these people," the LORD said to Moses, 'and they are a stiff-necked people. Now leave me alone so that my anger may burn against them and that I may destroy them. Then I will make you into a great nation.' But Moses sought the favor of the LORD his God. 'LORD," he said, "why should your anger burn against your people, whom you brought out of Egypt with great power and a mighty hand? Why should the Egyptians say, 'It was with evil intent that he brought them out, to kill them in the mountains and to wipe them off the face of the earth'? Turn from your fierce anger; relent and do not bring disaster on your people. Remember your servants Abraham, Isaac and Israel, to whom you swore by your own self: 'I will make your descendants as numerous as the stars in the sky and I will give your descendants all this land I promised them, and it will be their inheritance forever.' Then the LORD relented and did not bring on his people the disaster he had threatened."

Here, God is angry for the disobedience shown to him by His people, and their rejection of God, as evidenced by worshipping an idol.

> Deuteronomy 6:13-19 "Fear the LORD your God, serve him only and take your oaths in his name. Do not follow other gods, the gods of the peoples around you; for the LORD your God, who is among you, is a jealous

God and his anger will burn against you, and he will destroy you from the face of the land. Do not put the LORD your God to the test as you did at Massah. Be sure to keep the commands of the LORD your God and the stipulations and decrees he has given you. Do what is right and good in the LORD's sight, so that it may go well with you and you may go in and take over the good land the LORD promised on oath to your ancestors, thrusting out all your enemies before you, as the LORD said."

Judges 2:13-14 "Because they forsook him and served Baal and the Ashtoreths. In his anger against Israel the LORD gave them into the hands of raiders who plundered them. He sold them into the hands of their enemies all around, whom they were no longer able to resist."

Ezra 8:22 "I was ashamed to ask the king for soldiers and horsemen to protect us from enemies on the road, because we had told the king, 'The gracious hand of our God is on everyone who looks to him, but his great anger is against all who forsake him.'"

Numbers 11:1-17 "Now the people complained about their hardships in the hearing of the LORD, and when he heard them his anger was aroused. Then fire from the LORD burned among them and consumed some of the outskirts of the camp. When the people cried out to Moses, he prayed to the LORD and the fire died down. So that place was called Taberah, because fire from the LORD had burned among them. The rabble with them began to crave other food, and again the Israelites started wailing and said, 'If only we had meat to eat! We remember the fish we ate in Egypt at no cost—also the cucumbers, melons, leeks, onions and garlic. But now we have lost our appetite; we never see anything but this manna!' The manna was like coriander seed and looked like resin. The people went around gathering it, and then ground it in a hand mill or crushed it in a mortar. They cooked it in a pot or made it into loaves. And it tasted like something made with olive oil. When the dew settled on the camp at night, the manna also came down. Moses heard the people of every family wailing at the entrance to their tents. The LORD became exceedingly angry, and Moses was troubled. He asked the LORD, 'Why have you brought this trouble on your servant? What have I done to displease you that you put the burden of all these people on me? Did I conceive all these people? Did I give them birth? Why do you tell me to carry them in my arms, as a nurse carries an infant, to the land you promised on oath to their ancestors? Where can I get meat for all these people? They keep wailing to me, 'Give us meat to eat!' I cannot carry all these people by myself; the burden is too heavy for me. If this is how you are going to treat me, please go ahead and kill me—if I have found favor in your eyes—and do not let me face my own ruin." The LORD said to Moses: 'Bring me seventy of Israel's elders who are known to you as leaders and officials among the people. Have them come to the tent of meeting that they may stand there with you. I will come down and speak with you there, and I will take some of the power of the Spirit that is on you and put it on them. They will share the burden of the people with you so that you will not have to carry it alone.'"

Again, God is angry with the Israelites for all of their whining, complaining and disobedience.

> Numbers 12 "Miriam and Aaron began to talk against Moses because of his Cushite wife, for he had married a Cushite. 'Has the LORD spoken only through Moses?' they asked. "Hasn't he also spoken through us?" And the LORD heard this. (Now Moses was a very humble man, more humble than anyone else on the face of the earth.) At once the LORD said to Moses, Aaron and Miriam, 'Come out to the tent of meeting, all three of you.' So the three of them went out. Then the LORD came down in a pillar of cloud; he stood at the entrance to the tent and summoned Aaron and Miriam. When the two of them stepped forward, he said, 'Listen to my words: "When there is a prophet among you, I, the LORD, reveal myself to them in visions, I speak to them in dreams. But this is not true of my servant Moses; he is faithful in all my house. With him I speak face to face, clearly and not in riddles; he sees the form of the LORD. Why then were you not afraid to speak against my servant Moses?' The anger of the LORD burned against them, and he left them. When the cloud lifted from above the tent, Miriam's skin was leprous - it became as white as snow. Aaron turned toward her and saw that she had a defiling skin disease, and he said to Moses, 'Please, my lord, I ask you not to hold against us the sin we have so foolishly committed. Do not let her be like a stillborn infant coming from its mother's womb with its flesh half eaten away.' So Moses cried out to the LORD, 'Please, God, heal her!' The LORD replied to Moses, 'If her father had spit in her face, would she not have been in disgrace for seven days? Confine her outside the camp

> for seven days; after that she can be brought back.' So Miriam was confined outside the camp for seven days, and the people did not move on till she was brought back. After that, the people left Hazeroth and encamped in the Desert of Paran."

These examples are not inclusive. Next, we will look at some things that make Jesus angry.

Individual Reflection or Group Discussion

1. Look at current events using the newspaper, internet or other sources. List 3 current events that would stir God's anger.

2. Why would the things you have identified stir God's anger?

Chapter 11
The Anger of Jesus

"The real freedom of any individual can always be measured by the amount of responsibility which he must assume for his own welfare and security."

Robert Welch

"God is our refuge and strength, an ever-present help in trouble. Therefore we will not fear, though the earth give way and the mountains fall into the heart of the sea, though its waters roar and foam and the mountains quake with their surging." Psalm 46:1-3

Lesson Learned

I was working undercover and in plainclothes looking for prostitutes and drug dealers. I was in a city that had an abundance of both. I picked up a prostitute who looks to be all of 18 years old. We drove around discussing the details which were being recorded on a wire I am wearing that is being monitored by my back-up team. We go to a hotel room, and I give her the agreed upon amount of money. She begins to get undressed and is telling me to do the same thing. I am sitting on the edge of the bed wondering where my back-up team is. She asks me if I am a cop, and I deny it. I am now in my underwear and t-shirt and am thinking something has gone wrong with the wire I am wearing. I know many of these girls have their pimps follow them to assure the girls safety and to make sure they get paid.

Pimps have no reluctance to use violence. It is part of their trade and practice. Knowing this, I am getting a bit concerned not knowing where my back-up team is. I am seconds away from having to bust this girl myself. It turned out that my back-up team thought it would be funny to let me get almost completely naked before entering the room and busting her, which they finally did. They had a good laugh at my expense. They handcuffed me as well, in order to protect my identity. She went to jail, and I went to look for another prostitute.

Several weeks later I attended one of her court hearings as a witness. Her pimp also attended the hearing. She was fined and released. I spoke to her on the way out of the courthouse and encouraged her to break away from this lifestyle and her pimp. The pimp was not pleased with this. He confronted me on the steps outside the courtroom and threatened me. Another deputy was with me, who immediately began to slap this pimp with an open hand repeatedly until he was up against the wall of the building. I loved this guy. He was one of those real quiet guys, real low-key and soft-spoken but strong as an ox. After my fellow deputy reminded the pimp that we all knew where to find him, the pimp and the prostitute wandered off.

I would see this girl on the street occasionally and always encouraged her to leave the life she was living. She finally did and left town.

Lesson learned: A rule of life with people who are living in and practicing dark, illegal and criminal lifestyles is that they understand power. They know how to establish it within their own world through manipulation, coercion or force. Although the act of prayer is the most powerful thing that can be accomplished to mitigate evil on this earth, when God sticks us into the middle of a circumstance where it is clear that good and evil are clashing, we have a supernaturally charged responsibility to deal with it. And that may require violence on our part.

Jesus: The 1st Time

> John 2:14-16 "In the temple courts he found people selling cattle, sheep and doves, and others sitting at tables exchanging money. So he made a whip out of cords, and drove all from the temple courts, both sheep and cattle; he scattered the coins of the money changers and overturned their tables. To those who sold doves he said, 'Get these out of here! Stop turning my Father's house into a market!'"

Jesus was angry to the point of expressing his anger physically. He made whips for a reason; he probably used them on the vendors.

The 2nd Time: Three Years Later

> Matthew 21:12-13 "Jesus entered the temple courts and drove out all who were buying and selling there. He overturned the tables of the money changers and the benches of those selling doves. 'It is written,' he said to them, ''My house will be called a house of prayer,' but you are making it 'a den of robbers.'"

> Mark 11:15-19 "On reaching Jerusalem, Jesus entered the temple courts and began driving out those who were buying and selling there. He overturned the tables of the money changers and the benches of those selling doves, and would not allow anyone to carry merchandise through the temple courts. And as he taught them, he said, 'Is it not written: 'My house will be called a house of prayer for all nations'? But you have made it 'a den

of robbers.' The chief priests and the teachers of the law heard this and began looking for a way to kill him, for they feared him, because the whole crowd was amazed at his teaching. When evening came, Jesus and his disciples went out of the city."

Luke 19:45 "When Jesus entered the temple courts, he began to drive out those who were selling."

Matthew 16:23 "Jesus turned and said to Peter, 'Get behind me, Satan! You are a stumbling block to me; you do not have in mind the concerns of God, but merely human concerns.'"

Matthew 23:13-33 "'Woe to you, teachers of the law and Pharisees, you hypocrites! You shut the door of the kingdom of heaven in people's faces. You yourselves do not enter, nor will you let those enter who are trying to. 'Woe to you, teachers of the law and Pharisees, you hypocrites! You travel over land and sea to win a single convert, and when you have succeeded, you make them twice as much a child of hell as you are. 'Woe to you, blind guides! You say, 'If anyone swears by the temple, it means nothing; but anyone who swears by the gold of the temple is bound by that oath.' You blind fools! Which is greater: the gold, or the temple that makes the gold sacred? You also say, 'If anyone swears by the altar, it means nothing; but anyone who swears by the gift on the altar is bound by that oath.' You blind men! Which is greater: the gift, or the altar that makes the gift sacred? Therefore, anyone who swears by the altar swears by it and by everything on it. And anyone who swears by the temple swears by it and by the one who dwells in it. And anyone who swears by

> heaven swears by God's throne and by the one who sits on it. 'Woe to you, teachers of the law and Pharisees, you hypocrites! You give a tenth of your spices—mint, dill and cumin. But you have neglected the more important matters of the law—justice, mercy and faithfulness. You should have practiced the latter, without neglecting the former. You blind guides! You strain out a gnat but swallow a camel. 'Woe to you, teachers of the law and Pharisees, you hypocrites! You clean the outside of the cup and dish, but inside they are full of greed and self-indulgence. Blind Pharisee! First clean the inside of the cup and dish, and then the outside also will be clean. "Woe to you, teachers of the law and Pharisees, you hypocrites! You are like whitewashed tombs, which look beautiful on the outside but on the inside are full of the bones of the dead and everything unclean. In the same way, on the outside you appear to people as righteous but on the inside you are full of hypocrisy and wickedness. "Woe to you, teachers of the law and Pharisees, you hypocrites! You build tombs for the prophets and decorate the graves of the righteous. And you say, 'If we had lived in the days of our ancestors, we would not have taken part with them in shedding the blood of the prophets.' So you testify against yourselves that you are the descendants of those who murdered the prophets. Go ahead, then, and complete what your ancestors started! You snakes! You brood of vipers! How will you escape being condemned to hell?"

Jesus was expressing great anger towards these hypocrites and citing specific reasons. He took their rules and reasoning, turned it upside down, and threw it back in their faces.

Let's look at some other examples of anger and how we should be applying righteous anger to our daily lives.

Individual Reflection or Group Discussion

1. Identify three values within yourself that would align with those of Jesus, and like Jesus, would stir you to anger.

2. Why would the things you have identified stir Jesus' anger?

Consider the ways you would handle the following two scenarios:

- One of your best friends is having an affair and had confided this to you. You are good friends with this person and their mate. You love them both and enjoy their company. The friend of yours has met with you several times and described the affair in detail as well as the guilt they feel for betraying their mate. What is your advice to them? At what point would you tell their spouse about the affair?

- Imagine living in the End Times and experiencing the mark of the beast, in which, if you do not take this mark, you will not be able to buy goods or participate in commerce. Will you take the mark? Will it make you angry? What would Jesus' response to something like this be?

Chapter 12
The Heart of Righteous Anger

"All that is necessary for the triumph of evil is for good men to do nothing."

Edmund Burke

"Her (Israel's) priests do violence to my law and profane my holy things; they do not distinguish between the holy and the common; they teach that there is no difference between the unclean and the clean; and they shut their eyes to the keeping of my Sabbaths, so I am profaned among them. Her officials within her are like wolves tearing their prey; they shed blood and kill people to make unjust gain. Her prophets whitewash these deeds for them by false visions and lying divinations. They say, 'This is what the Sovereign Lord says' – when the Lord has not spoken. The people of the land practice extortion and commit robbery; they oppress the poor and needy and mistreat the alien, denying them justice. "I looked for a man among them who would build up the wall and stand before me in the gap on behalf of the land so I would not have to destroy it, but I found none. So I will pour out my wrath on them and consume them with my fiery anger, bringing down on their own heads all they have done, declares the Sovereign Lord." Ezekiel 22:26-31

Lesson Learned

It is a hot summer night and I decide to catch up on some paperwork and drive to my office which is an annex to the main building of my department. I unexpectedly find the external doors to these offices open, and quietly walk in. As I approach my office, I can hear familiar voices — that being our Narcotics Unit Supervisor, a guy who has a plethora of informants and operatives working undercover. He is talking to his support person who is a female civilian. It is very unusual for either one of them to be in these offices in the evening. It is clear to me they do not know I am present as their conversation never missed a beat. There are several walls and a hallway between us. As I begin my paperwork, I can hear a conversation that goes something like this:

Him: I do not have receipts for a lot of these expenses, and I don't remember how the money was spent.

Her: Well, we better come up with something, or we are going to be screwed when these guys come to look at the books. And, some of these expenses are just not going to fly.

Him: Alright, let's just make something up.

They are referring to an audit of the books that was coming on the heels of a large drug investigation our Narcotics Unit had conducted in which a number of people had been arrested and charged with various drug crimes. It had been discovered the main witness, an undercover agent supervised by this Narcotics Supervisor, had falsified a number of reports. Consequently, most of the charges against these people were being dropped. It was a great embarrassment not only to this Supervisor but to the department as well. Since much of the money used to fund these operations came from state funding, the state criminal division was coming in to look at the books.

My perception that night was that the Narcotics Supervisor and his support person were doctoring the books. I quietly left the office and spoke to my partner about what I had overheard.

He informed me that state criminal division agents were quietly coming to town to investigate this mess. Certainly, this conversation had relevance for those state agents.

Several weeks later, arrangements were made for me to meet these agents late at night in their hotel room. I shared the conversation I had overheard. They shared with me the rumors they had heard about this drug operation and advised me they were in town to investigate what had happened which included an audit of the books to examine where the state funding had been spent. They also advised me that I would likely never hear from them again.

Fast forward six months. By this time the investigation was complete and no criminal wrong-doing had been discovered — just gross incompetence. The books had been examined, and there were gaps found in the justification of money spent, however, there was no finding of criminal intent.

After the State completed their investigation, the Lieutenant who supervised the Narcotics Supervisor had an angry exchange with my partner that went something like this:

Lieutenant: Did you ever talk to those state agents that came here to investigate the Narcotics division?

Partner: No. I had nothing to do with that Narcotics investigation. (This was not true as he had spoken to the agents about what he had heard from street sources.)

Lieutenant: Well, somebody did, and it pisses me off! They accused my people of doctoring the books.

Partner: Well.....did they?

Lieutenant: I bet it was Hipp who talked to them! Was it?

Partner: I don't think Terry would do something like that.

This Lieutenant never came to me and asked me directly. However, shortly after the conversation the Lieutenant had with my partner, I found myself working a newly created overnight shift that was to specifically liaison with officers from other departments and back them up on calls. It was a public relations ploy aimed at reducing tensions that had built up between various departments, which was not uncommon then. Another officer was assigned to work this shift as well, which effectively broke up what had been an incredible partnership with the guy I had been working with for years. I and the other officer assigned to this shift worked out of separate vehicles.

Lessons learned: "And we know that in all things God works for the good of those who love him, who have been called according to his purpose." I knew I was being punished although this Lieutenant had no proof that I went to the state agents. Additionally, there were a lot of other officers who spoke to these agents and provided information more damaging than what I gave them. I had no reservations or regrets about speaking to them. After all, we were cops. We were the good guys. We shouldn't be breaking the rules. We enforce them. There were plenty of ways to creatively work the system without being dishonest or compromising integrity.

Standing up for the right thing often comes with a price. I tried to make the best of it. Outside of the difficult sleeping pattern, it wasn't bad. We saw plenty of action on this shift, and because we primarily responded as back up to other departments, there was very little paperwork. We also developed a great relationship with the chief cook of a restaurant who arrived each day at 4am to begin to prepare food. With great regularity, we visited this cook at 5am who served us a freshly cooked breakfast in a closed restaurant.

I was off this shift six months later, and shortly thereafter I received a phone call from a neighboring department inviting me to come and work for them as a detective. I accepted the invitation. The good fortune with my current department had seemingly run dry.

Other Examples of Biblical Anger

> Exodus 11 "Now the LORD had said to Moses, 'I will bring one more plague on Pharaoh and on Egypt. After

> that, he will let you go from here, and when he does, he will drive you out completely. Tell the people that men and women alike are to ask their neighbors for articles of silver and gold.' (The LORD made the Egyptians favorably disposed toward the people, and Moses himself was highly regarded in Egypt by Pharaoh's officials and by the people.) So Moses said, 'This is what the LORD says: 'About midnight I will go throughout Egypt. Every firstborn son in Egypt will die, from the firstborn son of Pharaoh, who sits on the throne, to the firstborn son of the female slave, who is at her hand mill, and all the firstborn of the cattle as well. There will be loud wailing throughout Egypt—worse than there has ever been or ever will be again. But among the Israelites not a dog will bark at any person or animal.' Then you will know that the LORD makes a distinction between Egypt and Israel. All these officials of yours will come to me, bowing down before me and saying, 'Go, you and all the people who follow you!' After that I will leave.' Then Moses, hot with anger, left Pharaoh. The LORD had said to Moses, 'Pharaoh will refuse to listen to you—so that my wonders may be multiplied in Egypt.' Moses and Aaron performed all these wonders before Pharaoh, but the LORD hardened Pharaoh's heart, and he would not let the Israelites go out of his country."

Moses is angry that Pharaoh has not let the people go as he knows this is God's will.

> 1 Samuel 17 "When David faced Goliath he said: 'Who is this uncircumcised Philistine that he should defy the armies of the living God?'"

I can hear the anger in David's voice. He must have been angry when he said these things about Goliath, a man so terrifying that he single-handedly held off a whole army for days.

> 2 Samuel 13 "In the course of time, Amnon son of David fell in love with Tamar, the beautiful sister of Absalom son of David. Amnon became so obsessed with his sister Tamar that he made himself ill. She was a virgin, and it seemed impossible for him to do anything to her. Now Amnon had an adviser named Jonadab son of Shimeah, David's brother. Jonadab was a very shrewd man. He asked Amnon, 'Why do you, the king's son, look so haggard morning after morning? Won't you tell me?' Amnon said to him, 'I'm in love with Tamar, my brother Absalom's sister.' 'Go to bed and pretend to be ill,' Jonadab said. 'When your father comes to see you, say to him, 'I would like my sister Tamar to come and give me something to eat. Let her prepare the food in my sight so I may watch her and then eat it from her hand.' So Amnon lay down and pretended to be ill. When the king came to see him, Amnon said to him, 'I would like my sister Tamar to come and make some special bread in my sight, so I may eat from her hand.' David sent word to Tamar at the palace: 'Go to the house of your brother Amnon and prepare some food for him.' So Tamar went to the house of her brother Amnon, who was lying down. She took some dough, kneaded it, made the bread in his sight and baked it. Then she took the pan and served him the bread, but he refused to eat. 'Send everyone out of here," Amnon said. So everyone left him. Then Amnon said to Tamar, "Bring the food here into my bedroom so I may eat from your hand.' And Tamar took the bread she had prepared and brought it to her brother Amnon in his bedroom. But when she

took it to him to eat, he grabbed her and said, 'Come to bed with me, my sister.' 'No, my brother!' she said to him. 'Don't force me! Such a thing should not be done in Israel! Don't do this wicked thing. What about me? Where could I get rid of my disgrace? And what about you? You would be like one of the wicked fools in Israel. Please speak to the king; he will not keep me from being married to you.' But he refused to listen to her, and since he was stronger than she, he raped her. Then Amnon hated her with intense hatred. In fact, he hated her more than he had loved her. Amnon said to her, 'Get up and get out!' 'No!' she said to him. 'Sending me away would be a greater wrong than what you have already done to me.' But he refused to listen to her. He called his personal servant and said, 'Get this woman out of my sight and bolt the door after her.' So his servant put her out and bolted the door after her. She was wearing an ornate robe, for this was the kind of garment the virgin daughters of the king wore. Tamar put ashes on her head and tore the ornate robe she was wearing. She put her hands on her head and went away, weeping aloud as she went. Her brother Absalom said to her, 'Has that Amnon, your brother, been with you? Be quiet for now, my sister; he is your brother. Don't take this thing to heart.' And Tamar lived in her brother Absalom's house, a desolate woman. When King David heard all this, he was furious. And Absalom never said a word to Amnon, either good or bad; he hated Amnon because he had disgraced his sister Tamar."

It is a wonder no one got killed in this creepy story. The act was clearly worthy of anger. It was rape and incest.

Acts 16:35-39 "When it was daylight, the magistrates

> sent their officers to the jailer with the order: 'Release those men.' The jailer told Paul, "The magistrates have ordered that you and Silas be released. Now you can leave. Go in peace.' But Paul said to the officers: 'They beat us publicly without a trial, even though we are Roman citizens, and threw us into prison. And now do they want to get rid of us quietly? No! Let them come themselves and escort us out.' The officers reported this to the magistrates, and when they heard that Paul and Silas were Roman citizens, they were alarmed. They came to appease them and escorted them from the prison, requesting them to leave the city."

Paul is angry about being unjustly accused, beaten and thrown in jail. He was denied due process as a Roman citizen. It appears he demanded a public apology and got it.

> 1 Samuel 11 "Nahash the Ammonite went up and besieged Jabesh Gilead. And all the men of Jabesh said to him, 'Make a treaty with us, and we will be subject to you.' But Nahash the Ammonite replied, 'I will make a treaty with you only on the condition that I gouge out the right eye of every one of you and so bring disgrace on all Israel.' The elders of Jabesh said to him, 'Give us seven days so we can send messengers throughout Israel; if no one comes to rescue us, we will surrender to you.' When the messengers came to Gibeah of Saul and reported these terms to the people, they all wept aloud. Just then Saul was returning from the fields, behind his oxen, and he asked, 'What is wrong with everyone? Why are they weeping?' Then they repeated to him what the men of Jabesh had said. When Saul heard their words, the Spirit of God came powerfully upon him, and he burned with anger. He took a pair

> of oxen, cut them into pieces, and sent the pieces by messengers throughout Israel, proclaiming, 'This is what will be done to the oxen of anyone who does not follow Saul and Samuel.' Then the terror of the LORD fell on the people, and they came out together as one. When Saul mustered them at Bezek, the men of Israel numbered three hundred thousand and those of Judah thirty thousand. They told the messengers who had come, 'Say to the men of Jabesh Gilead, 'By the time the sun is hot tomorrow, you will be rescued.' When the messengers went and reported this to the men of Jabesh, they were elated. They said to the Ammonites, 'Tomorrow we will surrender to you, and you can do to us whatever you like.' The next day Saul separated his men into three divisions; during the last watch of the night they broke into the camp of the Ammonites and slaughtered them until the heat of the day. Those who survived were scattered, so that no two of them were left together."

In this story, the Spirit of God produced the burning anger in Saul over a bully who was threatening his people.

About Anger

> Numbers 25:10-11 "The LORD said to Moses, 'Phinehas son of Eleazar, the son of Aaron, the priest, has turned my anger away from the Israelites. Since he was as zealous for my honor among them as I am, I did not put an end to them in my zeal.'"

Here, God's anger is dissipated through one man who was zealous for God.

> James 1:19-20 "My dear brothers and sisters, take note

> of this: Everyone should be quick to listen, slow to speak and slow to become angry, because human anger does not produce the righteousness that God desires."

This verse is talking about human anger not righteous anger. There is a difference.

> Mark 3:1-6 "Another time Jesus went into the synagogue, and a man with a shriveled hand was there. Some of them were looking for a reason to accuse Jesus, so they watched him closely to see if he would heal him on the Sabbath. Jesus said to the man with the shriveled hand, 'Stand up in front of everyone.' Then Jesus asked them, 'Which is lawful on the Sabbath: to do good or to do evil, to save life or to kill?' But they remained silent. He looked around at them in anger and, deeply distressed at their stubborn hearts, said to the man, 'Stretch out your hand.' He stretched it out, and his hand was completely restored. Then the Pharisees went out and began to plot with the Herodians how they might kill Jesus."

It appears Jesus is angry at the stubborn hearts that refused to answer his question. They knew the answer. They were hypocrites.

> Ephesians 4:26-27 "'In your anger do not sin': Do not let the sun go down while you are still angry, and do not give the devil a foothold."

This must refer to human anger, as righteous anger might last for days, and comes from the heart of God.

The Difference Between the Two

Any anger should be scrutinized to determine the roots of its character; those roots being in God or man. People are not nearly as complex is we try to make them. Anger is not a sin. It can become a sin depending on where it is taken or directed. Anger is a natural human expression and an appropriate emotional response to many things. The expression of human anger is almost always tied to some underlying emotional issue.

Human, or unrighteous anger, is usually self serving and sinful. It is often abusive and excessive. Most unrighteous anger can be resolved with the right tools.

There are clear directives how to align our relationships and what role anger should play in relationships within this book. Although many of the chapters speak to the authority that is in our lives, that advice is sound for dealing with relationships at large and anger.

Dealing effectively with angry people requires effective communication. A fact of violence is that when facing an agitated, angry or aggressive individual, professionals are encouraged to allow that person a three-minute vent by asking leading questions. This will usually reveal the underlying emotional issue that is driving the anger. When this principle is successfully applied to physically aggressive people, it reduces the risk of violence to almost zero.

Righteous anger can have the same or even greater emotional intensity that unrighteous anger has, and it can rise suddenly. The root and direction it takes will be different than unrighteous anger. Righteous anger reflects part of the nature and heart of God. Righteous anger usually will have the following characteristics.

- Righteous anger is always under control. (Psalm 78:38)

- Righteous anger is not a pleasurable experience, even to God. (2 Peter 3:9)

- Righteous anger is slowly provoked. It is thoughtful.

It does not have an emotional hair trigger attached to it. (Exodus 34:6)

- Righteous anger is lawfully expressed because it is based on God's spiritual laws. It is legal justice not vigilante justice. God is just. It is part of His nature. His anger is justified.

- Righteous anger is consistent with the holy and righteous character of God.

It should be clear from the following verses there is a distinction between unrighteous and righteous anger. Righteous anger would never be referenced alongside some of these other characteristics.

Ephesians 4:26-27 "'In your anger do not sin': Do not let the sun go down while you are still angry, and do not give the devil a foothold."

Ephesians 4:31 "Get rid of all bitterness, rage and anger, brawling and slander, along with every form of malice."

Colossians 3:8 "But now you must also rid yourselves of all such things as these: anger, rage, malice, slander, and filthy language from your lips."

Another Master List

By examining these stories and verses, we are able to compile a list of things that reveal the heart of righteous anger. These are issues that God gets angry about, Jesus gets angry about or men of God got angry about. The same things should stir up righteous anger in Christians.

- Perversion and sin. The men of Sodom were insisting on having sex with the angels.

- Not doing what God is asking.
- Doubting God's ability when He does ask someone to do something.
- Taking advantage of the widow and the fatherless.
- People pretending to be a prophet or some other instrument of God when they are not.
- Not following God's specific instructions.
- Following other gods.
- Idol worship.
- Godlessness and wickedness.
- Rejecting God.
- Disobedience.
- Ungrateful whining & complaining about what God is doing.
- Speaking against God's chosen leaders and criticizing them when the intent of doing so reflects personal motive.
- Turning the temple (house of worship) into a shady and unscrupulous marketplace.
- Hypocrisy.
- Stubborn hearts.

- Someone who is not letting others into the kingdom of heaven.

- Converting people away from God to be like themselves.

- Leading people to follow man-made tradition instead of God's word.

- Someone who is involving themselves in details to the point of ignoring what is really important in God's eyes.

- Someone who is keeping up appearances while their private world is corrupt.

- Someone who is acting spiritual in order to cover up sin.

- Someone who is pretending to have learned from the past, but their present behavior shows they have learned nothing.

- Someone who is clearly violating God's will.

- Someone who is evil and is threatening and intimidating God's people.

- Rape and other horrible violent crimes.

- Unjust accusations.

Look around. There are plenty of examples of this behavior going on all over the world. Sometimes it seems as though we have been bombarded through media with so many examples that we have become desensitized to the point of these things having little meaning – almost as if we just expect it.

These behaviors and the people who practice them should stir you up. We are to imitate God. These things touched the hearts of God, Jesus and great men of God. It also stirred them all to action. The framework for appropriate actions has already been built in previous chapters. The action that righteous anger should produce has to be prayerfully considered and acted upon obediently. Confrontation of some type may be required and probably more often than many Christians are comfortable with.

Individual Reflection or Group Discussion

1. Can we expect more or less of this type of behavior as we move toward the end of this age?

2. What are you going to do about it?

3. Do you think violence is ever justified in situations that produce righteous anger?

Chapter 13
When is Violence Justified?

> "The safety and happiness of society are the objects at which all political institutions aim, and to which all such institutions must be sacrificed."
>
> **James Madison**

> "'Who is this uncircumcised Philistine that he should defy the armies of the living God?' David said to the Philistine, 'You come against me with sword and spear and javelin, but I come against you in the name of the LORD Almighty, the God of the armies of Israel, whom you have defied. This day the LORD will deliver you into my hands, and I'll strike you down and cut off your head. This very day I will give the carcasses of the Philistine army to the birds and the wild animals, and the whole world will know that there is a God in Israel. All those gathered here will know that it is not by sword or spear that the LORD saves; for the battle is the LORD's, and he will give all of you into our hands.'" 1 Samuel 16:26, 45-47

Lessons Learned

It is a hot August night, and I am in an area working with my partner who is in a separate car. It is a slow, lazy night and we were just cruising through several cities. We overheard a police radio transmission with another agency indicating there were several suspects in a large grocery store who were hiding up in the ceiling. Apparently a shopper noticed a leg poke through one of the false ceiling tiles near closing time. The store was vacated and closed by the local police who were about to search the store. We arrived to assist them. They asked us to search the liquor store, which was connected to the grocery store but separated by a wall. These two stores shared a common ceiling. I grabbed my shotgun as had my partner, and we went into the liquor store. What we did not know is that the officer who let us into the front of the liquor store locked the door behind us.

My partner and I split up and began to check the aisles of the liquor store and after seeing nothing obvious began to slowly work our way down separate isles towards the enclosed coolers at the other end of the store. As I got near the end of an aisle I saw a man directly in front of me looking at me through the cooler. I immediately stood up with my shotgun aimed at him and commanded him to freeze. He quickly disappeared. I yelled to my partner that a suspect was back in the cooler area. We quickly found the door to the back area of the liquor store and made entry through it — something we had done with some regularity in the line of duty and something we had practiced many times together.

All we knew was that someone was back there who should not be there and that person had ignored my orders that were backed up by a badge and a shotgun. We had no idea if he was armed or not. As we began to search the back room and cooler, we quickly discovered the man in a small closet. He was ordered out of the closet, and he complied. As I got a good look at him my heart raced even faster. He was well over 6 feet tall and had biceps that seemed to rival the size of my head. He was ordered to show his hands, and he did so. He was ordered to lie on the ground but instead of complying, he began to argue with us — denying any wrong doing. This went on for a full minute as he began to pace around. This turned into a bizarre dance ritual as we moved in concert with his movements, all the while keeping him in front of us.

My thoughts: Here is a guy with two cops pointing shotguns at him, ordering him to the ground, and he wants to walk around and argue about it? We might be in trouble here. We could not justifiably shoot him as he did not have any visible weapons. My partner suddenly lunged at him with the full force of his body, slamming the stock of his shotgun into the suspect's chest. The force was so great it broke the stock off of the shotgun. The suspect just stood there and looked at us. This moment seemed to freeze in time. Now, I was no longer wondering if we were in trouble; I knew we were.

The suspect grabbed what was left of my partner's shotgun, and they began to fight over control of it. I was useless to help as long as I still had my shotgun in my hands, but I did not want to put it down for fear of the suspect possibly getting a hold of it. I put it on the floor and kicked it across the room as far as I could. I jumped in to assist my partner in the struggle only to find myself with the barrel of the shotgun inches in front of my face. I was now looking down the barrel of the shotgun. I could not see whose hands had control of the trigger area as they were sandwiched between the bodies of my partner and this suspect. I was quite sure I was going to die. I used all of my strength to push the barrel away from my face, and eventually we wrestled the shotgun away from the suspect. I tossed what was left of it as far as I could across the room. Now, we had two loose shotguns in a room with an assaultive suspect who was not afraid to try and take a gun away from an officer. The fight was on. We bounced off of shelves and racks and walls breaking liquor bottles along the way. We could not restrain or control this man.

In the meantime, some of the officers maintaining a perimeter on the outside of the building could hear this altercation taking place. There is no other situation in law enforcement that collectively bands officers together with great determination, courage, strength and focus as another officer needing help. I could hear several officers trying to break through the locked external back door to no avail. I could hear them yelling on their radios that we needed assistance inside the liquor store. Unknown to us at the time, the front door had been locked behind us when we entered the store. After several minutes of an all-out brawl with this suspect, I finally got behind him and jumped on his back performing a choke-hold which rendered him monetarily unconscious. This allowed us to get him to the ground, but he quickly gained consciousness and began to struggle again while we attempted to handcuff him.

The officers outside were trying to locate the key to the front door. Having little success, one of the officers finally took his flashlight to the front plate-glass window breaking it to gain entry. This brave officer ended up taking a dozen stitches in his forearm in his attempt to get to us. By the time these officers reached us, we had one of the prone suspect's hands cuffed and were struggling to get his other arm out from under his chest. One of the assisting officers kicked the suspect several times in the face which allowed us to get his other arm out from under him and his remaining hand cuffed. These officers knew him by name. He had just been released from the state penitentiary several months before. He must have eaten weights for breakfast. His partner in crime had been arrested in the grocery store without incident and had already admitted to planning a burglary after all the shoppers and employees had left. They thought hiding in the ceiling until the store was closed was a good idea.

As this was not our official jurisdiction and technically we were assisting these officers, they were responsible to take custody of the suspects. We, however, would have to write a report as to our involvement in this incident.

There is often a big "exhale" after an event like this in which officers hang around for a while and collect evidence, discuss what happened, or just unwind. I noticed my partner was coughing excessively. I figured it was due to the altercation and that he was winded — probably charged up with adrenaline. I offered to take my car and drive us to the local police station to write our report. Several blocks away from the scene he suddenly grabbed his chest, looked at me and struggled to get the word "Doctor" out of his mouth. He lost consciousness and promptly collapsed in the passenger seat.

I grabbed him and began yelling at him and shaking him. I immediately got on the radio and advised a dispatcher I was heading to the hospital, which was a few miles away, with an injured officer. I assumed my partner had experienced a heart attack since he had grabbed his chest. As I raced toward the hospital, lights on and siren screaming, I continued to yell at him; "Stay with me!" "Hang on!" "You are not going to die on me!" I remember saying a frenzied prayer. The doctors were waiting at the emergency room entrance as I speed up to it and screeched to a halt.

It turned out that in the scuffle, my partner had taken a strike to the front of his neck. This area is vulnerable with many small bones and when struck or injured the airway can swell shut. The injured party either dies from suffocation or the airway relaxes and begins to open back up depending on the severity of the injury. My partner's airway was opened by the doctors. He was sore for a while and had a few days off. He could have died. God answered my prayer for him.

Lessons learned: We had to take natural action to contain the evil that was being manifested through another human being. While doing so, I believed he would have killed us had he gotten control of that shotgun. There was no negotiating with him. He would not comply with legal directives or orders. There were injuries that resulted from the incident. Prayer was coupled with weapons and violent action on our part in order to contain this individual. It took superior force, not equal force, to subdue this individual.

The Next Logical Question

God's righteous anger killed a lot of people. Jesus took whips to people in righteous anger. Saul and David killed in righteous anger. Is violence ever justified in situations which stir up righteous anger?

This question can be complicated or relatively simple to deal with. It all depends how you look at it.

I have had the privilege of providing protection for a number of high-profile people. People with an extraordinary amount of power, fame or money live in a world far different from most of us. This was not the case with Walid Shoebat, a former Palestinian terrorist who had converted to Christianity and had been invited to speak at a conference. Mr. Shoebat had real threats to be concerned about. There were people who wanted to kill him. Because of this, we watched him and those who interacted with him very closely.

As we sat and had lunch together in our designated safe room, a message was sent to him by one of the conference facilitators. Although he had spoken in the morning about his conversion to Christianity, the message was requesting Mr. Shoebat address more fully his conversion experience and his relationship with Jesus in light of his political upbringing and specific Bible verses. I will always remember his response: "Why is it that people always need to make things complicated? Accepting Christ as my Lord and Savior was not complicated. The word of God is not complicated. It was not written for theologians and scholars. It was written for the fisherman and the prostitute."

In that context, let's keep the discussion about justified violence simple. In earlier chapters of this book we have considered the following:

- Satan is trying to devour Christians, and he often manifests himself through human beings.

- There is a call to action from Jude, who with great

urgency asks us to fight for the faith, to fight for our brothers and sisters, to fight for the souls of the lost, and to hate sinful attitudes and behavior.

- God has established relational authority.

- There is ungodly, harsh and incompetent authority. We have instructions from the word of God for dealing with it. Sometimes it requires confrontation.

- There are sure things that can be expected as we move toward the end of this age and none of them look pleasant.

- There are many examples of God's children having to confront and fight through difficulties using His supernatural power, provision and protection alongside their own faith and action.

- The God-given, hard-wired intuition and the fight or flight response we all have within us. God put these there so we could sense danger and survive an attack.

- The notion of passivity in the face of evil.

- Things that should produce righteous anger within us.

Is there Righteous and Unrighteous Violence?

Much like the contrast between righteous and unrighteous anger, there are differences between righteous and unrighteous violence. There are sufficient examples of both righteous and unrighteous violence in the Bible. We will not recount them all here, for their characteristics are very similar to those of anger.

Examples of righteous and unrighteous violence can be found in Genesis.

Unrighteous violence fueled by intense jealousy looked like this.

> Genesis 4:2-8 "Now Abel kept flocks, and Cain worked the soil. In the course of time Cain brought some of the fruits of the soil as an offering to the LORD. And Abel also brought an offering—fat portions from some of the firstborn of his flock. The LORD looked with favor on Abel and his offering, but on Cain and his offering he did not look with favor. So Cain was very angry, and his face was downcast. Then the LORD said to Cain, 'Why are you angry? Why is your face downcast? [7] If you do what is right, will you not be accepted? But if you do not do what is right, sin is crouching at your door; it desires to have you, but you must rule over it.' Now Cain said to his brother Abel, "Let's go out to the field." While they were in the field, Cain attacked his brother Abel and killed him."

Righteous violence is fueled by the evil, wickedness, corruption and violence of others. The actions and behavior of others are so disgustingly contrary to the nature of God; action is required – because the justice of God requires action.

> Genesis 6:5-13 "The LORD saw how great the wickedness of the human race had become on the earth, and that every inclination of the thoughts of the human heart was only evil all the time. The LORD regretted that he had made human beings on the earth, and his heart was deeply troubled. So the LORD said, 'I will wipe from the face of the earth the human race I have created—and with them the animals, the birds and the creatures that move along the ground—for I regret that I have made them.' But Noah found favor in the eyes of the LORD.

> This is the account of Noah and his family. Noah was a righteous man, blameless among the people of his time, and he walked faithfully with God. Noah had three sons: Shem, Ham and Japheth. Now the earth was corrupt in God's sight and was full of violence. God saw how corrupt the earth had become, for all the people on earth had corrupted their ways. So God said to Noah, 'I am going to put an end to all people, for the earth is filled with violence because of them. I am surely going to destroy both them and the earth.'"

See the difference?

If we did not live in a fallen world due to Satan's presence and man's sin, there would be no evil or violence. But evil does exist, and it usually manifests itself through people. God's righteous and just nature requires a response to it.

But I Thought that We Don't Fight with the Weapons of this World

> 2 Corinthians 10:3-6 "For though we live in the world, we do not wage war as the world does. The weapons we fight with are not the weapons of the world. On the contrary, they have divine power to demolish strongholds. We demolish arguments and every pretension that sets itself up against the knowledge of God, and we take captive every thought to make it obedient to Christ. And we will be ready to punish every act of disobedience, once your obedience is complete."

> Ephesians 6:10-18 "Finally, be strong in the Lord and in his mighty power. Put on the full armor of God, so that you can take your stand against the devil's schemes. For our struggle is not against flesh and blood, but against

> the rulers, against the authorities, against the powers of this dark world and against the spiritual forces of evil in the heavenly realms. Therefore put on the full armor of God, so that when the day of evil comes, you may be able to stand your ground, and after you have done everything, to stand. Stand firm then, with the belt of truth buckled around your waist, with the breastplate of righteousness in place, and with your feet fitted with the readiness that comes from the gospel of peace. In addition to all this, take up the shield of faith, with which you can extinguish all the flaming arrows of the evil one. Take the helmet of salvation and the sword of the Spirit, which is the word of God. And pray in the Spirit on all occasions with all kinds of prayers and requests. With this in mind, be alert and always keep on praying for all the Lord's people."

These verses are true and the specific words the authors chose to use are war-like, but they must be kept in context. Successful warfare is best fought and usually won through superior tactics, one of which is using the appropriate weapon for the task at hand. Using another analogy, the proper tool needs to be chosen for the job at hand. You do not use a hammer when a saw is needed. If you use the hammer, the results are going to be less than acceptable. The same goes for spiritual warfare.

There is a natural world. We live in it. God created it. It has natural laws, and we use natural tools and abilities to negotiate our way through it.

There is a spiritual world most people do not see, and one aspect of that world is that it is inhabited by angels and demons. They are around us everywhere.

> Revelation 12:9 "The great dragon was hurled down—that ancient serpent called the devil, or Satan, who

> leads the whole world astray. He was hurled to the earth, and his angels with him."

Man and woman are God's creation, and they are both natural and spiritual. The body is natural. The soul and spirit is spiritual. The body and mind is intricately connected to the soul and spirit. Therefore, the natural and the spiritual are interconnected in human beings, so naturally much of what they do on earth has natural and spiritual implications.

> Genesis 1:26 "Then God said, 'Let us make man in our image, in our likeness, and let them rule over the fish of the sea and the birds of the air, over the livestock, over all the earth, and over all the creatures that move along the ground.'"

From The Spirit of the Disciplines by Dallas Willard: "We were created to govern the earth with all its living things - and to that specific end, we were made in divine likeness. Evil did not originate on planet earth. Before God created earth, he had already populated the universe with other rational beings. The Bible calls these beings "angels," and names several different orders. They are simply another form of living creature that has come from the hand of God. The angels, like mankind, were created with free will, and were subject to the same conditions regarding their eternal life. The most prominent of these chose to rebel against God. God could have destroyed Satan when he first rebelled. But the rest of His creatures would not have understood, not having seen the consequences of Lucifer's course of action. Instead, God allowed Satan to demonstrate what the universe would be like under his authority. The results are written across the pages of human history. When the demonstration is complete, God will safely be able to eliminate Satan without running the risk that His other creatures will serve Him out of fear. Satan is a defeated foe. He knows that he will soon be destroyed, and the universe cleared of the effects of his rebellion. It is sheer desperation that causes him to continue to fight against God. Sin has so thoroughly warped Satan's character that he is beyond the point of no return as far as repentance is concerned. Bitterness, hatred, and selfishness are the only plants that grow in his heart. His hatred for mankind is intensified as he sees men and women return to God and receive the forgiveness that he too at one time could have received. Adam and Eve gave their obedience to Satan, and he was quick to proclaim his dominion over planet earth. From this geographical location he would continue his war against God. The apostle Paul later described him as the 'god of this world'."

> 2 Corinthians 4:4 "The god of this age has blinded the minds of unbelievers, so that they cannot see the light of the gospel of the glory of Christ, who is the image of God."

If you believe what you have just read, it is unarguable; the natural and the spiritual are intricately linked.

Angels, Demons, Spiritual Tools and Spiritual Authority

> Psalm 91:9-13 "If you say, 'The LORD is my refuge,' and you make the Most High your dwelling, no harm will overtake you, no disaster will come near your tent. For he will command his angels concerning you to guard you in all your ways; they will lift you up in their hands, so that you will not strike your foot against a stone. You will tread on the lion and the cobra; you will trample the great lion and the serpent."

There are many references to angels and demons in the Bible that stand as a testament to their attributes, characteristics, powers and mission. There are good books available on the subject of angels and demons. For our purposes, we are simply acknowledging that they exist and are active around us. Angels are God's messengers and servants who carry out His will on earth. Demons are Satan's recruits whose goal is to do everything they can do to deter Christianity and the work of God. They are both worthy of study. Demons are the enemy, and it is good to know the methods and ways of the enemy. Angels are at your call, a prayer away.

In considering how we should respond to evil around us, let's look at one example of demon possession that is described in Matthew:

> Matthew 8:28-32 "When he arrived at the other side in the region of the Gadarenes, two demon-possessed men coming from the tombs met him. They were so violent that no one could pass that way. 'What do you want with us, Son of God?' they shouted. 'Have you come here to torture us before the appointed time?' Some distance from them a large herd of pigs was feeding. The demons begged Jesus, 'If you drive us out, send us into the herd of pigs.' He said to them, 'Go!' So they came out and went into the pigs, and the whole herd rushed down the steep bank into the lake and died in the water."

There is a lot of revealing information contained within these few verses.

- Demons can possess people.
- Demons can cause people to be violent.
- The violence can be so great it is a risk to other people.
- The primary tactic of Jesus when confronting demons directly was to use divine authority and divine violence.

- Jesus used the right tool for the job. He used spiritual weapons to deal with a spiritual root problem, which was demonic.

- Jesus actually had to tell them to leave. The demons did not flee just because of Jesus presence. But, it is also clear they knew who Jesus was. Jesus' presence could be felt and was known by them.

- Jesus never negotiated or had lengthy conversations with demons, and he never showed them compassion or weakness.

- Satan and his demons have tremendous power on earth, but they have no authority over Christians. Jesus took care of this when he died on the cross.

Matthew 16:18 "And I tell you that you are Peter, and on this rock I will build my church, and the gates of Hades will not overcome it."

John 14:12 "Very truly I tell you, whoever believes in me will do the works I have been doing, and they will do even greater things than these, because I am going to the Father."

Revelation 1:17-18 "When I saw him, I fell at his feet as though dead. Then he placed his right hand on me and said: 'Do not be afraid. I am the First and the Last. I am the Living One; I was dead, and now look, I am alive forever and ever! And I hold the keys of death and Hades."

Matthew 10:1, 5-16 "He called his twelve disciples to him and gave them authority to drive out evil spirits and to heal every disease and sickness....'Do not go among the Gentiles or enter any town of the Samaritans. Go rather to the lost sheep of Israel. As you go, preach this message: The kingdom of heaven is near. Heal the sick, raise the dead, cleanse those who have leprosy, drive out demons. Freely you have received, freely give. Do not take any gold or silver or copper in your belts; take no bag for the journey, of extra tunic, or sandals or a staff; for the worker is worth his keep. Whatever town or village you enter, search for some worthy person there and stay at his house until you leave. As you enter the home, give it your greeting. If the home is deserving, let your peace rest on it; if it is not, let your peace return to you. If anyone will not welcome you or listen to your words, shake the dust off your feet when you leave that home or town. I tell you the truth, it will be more bearable for Sodom and Gomorrah on the day of judgment than for that town. I am sending you out like sheep amongst wolves. Therefore be as shrewd as snakes and as innocent as doves.'"

Mark 11:23 "Truly I tell you, if anyone says to this mountain, 'Go, throw yourself into the sea,' and does not doubt in their heart but believes that what they say will happen, it will be done for them."

Matthew 17:20 "Truly I tell you, if you have faith as small as a mustard seed, you can say to this mountain, 'Move from here to there,' and it will move. Nothing will be impossible for you."

Here is how all of this works.

There are natural laws which are sure and certain, like putting your hand on a hot stove. The promises of the Bible are spiritual laws, which are eternal. These promises are surer than natural law. If you have certainty that you will burn your hand if you it into a flame, you can be more certain that all the promises of the Bible are there for the taking, and the principles are certain – overseen and supervised by God's perfect will. Your job as a Christian is to know what the Bible says and then invoke it into your daily life, leaving the results up to God.

As a Christian, Jesus lives inside of you. He and the Father (God) are one. As a child of God through Jesus, you have access to the same power Jesus used while he walked the earth. This is part of the legal covenant you have with God through Jesus.

The key to accessing that power is faith. Faith is like a muscle. You work it and train it to get it to grow. The more it grows, the more comfortable you become taking on different tasks that require more muscle. Notice faith, which is spiritual, has a natural parallel principle.

Your mere presence can shift and change things wherever you are because where you are, so is Jesus. You invoke these promises, just like Jesus did. The promises of the Bible go far, far beyond what is presented here.

Merging Natural & Spiritual Weapons

Satan is intent on destroying Christians as discussed in the Introduction of this book. His armies of demons are also intent on keeping the unsaved away from Christianity.

Let me change the story in Matthew 8 in order to make a point. Imagine someone approached these demon possessed men who was not a Christian and killed them both by bow and arrow. Are they dead? Of course they are — in the natural world. A bow and arrow are some of the right tools for killing someone in the natural world. Their bodies are dead, but their spirits and souls have moved on into the spiritual world because the spirit and soul inhabit the body. The only reason Jesus didn't kill these men was because of his compassion for mankind and his mission — to save the world. He cast out the demons thereby giving them the opportunity of salvation.

Now, consider a spiritual tool being used as the sole tool on a natural problem. My house is on fire, and I command it to cease then get on my knees and pray that God put it out. Can God accomplish these things? Of course, He can. There are many, many stories of God's supernatural resolution to a natural problem within the breath of a prayer.

Is this God's usual way of dealing with a natural problem? No. If it was, there would be no need for fire departments. I need to pray while I am calling the fire department, and then grab my house hose or fire extinguisher. This is God-given common sense.

We need to use the right tool for the problem being presented.

Notice that Jesus did not ask God to remove the demons. He did it himself through spoken word. The Bible reference to moving mountains does not suggest I come to God and ask (pray) that the mountain be moved. It tells me to speak directly to the mountain. This is not some complex verse filled with imagery and hidden meaning about persistent prayer. There is a lot of straight-forward direction about prayer in the Bible, so there is no need for the Bible to be a mystery in these verses about moving mountains.

These are God's spiritual laws, enacted on by Christians through the promise and power of Jesus Christ.

> James 5:13-16 "Is anyone among you in trouble? Let them pray. Is anyone happy? Let them sing songs of praise. Is anyone among you sick? Let them call the elders of the church to pray over them and anoint them with oil in the name of the Lord. And the prayer offered in faith will make the sick person well; the Lord will raise them up. If they have sinned, they will be forgiven. Therefore confess your sins to each other and pray for each other so that you may be healed. The prayer of a righteous person is

powerful and effective."

I hope at this point it is obvious that the spiritual world and the natural world are inextricably linked. A natural tool will work with a natural problem. A spiritual tool will with work with a spiritual problem. Humans are a combination of the natural and spiritual, therefore circumstances and situations they create or find themselves in can be both natural and spiritual with angels, demons and the promises of scripture present to influence the outcomes.

When is Violence Acceptable?

In my view, the debate over the use of violence based on what the Bible says has been put into the wrong context. It is not an all or nothing proposition, nor is it complex. Many of the verses like that of 2 Corinthians 10:3-6 and Ephesians 6:10-18 are being used as the theological foundation for never using violence in this natural world.

> 2 Corinthians 10:3-6 "For though we live in the world, we do not wage war as the world does. The weapons we fight with are not the weapons of the world. On the contrary, they have divine power to demolish strongholds. We demolish arguments and every pretension that sets itself up against the knowledge of God, and we take captive every thought to make it obedient to Christ. And we will be ready to punish every act of disobedience, once your obedience is complete."

> Ephesians 6:10-18 "Finally, be strong in the Lord and in his mighty power. Put on the full armor of God, so that you can take your stand against the devil's schemes. For our struggle is not against flesh and blood, but against the rulers, against the authorities, against the powers of this dark world and against the spiritual forces of evil in the heavenly realms. Therefore put on the full armor of God,

> so that when the day of evil comes, you may be able to stand your ground, and after you have done everything, to stand. Stand firm then, with the belt of truth buckled around your waist, with the breastplate of righteousness in place, and with your feet fitted with the readiness that comes from the gospel of peace. In addition to all this, take up the shield of faith, with which you can extinguish all the flaming arrows of the evil one. Take the helmet of salvation and the sword of the Spirit, which is the word of God. And pray in the Spirit on all occasions with all kinds of prayers and requests. With this in mind, be alert and always keep on praying for all the Lord's people."

However, these verses are recommending the appropriate spiritual tools to deal with a spiritual problem in the spiritual world. These are the tools and tactics Christians should be employing in the larger context of Satan's work in the church and the world at large — amongst leaders, and with their own family and neighbors. Christians should invoke these tools every day in specific situations through prayer, faith and spoken word.

In the natural, there is ample justification for using violence as a means of defending oneself or loved ones found the Bible. Using violent means as a form of self defense is also justified in almost every nation on earth.

Both Christian and unsaved military and law enforcement personnel take (kill) natural life in the context of protection and defense of people groups. This is sanctioned and ordained by God (see previous chapters).

Under international law, personal self-defense is a well-established human right and is an important foundation of international law itself as well as the Constitution of America. From 1893 to 1896, the United States Supreme Court handed down a series of decisions involving self-defense and the carrying and use of firearms for self-defense. These cases laid the foundation for a 1921 opinion, authored by Justice Oliver Wendell Holmes, which became the most important armed self defense case in American legal history, upholding and extending the right to armed self-defense.

Self-defense is a legal protection for the use of force — even deadly force to protect one's life or the life of a third party. The concept has roots back to Roman law and English Common Law, and, in the United States, has been refined over a series of historic self-defense cases in the Supreme Court. In many cases, but not all, the issue of self-defense has been connected with shooting deaths and the right to bear arms. While the Supreme Court has outlined principles governing self-defense as a legal concept, individual states are given the responsibility to legislate the specific limits of self defense within their own jurisdictions.

> Nehemiah 4 "When Sanballat heard that we were rebuilding the wall, he became angry and was greatly incensed. He ridiculed the Jews, and in the presence of his associates and the army of Samaria, he said, "What are those feeble Jews doing? Will they restore their wall? Will they offer sacrifices? Will they finish in a day? Can they bring the stones back to life from those heaps of rubble—burned as they are?" Tobiah the Ammonite, who was at his side, said, "What they are building—even a fox climbing up on it would break down their wall of stones!" Hear us, our God, for we are despised. Turn their insults back on their own heads. Give them over as plunder in a land of captivity. Do not cover up their guilt or blot out their sins from your sight, for they have thrown insults in the face of the builders. So we rebuilt the wall till all of it reached half its height, for the people worked with all their heart. But when Sanballat, Tobiah, the Arabs, the Ammonites and the people of Ashdod heard that the re-

pairs to Jerusalem's walls had gone ahead and that the gaps were being closed, they were very angry. They all plotted together to come and fight against Jerusalem and stir up trouble against it. But we prayed to our God and posted a guard day and night to meet this threat. Meanwhile, the people in Judah said, "The strength of the laborers is giving out, and there is so much rubble that we cannot rebuild the wall." Also our enemies said, "Before they know it or see us, we will be right there among them and will kill them and put an end to the work." Then the Jews who lived near them came and told us ten times over, 'Wherever you turn, they will attack us." Therefore I stationed some of the people behind the lowest points of the wall at the exposed places, posting them by families, with their swords, spears and bows. After I looked things over, I stood up and said to the nobles, the officials and the rest of the people, "Don't be afraid of them. Remember the Lord, who is great and awesome, and fight for your families, your sons and your daughters, your wives and your homes.' When our enemies heard that we were aware of their plot and that God had frustrated it, we all returned to the wall, each to our own work. From that day on, half of my men did the work, while the other half were equipped with spears, shields, bows and armor. The officers posted themselves behind all the people of Judah who were building the wall. Those who carried materials did their work with one hand and held a weapon in the other, and each of the builders wore his sword at his side as he worked. But the man who sounded the trumpet stayed with me. Then I said to the nobles, the officials and the rest of the people, 'The work is extensive and spread out, and we are widely separated from each other along the wall. Wherever you hear the sound

> of the trumpet, join us there. Our God will fight for us!' So we continued the work with half the men holding spears, from the first light of dawn till the stars came out. At that time I also said to the people, 'Have every man and his helper stay inside Jerusalem at night, so they can serve us as guards by night and as workers by day.' Neither I nor my brothers nor my men nor the guards with me took off our clothes; each had his weapon, even when he went for water."

In Nehemiah 4, we see God's people using both spiritual and natural tools, tactics and strategy to deal with what would seem to most people to be a natural problem — an enemy of people in the natural world. I think this is the model for all Christians when dealing with significant threat.

Can I Use Violence as a Tool When I am Moved to Righteous Anger?

Unfortunately, there are far too many examples of whackos that have killed people in the name of God and mentally ill people who have heard voices from God or Satan telling them to kill people — including their own families at times. This is demonic.

Field Trip: Sin Is Sin?

Before I go any further, let me establish something very clearly. I am using homosexuality as a forthcoming example of something that might stir people to righteous anger. However, in the example I use, it also stirs someone to take the wrong action — unrighteous violence. The Bible describes homosexuality as sin. I am not picking on homosexuals. I am not suggesting homosexuality is a greater sin than another.

> 1 John 3:4 "Everyone who sins breaks the law; in fact, sin is lawlessness."

Romans 6:23 "For the wages of sin is death, but the gift of God is eternal life in Christ Jesus our Lord."

James 2:10-11 "For whoever keeps the whole law and yet stumbles at just one point is guilty of breaking all of it. For he who said, 'Do not commit adultery,' also said, "Do not murder.' If you do not commit adultery but do commit murder, you have become a lawbreaker.'

To God, all sin is equal before Him because it falls short of His perfection – which is His nature. Clearly, sin is punishable by death, and we are saved by God's grace and mercy through Jesus Christ. However, God is also just. Therefore, He is fully aware that different sins have different effects and will carry different consequences.

John 19:11 "Therefore the one who handed me over to you is guilty of ***a greater sin.***"

2 Peter 2 "But there were also false prophets among the people, just as there will be false teachers among you. They will secretly introduce destructive heresies, even denying the sovereign Lord who bought them—bringing swift destruction on themselves. Many will follow their depraved conduct and will bring the way of truth into disrepute. In their greed these teachers will exploit you with fabricated stories. Their condemnation has long been hanging over them, and their destruction has not been sleeping. For if God did not spare angels when they sinned, but sent them to hell, putting them in chains of darkness to be held for judgment; if he did not spare the ancient world when he brought the flood on its ungodly people, but protected Noah, a preacher of righteousness, and seven others; if he condemned

the cities of Sodom and Gomorrah by burning them to ashes, and made them an example of what is going to happen to the ungodly; and if he rescued Lot, a righteous man, who was distressed by the depraved conduct of the lawless (for that righteous man, living among them day after day, was tormented in his righteous soul by the lawless deeds he saw and heard)— if this is so, then the Lord knows how to rescue the godly from trials and to hold the unrighteous for punishment on the day of judgment. This is especially true of those who follow the corrupt desire of the sinful nature and despise authority. Bold and arrogant, they are not afraid to heap abuse on celestial beings; yet even angels, although they are stronger and more powerful, do not heap abuse on such beings when bringing judgment on them from the Lord. But these people blaspheme in matters they do not understand. They are like unreasoning animals, creatures of instinct, born only to be caught and destroyed, and like animals they too will perish. They will be paid back with harm for the harm they have done. Their idea of pleasure is to carouse in broad daylight. They are blots and blemishes, reveling in their pleasures while they feast with you. With eyes full of adultery, they never stop sinning; they seduce the unstable; they are experts in greed—an accursed brood! They have left the straight way and wandered off to follow the way of Balaam son of Bezer, who loved the wages of wickedness. But he was rebuked for his wrongdoing by a donkey—an animal without speech—who spoke with a human voice and restrained the prophet's madness. These people are springs without water and mists driven by a storm. ***Blackest darkness is reserved for them.*** For they mouth empty, boastful words and, by appealing to the lustful desires of sinful human nature, they entice people who are just escaping from those who live in error. They promise them freedom, while they themselves are slaves of depravity—for 'people are slaves to whatever has mastered them.' If they have escaped the corruption of the world by knowing our Lord and Savior Jesus Christ and are again entangled in it and are overcome, they are worse off at the end than they were at the beginning. It would have been better for them not to have known the way of righteousness, than to have known it and then to turn their backs on the sacred command that was passed on to them."

Jude 1:13 "They are wild waves of the sea, foaming up their shame; wandering stars, ***for whom blackest darkness has been reserved forever."***

These passages serve several purposes.

1. They demonstrate a clear relationship between how people live, believe, reward and punishment.

2. The highlighted areas indicate there are some "degrees" of sin, at least in terms of consequences. The severity of consequences for different types of behavior has been well established around the world through the use of criminal codes and statutes.

3. They demonstrate some of the behaviors that should stir righteous anger.

4. They seem to indicate the sin of deceiving God's Church through false teaching, among other things,

is a serious sin with a "blackest darkness" for those engaged in it.

5. Some actions, both in the natural and in the spiritual, have greater consequences than others.

Galatians 6:7-8 "Do not be deceived: God cannot be mocked. A man reaps what he sows."

Back To The Point

We have people like Eric Rudolph, who killed two people and injured at least 150 others through the use of explosives at clinics that were performing abortions and at the Olympic Games in 1996. He eventually released a statement which indicated he saw himself as an anti-abortion and anti-gay activist. We can use Mr. Rudolph as an example of how NOT to proceed under the guise of Biblical justification for violence.

Although Mr. Rudolph could make a case for righteous anger based on abortion and homosexuality, those behaviors were not landing on his doorstep. No one was requiring him to have an abortion which would be a clear violation of God's word. No one was requiring him to practice homosexuality which is also something spoken about clearly in God's word. Abortion and homosexuality were not threatening his life or his loved ones. Abortion and homosexuality are legitimized through the law, but the law does not require people to participate. It is a choice.

His appropriate response to these issues should have been through protest, civil disobedience, personal influence, and prayer or by joining like-minded organizations. All of these actions would be fueled by righteous anger.

Let's change Mr. Rudolph's situation. Let us imagine for a moment that the US government has passed a law or the President has established an executive order compelling Mr. Rudolph (and others) to participate in homosexual behavior and for his wife to have an abortion. Additionally, enforcement procedures are being executed throughout the country, which means at some point, Mr. Rudolph will be confronted directly and forced to participate or suffer. These are entirely different circumstances than those under which he took his actions. Would a scenario like this give a person the Biblical right to seek out and kill those who created the laws or those who might be involved in the enforcement of these orders?

If we look to the Bible for an answer, at least on the surface, we might expect Saul or David to go find these people and kill them. We might expect God to make them suffer terribly or just kill them outright. We would expect Jesus to confront them with a forceful truth driven by compassion for their souls. Shadrach, Meshach, and Abednego would have respectfully refused to obey.

We can agree in our imaginary scenario that these laws violate God's word, therefore we should be moved to righteous anger, and we should not participate in them. We should do what we can to push back with both spiritual and natural tools. But until there is a viable, imminent threat to life – or at least the perception thereof — you will not find examples in the Bible that will justify Mr. Rudolph's behavior.

Planning for It

If we use something like hurricane Katrina as an example, we saw a lot of people taking the risk of living in a part of the country that is on average eight feet below sea level. Next, consider any hurricane, or a collapse of the elaborate pumping stations, or a collapse of levees. There is a risk of flooding from a variety of sources. From this aspect alone I would consider owning a blow-up raft just in case something happens. I might also have on hand a few emergency supplies and a flashlight. With these simple precautions I can survive and escape. This seems to be obvious.

If you have faith in government, consider the average police response time in the US is over 6 minutes. The average violent encounter is less than 2 minutes. Do the math. Government and law enforcement officials may be well-intended, but their resources are limited. If someone tries to hurt you or take your property, you are on your own.

I am not predicting anything. I am not qualified to do so. All I have to do is to look at the list of things that the Bible predicts are coming my way and consider the possible outcomes to realize I need to do some planning.

I could be betrayed by brother, father, children, friends or relatives and be handed over to authorities to be put to death. If I am alive and refuse the Mark of the Beast, how am I going to eat? The global financial meltdown should have taught us that things can change overnight. What if there is a panic and stores have sold out of all their goods within hours? What if our supply and delivery system breaks down? What if there is widespread panic and people start looting just to survive? Famine? Earthquake? Flood? A war zone? Wickedness? No love? Great distress? Increased martyrdom of Christians? The list goes on and on. It is all there for us to consider. Why do you think God decided we should know all of this?

The only wild card remaining is the timing of this. We do not know the exact day, but we do know the season.

The Bottom Line

When persecuted specifically in the name of Jesus, submit. This is what Jesus and the disciples did. Even then, keep in mind that Jesus and the disciples had a different mission than most of us. Jesus came to be obedient by doing exactly what God told him to do which required great discipline, suffering and a horrid death in order to defeat Satan once and for all in the spiritual realm. The disciples' primary mission was to spread the gospel throughout the world by planting churches and overseeing the beginnings of the New Testament church.

Let me be clear. All Christians have parallel responsibilities in the big picture. Some of us are bookkeepers, small business owners, CEO's, soldiers, police officers, waitresses or plumbers. Our mission is to also spread the gospel through the way we live in the places God has planted us in. Jesus could have destroyed anyone who came against him, and the disciples could have called upon thousands of followers. They didn't. It would have subverted their primary mission.

If your primary mission from God is to be a martyr then you would be exemplifying their behavior. If you are a soldier, you will not imitate this behavior when the enemy tries to kill you or take you into custody. If you are a Christian, you will fight for the privilege of influencing a few more people toward the kingdom of God because you would like to see them in eternity.

If ungodly laws are requiring you to submit to unscriptural behavior, refuse to participate.

When evil is manifesting itself through other people, and the threat of death, injury, loss of property or other criminal acts are being brought to bear on you or those you protect; fight with natural and spiritual weapons.

It might be easier to view it like this:

- In personal matters, love the enemy.

- In spiritual matters, use the weapons of spiritual warfare.

- In physical matters, fight!

The best thing you can do right now is to submit all of what you are reading here to prayer. Read the Bible and continue to develop an intimate relationship with Jesus as you consider these issues.

Let's bring this full circle.

Individual Reflection or Group Discussion

You are living in the End Times, and you are experiencing the list of things found in Chapter 9.

1. What are your plans for pushing back in the natural and spiritual?

2. What are your plans for surviving any of those things should you find yourself in the midst of them?

3. Will these things stir you to righteous anger?

4. At what point will any of these things create a scenario where there is imminent threat to you or a loved one?

Chapter 14
Now What?

"Having heard all of this, you may choose to look the other way but you can never say again that you did not know."

William Wilberforce

Let's summarize Sections 1, 2 & 3 of this book.

Overview

- The world's perception of Christians, is that they are weak. This view is not completely unjustified.

- Satan is trying to devour Christians and he often manifests evil through human beings.

- Evil understands one thing — an overwhelming amount of natural and spiritual power. It manipulates grace, mercy, kindness and the gifts of the Spirit to its own liking and advantage.

- There is a call to action from Jude, who with great urgency asks us to fight for the faith, to fight for our brothers and sisters, to fight for the souls of the lost, and to despise sinful attitudes and behavior.

- God has established relational authority and gives us instructions regarding how we interact within those relationships.

- There is ungodly, harsh and incompetent authority. We have instructions from the word of God for dealing with it. Sometimes it requires confrontation.

- There are sure things that can be expected as we move toward the end of this age, and none of them look pleasant.

- The Bible contains many examples of God's children having to confront and fight through difficulties using His supernatural power, provision and protection alongside their own faith and action.

- We all have God-given intuition and the fight or flight response within us. God put these there so we could sense danger and survive an attack.

- The general notion of passivity in the face of evil is bad theology and needs to be put into proper context.

Living Through the End of the Church Age

If you are alive, these are the things you will have to figure out how to live through.

- Great deceit. Many will come claiming, "I am Christ". There will be false prophets who will perform great signs and miracles to deceive the elect.

- Wars and rumors of wars.

- Nation will rise against nation. Kingdom will rise

against kingdom.

- Brother will betray brother — often leading to death.

- A Father will betray his child.

- Children will rebel against their parents and have them put to death.

- You will be betrayed by friends and relatives.

- Famines.

- Earthquakes.

- You will be handed over to be persecuted and put to death. You will stand before governors and kings as witnesses.

- You will be hated by all nations.

- Many will turn from the faith and will betray and hate each other. All men will hate you.

- There will be an increase in wickedness.

- The love of most will grow cold.

- There will be great distress.

- Men will faint in terror.

- The sun and moon will not give light, the stars will fall and heavenly bodies will be shaken. Nations will be in anguish and perplexity at the roaring and tossing of the sea.

- It will be like in the days of Noah.
- Counterfeit Worldwide Peace & Safety.
- The Great Falling Away.
- The Great Harvest.
- The Antichrist coming forth with deceitful diplomacy.
- The Evil 10-Nation Federation.
- The False Prophet rising up.
- The Middle East and Israel having a false peace.
- The city of Babylon being re-established.
- The Jerusalem Temple being rebuilt.
- The Antichrist demanding worship.
- The Two Witnesses coming forth.
- The 144,000 Israelites being sealed.
- Michael standing up against Satan.
- All Nations gathered against Jerusalem.
- An increased martyrdom among Christians.
- Israel's strength being shattered.
- A time of previously inconceivable lawlessness and unrighteousness.

1st Seal: The Antichrist's conquest of political and economic aggression.

2nd Seal: Military conflict, world war and violence among men.

3rd Seal: Economic crisis and famine.

4th Seal: 25% of the earth's population dies by sword, famine, plague and wild beasts of the earth.

5th Seal: The Martyrs ask the Lord for judgment and justice regarding their own deaths and are told more of their brothers that are still alive will be martyred first, as they were.

6th Seal: Great earthquake, the sun turns black, the moon turns red and stars fall to the earth.

7th Seal: Releases the Seven Trumpets

1st Trumpet: Hail and fire mixed with blood which burns up a third of the world's plant life.

2nd Trumpet: Something described similar to a meteor hits the oceans causing the destruction of one third of all sea life, ships and the sea itself.

3rd Trumpet: Similar to the 2nd Trumpet, this affects one third of the rivers and springs, and more people die as a result.

4th Trumpet: One third of the moon and stars and sun are affected to the point that one third of the day and night is complete darkness.

5th Trumpet: Locusts are given the power of scorpions to torture, but not kill those who do not have the seal of God on their foreheads. The agony is so great the victims of these locusts will seek death.

6th Trumpet: An army of two hundred million mounted troops are released and use fire, smoke and sulfur to kill one third of all mankind.

Between the 6th and 7th Trumpets living Christians are sealed and appear with God. The Rapture has taken place.

If you have not been saved and redeemed, you will further experience these things.

7th Trumpet: Releases the Seven Angels with Seven Plagues, or Bowls of Wrath. It also signifies the beginning of the 2nd Coming.

1st Bowl: Ugly and painful sores break out on those with the mark of the beast.

2nd Bowl: The Sea becomes like blood and everything living thing in it dies.

3rd Bowl: The rivers and springs follow suit.

4th Bowl: The sun heats up to the point of scorching people.

5th Bowl: There is great darkness and some type of intensification of the sores.

6th Bowl: The Euphrates River dries up and the armies are gathered for the battle of Armageddon.

7th Bowl: An earthquake beyond what history has ever experienced. Hundred pound hailstones fall from the sky.

Righteous Anger

The Bible leads us to believe that as these things begin to take place, there will be an increase in the persecution of Christians. It is hard to fathom how some of these things could take place without direct governmental action and enforcement. However, please keep in mind that Satan's primary weapon is deceit.

Consider the slow decline of values and morals worldwide. This has come gradually, not by storm. A number of conservatives believe at some point their rights, their freedoms and their guns are going to suddenly yanked away from them. This is certainly possible and we have historical examples of this. But it is also possible these things will come to pass subtlety and slowly, which might be more in line with Satan's nature.

Regardless, as these things do come to pass there must be some type of continuum. As we move across that continuum we should be stirred to righteous anger about some of the things we see, hear about or experience. We have been desensitized to some degree through constant media bombardment. Many of these things will come from the hands of men.

- Perversion and sin.
- Disobedience to God.
- Doubting God's ability.
- Taking advantage of the widow and the fatherless.
- False prophets and false messengers.
- Not following God's specific instructions.
- Following other gods.
- Idol worship.
- Godlessness and wickedness.
- Rejecting God.
- Disobedience.
- Ungrateful whining & complaining about what God is doing.
- People who speak against God's chosen leaders and criticize them when the intent of doing so reflects personal motive.
- Turning the temple (house of worship) into a shady and unscrupulous marketplace.
- Hypocrisy.

- Stubborn hearts.

- People who are not letting others into the kingdom of heaven.

- People who convert others away from God to be like themselves.

- Leading people to follow man-made tradition instead of God's word.

- People who involve themselves in details to the point of ignoring what is really important in God's eyes.

- People who keep up appearances while their private world is corrupt.

- People who are acting spiritual in order to cover up sin.

- People who are pretending to have learned from the past, but their present behavior shows they have learned nothing.

- People who are clearly violating God's will.

- People who are evil and are threatening and intimidating God's people.

- Rape and other horribly violent crimes.

- Unjust accusations.

Characteristics of Righteous Anger

We are to imitate God. The action that righteous anger produces needs to be prayerfully considered and acted upon obediently. Confrontation of some type may be required, and probably more often than many Christians are comfortable with.

- Righteous anger is always under control.

- Righteous anger is not a pleasurable experience, even to God.

- Righteous anger is slowly provoked. It is thoughtful. It does not have an emotional hair trigger attached to it.

- Righteous anger is lawfully expressed because it is based on God's spiritual laws. It is legal justice, not vigilante justice. God is just. It is part of His nature. His anger is justified.

- Righteous anger is consistent with the holy and righteous character of God.

Justifiable Violence

If you are a Christian, you will fight for the privilege of influencing a few more people toward the kingdom of God, because you would like to see them in eternity.

- When persecuted specifically in the name of Jesus, submit.

- If ungodly laws are requiring you to submit to unscriptural behavior, refuse to participate.

- When evil is manifesting itself through other people and the threat of death, injury, loss of property or other criminal acts are being brought to bear on you or those you protect, fight with natural and spiritual weapons.

- In personal matters, love the enemy.

- In spiritual matters, use the weapons of spiritual warfare.

- In physical matters, fight!

The Spiritual & Natural

> Hebrews 13:2 "Be not forgetful to entertain strangers: for thereby some have entertained angels unaware."

The natural world and the spiritual world are intricately linked. There are many references to angels and demons in the Bible that stand as a testament to their attributes, characteristics, powers and their mission. Biblical descriptions and characteristics of angels and demons are provided below; with little or no commentary.

Excerpts from Billy Graham's book Angels:

Angels

- Angels were created by God. Angels are non-material. They have the ability to change their appearance and shuttle in a flash from heaven to earth. They do not possess physical bodies although they may take them on for certain tasks. Even one angel is indescribably mighty as though an extension of the arm of God.

- The chief business of angels is to carry out God's orders in the world. Angels intervene in the affairs of nations and execute judgment on them. God has countless angels at His command.

- God has commissioned them to aid His children in the struggle against Satan. They guide, comfort and provide for the people of God in the midst of suffering and persecution. If you are a believer, expect powerful angels to accompany you in your life experiences.

- Angels belong to a different dimension. The limitations are different than God has imposed on the natural order. Angels have a higher knowledge, power and mobility than us. Angels speak. They appear and reappear. They feel with apt sense of emotion. While angels may become visible by choice, we generally can't see them any better than we could the dimensions of a nuclear field for instance. They meet a need - then they are gone. They cannot fail.

- The enemies of Christ who attack us incessantly would often be thwarted if we could grasp God's assurance that His mighty angels are always nearby, ready to help. The most important characteristic of angels is that they work on our behalf. Angels are watching; they make our path. They superintend the events of our lives and protect the interest of the Lord God, always working to promote His plans to bring about His highest for us.

Demons

- Daniel 10 dramatically reveals the constant and bitter conflict between holy angels and the angels of darkness. The angels who fell had sinned against God. The greatest catastrophe in the history of the universal creation was Lucifer's defiance of God and the consequent fall of perhaps 1/3 of the angels who joined him.

- These fallen angels constitute a mighty force capable of wreaking havoc among individuals, families and nations. They are dangerous, viscous, and deadly. They want you under their control and will pay any price to get you. They are dedicated to the spirit of destruction.

Satan and his followers' primary endeavor is to destroy faith in the world.

- Satan has great power. He is cunning and clever having set himself against God and His people. He will do everything in his power to hold people captive in sin and to drag them down to the prison of eternal separation from God. He forever tries to discredit the truthfulness of the Word of God; he coaxes men to deny the authority of God; he persuades the world to wallow in the deluding comforts of sin. Satan often works by interjecting a question to raise doubts. Satan's strategy is to persuade us to rationalize.

- Satan always directs his sharpest attack at his victim's weakest point. He knows where the Achilles' heel is, and he does not fail to strike at the most opportune time.

- These fallen spirits do not abound in knowledge. Satan himself is far from excelling in knowledge. He may be curious and insidious, but he is certainly not wise and prudent. We give him credit for wisdom he does not deserve. Devils are not at strife with each other. Satan desires his empire to live in peace and security. Demons do not have the ability to be in more than one place at a time. They are neither omnipotent nor omnipresent. They cannot read our minds. They need to be spoken to directly, out loud.

- These spirits can assume all shapes, change the appearances of subjects on which they operated, or suddenly convey one thing away and substitute another in its place.

- They can imitate the servants of God but not duplicate them. They can make counterfeit miracles to draw attention off the real miracle.

- These spirits can oppress and possess people. Symptoms of demon possession are a continuing state or presence of an evil entity that is not "of the person". Different from demonic oppression, a continuing state of severe assault by an external entity, but the person retains control of the behavior and the body.

- Persons become demon possessed by not having control over his/her spirit. Their minds are focused on the wrong things, they are not keeping the body in the will of God, they are not filling life with the things of God, their sins are not taken care of, they worship false gods, they have no faith in a true God, and they fellowship with demons. These are all doors to demonic influence, oppression or possession.

- The chief characteristic of possession is a distinct "other personality" within. The demons have a longing to possess a body. It seems to bring them some relief, and they enter the bodies of animals as well as humans. There is sometimes great changes in the demon possessed person's behavior. There may be great rage and violent behavior. Sometimes there is physical sickness and/or handicaps. They can cause many kinds of insanity. They can break down and manipulate a body. They can cause the body to dry up and wither away. Any number of demons can possess an unsaved person. When an unclean spirit goes out of a man, it seeks another place to rest, preferably people nearby. Demons harm the body they enter physically. Demons talk using the organs of speech and show evidence of desire, fear and personality.

- Demons will sometimes say wrong and evil things about Jesus. They fear Jesus. They do not like to hear the truth from the Word of God. Jesus was never overmatched. He cast out demons with a divine violence. Devils do not like to be interfered with. They have nothing to do with Jesus nor do they want anything to do with Him. Jesus' presence was a torment to them. The Lord never wasted words. He did not scream or chatter. Jesus cast out the spirits with His word. He simply told them to, "Go". "Come out of the man, thou unclean spirit." These are not empty words. They are connected with inward thoughts.

Individual Reflection or Group Discussion

Write a personal Vision and Mission Statement for you or your group that is consistent with the principles thus far presented in this book.

A Vision Statement will describe how the future should be. A Mission statement describes how you will get there. Here are my company Assault Prevention's Vision and Mission Statements:

Vision: To connect our talents and services with practical outreach that meets human needs with the grace of God. To restrain evil that promotes violence, death and comes against the kingdom of God.

Mission: Assault Prevention is committed to enhancing the ability of individuals, organizations and communities to build a protective perimeter around their personal and corporate lives. We will use our expertise to assess and evaluate real risk, craft practical recommendations and plans to mitigate risk, and present appropriate information through education.

Every corporate decision I make is driven by our Vision and Mission Statements.

Your Vision Statement should reflect how you would like things to look in the future in regards to what you have read and discussed so far. Your Mission Statement should be a general outline of how you plan to get there.

One of the reasons I have provided the Individual Reflection or Group Discussion section at the end of each chapter is to encourage you to take some action that will eventually move you toward preparation for things to come — whether it be for you, your children or your children's children. Reading a book is simple. Taking action requires some degree of commitment. The amount of action and detail you commit to is entirely up to you, but it should be clear by now that you need to do something.

Most people, presumably, wear a seat belt because statistics show that the risk of death and injury fall dramatically if a seat belt is worn. The one-year odds of death in a car accident are 1 in 6,535. Lifetime odds are 1 in 84. But, you still wear a seat belt just in case. Your one-year odds of death from an assault are 1 in 25,263. Lifetime odds are 1 in 217. But, you don't purposely walk the streets in crime-ridden neighborhoods after dark.

Now, consider all the things you will experience with the Birth Pangs, Increased Labor Pangs and Tribulation. Don't you think some planning is prudent? The Vision and Mission Statement will get you there.

SECTION FOUR:
LIVING THROUGH IT

I do not have any special revelation as to how this all plays out or even exactly how it looks. I am not making any great predictions. I am asking you to simply ask "what if?"

- What if all these things come to pass, and it is in your lifetime?

- What if even as a Christian, you have not been raptured out of here before these things some to pass?

- What if you have to figure out a way to live through any, some or most of it?

- What if you are a person who is wired in a manner that Jude resonates within you?

- What if you are the person who will fight for the opportunity to plant a few more seeds and influence a few more people toward salvation and the Kingdom of God?

- What if your friends, family, children, parents or even your own government comes against you?

- What if you find yourself in a war-torn area or a place where great natural catastrophe and devastation has taken place?

- What if evil is roaming the earth like it never has before?

At the risk of being cliché, you must have a solid foundation in order to build anything that is going to work well. What follows will give you a basic understanding of things you will need to know to live through it — basic self defense, emergency planning, criminal behavior, how to choose a firearm and several other topics.

If you think that simply buying a gun will suffice, you are sadly mistaken. Conversely, you do not need to turn this information into extravagant actions or take things over the top by building a bomb shelter in your home or buying three years worth of food. I am somewhat confused by those people who have amassed thousands of rounds of ammunition. Really? Think about it. Under what scenario would anybody be shooting thousands of rounds of ammunition?

I would encourage you to take the prudent approach. You do not need to invest a great amount of time or money. Take some simple actions towards preparation.

Under extreme survival conditions you should be asking these four questions:

1. Will there be air available?

2. Will there be water available?

3. Will there be food available?

4. Will I be a target?

Chapter 15
Personal Safety – The Big Picture

"Insisting on perfect safety is for people who don't have the balls to live in the real world."

Mary Shafer

"'Lord, if it's you,' Peter replied, 'tell me to come to you on the water.' "Come,' he said. Then Peter got down out of the boat and walked on the water to Jesus. But when he saw the wind, he was afraid and, beginning to sink, cried out, 'Lord, save me!' Immediately Jesus reached out his hand and caught him. 'You of little faith,' he said, 'why do you doubt?'" Matthew 14:28-31

Lessons Learned

"Lady! Put the knife down!"

I had developed a reputation amongst my peers as being exceptionally qualified to deal with domestic disturbances. I didn't really think I was, but as the years slid by and the domestic calls piled up, I did notice a lot of officers had difficulty connecting on any emotional level with these people who allegedly loved each other at one time but now were either physically or emotionally battering each other. All I did was try to empathize with the people involved.

The net result of this skill I seemed to have acquired was that if there was a domestic disturbance call in my jurisdiction, and I was on duty, inevitably I was asked by responding officers to join them. At first I took this as a compliment but then began to dread it. It has been widely accepted amongst law enforcement personnel that domestic calls pose one of the most dangerous situations for officers. A lot of officers get assaulted during disturbance calls, and domestics are one type of disturbance call. Domestic disturbance calls are fueled with intense emotion, alcohol, drugs, mental illness or some other type of dysfunction. Often, these situations deteriorate into domestic abuse. Domestic abuse calls were relatively straight-forward. Once we determined who hit who, the initiator was arrested and taken to jail. This was the law.

Prior to that law being passed, officers had to be creative in their attempts to be peacemakers. A common tactic was to separate the people who were fighting and talk to them in an attempt to figure out what was going on. Next, officers would encourage one of the people to go stay with a friend, relative or overnight at a hotel. Police officers know that things usually look different to people the next day. Prior to the law being changed, I recall an old officer who was close to retirement telling the abusive husband who had hit his wife to do it again after we left, and that would solve things. I could not believe what I was hearing. After redressing his expert advice to the husband, I confronted him outside of the residence and then had a chat with my supervisor the next day. He was transferred to a desk job and served civil papers after that. There are idiots in law enforcement just like in any other profession. By and large, the majority of officers I met were exceptional, but there are always a few knuckleheads in every crowd.

I had been asked by fellow officers to join them on a domestic abuse call during the middle of a slow evening shift. When I arrived, they had already separated the warring parties. I went into the living room to speak to the female. All I did was ask leading questions and listen. Most of these people just needed to v the moment. After spending about ten minutes with her, I ch with my colleagues to see what the plan was. Since there we accusations or signs of physical assault, they had convince slightly inebriated husband into staying at a hotel overnight. turned to the wife to advise her. She seemed to have fully vent her emotional bank and asked if she could retrieve her cigarettes from the kitchen. I agreed and followed her there.

I did not notice that the other officers were escorting the husband to the kitchen to get his cigarettes before he left. This kitchen was small, U-shaped with a table in the middle, leaving very narrow walkways between the table and counters. Suddenly, the wife grabbed a knife from a drawer and headed directly toward me, knife outstretched in a threatening manner. "Lady! Put the knife down!" She kept coming. There was no time and no room to pull my handgun. Instinctively, I kicked her arm when she was within range. I do not remember even thinking about it. My boot connected with her forearm and the knife went flying across the kitchen. She went to jail for assault.

Lesson learned: Prior planning, preparation or training is the best method of preparing to deal with the real thing. My brain, in an instant, decided a kick was the best way to deal with this particular threat in this environment under these specific circumstances. This principle served me well throughout my career and saved my life more than once.

Getting a Grip on the Big Picture

Early one morning several years after 9/11, I sat behind a large truck at a stoplight in a major urban business district and found myself thinking about the truck exploding. I looked around at the sidewalks full of people hustling to work and the streets crowded with vehicles during the early morning rush hour. I observed two tall buildings on either side of the street; one appeared to have an almost complete glass exterior. I estimated that if the truck did explode, the resulting damage and loss of life would be horrific. I had absolutely no credible reason to think the truck in front of me was filled with explosives. Why would I have such a thought?

If you ever find your imagination wandering off into thoughts like these you are not alone. Terrorism has come to America and the world at large. Barely a day goes by now in which the media is not reporting something related to terrorism. It has become integrated into our everyday life.

If you struggle to understand some of the more despicable acts you hear about one of the first things you should consider when it comes to violence is the "big picture". If your world is so small that it is a challenge to see beyond your own doorstep, making sense of violence will be difficult. I encourage you to take a broader view of violence and the factors that contribute to it. Therein lays the ability to begin to objectively plan for your own personal safety.

The United States is arguably the greatest country on earth, but it becomes more deeply divided each day with changing demographics and clashing cultures. Although the figures represented below will change year by year, please consider the primary effects that these things produce:

- The aftermath of 9/11 and terrorism has produced a psyche of fear.

- There is a huge gap between the rich and poor. The world's median per capita income per year is approximately $7,000 but only 19% of the world's population lives in countries where it is this high. For most, it is closer to $1,700 per year.

- Approximately 12% of U.S. citizens live below the poverty line.

- Minorities are disproportionately affected by poverty, prison and drugs. Racial inequality is alive.

- Poor and minority children go to worse schools, have less expected of them, are taught by less knowledgeable teachers, and have the least power to alter bad situations.

- An estimated 32 million adults in the USA are functionally illiterate.

- Numbers change year by year, but in 2008, over 7.3 million people were on probation, in jail or prison, or on parole. This represents 3.2% of all U.S. adult residents or 1 in every 31 adults.

- A 2010 report from the United Nations Office on drugs and crime indicates a shift in drug abuse toward new drugs and new markets in developing countries, although rich countries still have a wide lead in drug consumption statistics. Amphetamine, ecstasy and prescription drug use is on the rise. The use of illegal drugs in our society is a business approaching $100 billion in annual volume.

- The actual lifetime divorce rate for marriages is probably somewhere between 15-30% not the 50% often quoted.

- The National Center for Health Statistics report that nearly 40 percent of babies born in the United States in 2007 were delivered by unwed mothers. The 1.7 million out-of-wedlock births, of 4.3 million total births, marked a more than 25 percent jump from five years before.

- There was an explosion of gang activity between the 1970's and 1990's amounting to a 640% increase in about 25 years. Gangs, who primarily make money from drug activity, are now an integrated part of our culture.

- Prudent economists know the US is bankrupt, and there is a real danger of a global financial collapse based on debt and credit.

- Terrorism is not going away. Over 11,000 terrorist incidents occurred worldwide in 2005, nearly four times the total in 2004 according the State Department. According to Rand, in 1995 there were approximately 268 international and domestic terror incidents.

- The United States has 5% of the world's population yet consumes approximately 25% of the world's energy.

- How many countries hold an endearing view of Americans?

Facts like these, along with the volatile economic and structural problems around the world have left us living in a world of violence, intimidation, chaos and confusion. All of these factors add stress to the lives of people who feel they are powerless in effecting any significant change. This leaves many frustrated and without hope — for some that will lead to violence. These things create pressure in people's minds and hearts. When enough pressure is created in anyone's life, they either change something or burst – just like a balloon. Often times the bursting balloon comes out in aggressive, inappropriate or violent behavior.

I am living below poverty level. I have been tossed around by the system because I am a minority. I feel powerless to make changes. I am functionally illiterate. I have been incarcerated twice for stealing to support my kids who have no mother. I live in a drug-infested neighborhood and am a former gang member. Am I more prone to violence than the person who has none of these characteristics? I hope you get the point.

In this new era, we are encouraged by government officials to go about our lives as if they are the same as before. I beg to differ. Our lives are not the same. To suggest they are is naïve. We live in a more dangerous world that is constantly evolving. If you honestly believe that the police or the government can protect you from violence, you are sadly mistaken. These agencies are well-intended and will do what they can, but they have limited resources and cannot be present everywhere violence erupts. The average violent encounter is less than two minutes. The average police response in the US is over six minutes. You do the math.

Evaluating Personal Risk Requires a Paradigm Shift

High-profile kidnappings, sexual assaults, child and elder abuse are a handful of crimes that get a lot of attention from the media. Often, these cases are the catalyst for changes in the law or procedural changes regarding the manner in which the offenders responsible for these crimes are sentenced or treated. Mass school shootings have sparked a debate over whether school personnel should be armed. These crimes create intense emotion and often result in change. There are schools with metal detectors which were unheard of years ago. How do you evaluate real risk and take proactive steps toward building a safer life or community?

During the evening rush hour on August 1, 2007, the I-35W Mississippi Bridge in Minneapolis, Minnesota collapsed in catastrophic failure. Thirteen people were killed and approximately 145 people were injured. In January 2008, the NTSB (National Transportation Safety Board) suggested the bridge collapse may have originated with the failure of gusset plates that were too thin. By June 16, 2008, the Minnesota Department of Transportation had announced it would replace or rehabilitate 120 bridges throughout Minnesota by the year 2018 to the tune of $2.5 billion. Is this expense necessary or is it a knee-jerk reaction based on emotion from the bridge collapse?

According to the 9/11 Commission Report: "At 8:46 on the morning of September 11, 2001, an airliner traveling at hundreds of miles per hour and carrying some 10,000 gallons of jet fuel plowed into the North Tower of the World Trade Center in Lower Manhattan. At 9:03, a second airliner hit the South Tower. The Twin Towers, where up to 50,000 people worked each day, both collapsed less than 90 minutes later. At 9:37 that same morning, a third airliner slammed into the western face of the Pentagon. At 10:03, a fourth airliner crashed in a field in southern Pennsylvania. It had been aimed at the United States Capitol or the White House, and was forced down by heroic passengers armed with the knowledge that America was under attack. More than 2,600 people died at the World Trade Center; 125 died at the Pentagon; 256 died on the four planes. The death toll surpassed that at Pearl Harbor in December 1941. This immeasurable pain was inflicted by 19 young Arabs acting at the behest of Islamist extremists headquartered in distant Afghanistan. Some had been in the United States for more than a year, mixing with the rest of the population. Though four had training as pilots, most were not well-educated. Most spoke English poorly, some hardly at all. In groups of four or five, carrying with them only small knives, box cutters, and cans of Mace or pepper spray, they had hijacked the four planes and turned them into deadly guided missiles."

The Department of Homeland Security, formed as a direct result of these attacks, released the following on 04/11/02: "Immediately following the tragic events of September 11, departments and agencies from across the federal government took steps to strengthen the safety and security of the American people. At the Federal level, a total of $10.6 billion from the Fiscal Year 2002

Emergency Budget Supplemental was dedicated to homeland security." The list of activities these funds were dedicated to is much too lengthy to list here. Suffice it to say there were significant changes that took place on many levels and serious funding dedicated towards those changes. Was all of this expense necessary, or was it over-reaction based on the violent acts of a few people?

Educated professionals have been warning of oil demand outstripping oil production for many, many years. A decade ago, crude was priced at $13.00 - $14.00 per barrel. In recent years it has hovered as high as $130.00 - $135.00 per barrel. A decade ago much of the alternative energy research and development was being explored by small companies. Per the American Petroleum Institute, between 2000 and 2005, oil and gas industry investment in emerging energy technologies was approximately 98 billion dollars. When gas prices soared in 2008, there was intense pressure from stockholders and legislators on oil companies to invest significant profits into alterative energy development and resources. Initially, they did, or at least their public relations departments led us to believe they were. Then gas prices dropped, and the urgency to invest in alternative energy dropped as well.

Dr. Peter Sandman is the creator of the "Risk = Hazard + Outrage" formula for risk communication. Essentially, the formula works like this: Outrage and hazard do not carry equal weight. When hazard (real risk) is high and outrage (emotion) is low, people under-react based on their perception that everything is okay. When hazard (real risk) is low and outrage (emotion) is high, most people over-react based on their perception things are not okay. Real risk will not necessarily be the determining factor that motivates people toward action. It is the emotion that outrage produces.

In the examples above:

- The bridge collapse may have exposed a real hazard, previously unknown, which is being addressed. We can be certain, due to the intense emotion surrounding the bridge collapse, officials will err on the conservative side of safety when evaluating bridge design.

- Swift action and a lot of money was spent post 9/11. Most people were outraged over these attacks.

- The alternative energy solution is still developing, but it is clear people are moved toward outrage when the price of gasoline reaches a certain level.

As someone who has been preaching a proactive approach to personal safety for many years, I have made some interesting observations. Most people do not take action in regards to their personal safety unless they are significantly motivated. It is fear or outrage that usually motivates people to take action, not necessarily the actual hazard. Some organizations will wait until a lawsuit requires them to take action or a violent act in their community demands attention.

Example: Several employees of a company have complained informally about being approached by strangers in the parking ramp. Nobody takes any proactive action. Eventually, an employee of the company is sexually assaulted in the parking ramp. It is perfectly understandable and natural that other employees are outraged and frightened as a result of the incident. They press for changes in security at the parking ramp. The company hires a private security firm to patrol the ramp for $100,000 annually. Would some of this money be better spent by the company offering self-defense training to all employees? How about changing company policy so employees are able to possess pepper spray for defensive purposes?

Over the years I have been asked to present information to countless safety committees, administrators, politicians and decision-makers. Many of these invitations are generated by someone who believes in the benefits of proactive safety planning and perceives a benefit to their community. The people who initiate these things are not necessarily decision-makers. Therefore, some of the presentations fall on deaf ears as the invitation to me has been crafted only to pacify the initial requestor. Public outrage drives decision-making and behavior.

Community is defined by any group that has a particular mission–a company, corporation, association or organization. It is a place where a group of individuals spend a considerable amount of time with others. What "communities" do you belong to? Are those communities safe? What real hazards are experienced with some frequency? Are the decisions regarding safety based on emotion or solid research and information?

Taking the Holistic Approach

Most people's goals when it comes to personal safety are to keep themselves and their loved ones out of harm's way. Martial arts, self defense courses and handgun ownership seems to be the American way of personal protection. However, does owning a handgun or participating in a martial arts course have real-world application?

I have studied a number of martial arts disciplines, and I am a handgun permit holder. Let's be clear. Martial arts, gun clubs and self defense programs are great disciplines and wonderful sports. Most of these programs teach discipline and build character. They provide good exercise, teach social skills and expand knowledge. Some studies suggest martial arts may even reduce hostility. For the disciplined and committed enthusiast, these activities will certainly provide excellent self defense skills but with significant cost. Are the things they teach applicable to real-life violence?

- When, during your martial arts class or self defense seminar, did anyone swing a chair at your head, try to push you forcefully into a car or wake you in the middle of the night with a knife to your throat? These are examples of real-life violence.

- Do traditional martial arts and self defense programs understand the relationship that exists between the brain and the body under high stress?

- Is the gun club able to appropriately identify the primary characteristics of violent crime?

- Does the gun club acknowledge that most self defense shootings occur in low or no-light conditions?

- Do any of these programs know what criminals look for in victims?

- Does the self defense program understand the recognizable clues of body language?

- Do they practice the art of interpersonal communications and de-escalation?

- Do they give any thought to unexpected emergencies and emergency planning?

Most of these issues are not even discussed, much less part of their curriculums. Unfortunate, as these issues are all vital in today's widening concerns about what personal safety entails. For all practical purposes the dojo as we know it is dead.

There is value in learning how to shoot a handgun and under what conditions it might be appropriate and legal. But the core of personal safety is not in learning how to shoot or a plethora of defensive techniques. The essence of personal safety is cognitive. How the brain recognizes, processes, interprets and acts on information will always trump technique. For it is there, in the decision-making process, that outcomes are formed. Having fed the appropriate information into your brain, that decision-making process is almost automatic and the outcomes are seamless.

Research into violent crime and interviews with victims reveal many violent encounters can be avoided by knowing what to look for. Anyone interested in their own personal safety should be prepared to respond to unexpected violence with strategies and techniques that are simple yet very effective should they find themselves in a situation that they cannot immediately escape.

Martial arts styles emphasize motor skills, often employing techniques which require fine and complex motor skills which are unavailable to most people when placed in high-stress situations. A good self-defense program should focus on motor skills the average person can remember and quickly perform in unexpected situations. There needs to be an emphasis on gross motor skills which are available to most people when under high stress. The high stress that comes with unexpected threat is often referred to as the Flight or Fight Syndrome.

You must also recognize how the brain works. When confronted with any task, the brain "scrolls" through its data base to find applicable principles to apply to the task. If there is nothing in the brain's data base that is applicable, the brain stalls and does not know what to do. Here is where preparation becomes critical.

This leads to the question — what type of training will best serve an individual in regards to personal safety?

Many states are now considering passing legislation commonly referred to as the "Castle Law" or "Castle Doctrine". Generally, these laws provide a legal standing for civilians not to retreat when confronted by an assailant. It also allows for reasonable force in defense of one's own life or that of another's. In addition, it will often remove civil liability for the outcome of such an event. In some states, this law is reserved for the home. In other states, it extends outside of the home. Civilians who live in states where this concept is law can stand their ground rather than retreating using reasonable force.

When planning for your own safety, your loved ones or that of your organization or community, please consider taking a holistic view by looking for a self defense style, system or course that will answer the following questions:

- What is reasonable force? Here is another shortcoming in traditional training. They do not teach the participant what is reasonable.

- What does the law allow me to do?

- What legal obligations do I have?

- Are there policies in my work environment that restrict my legal abilities?

- What is it that I really need to protect myself from?

- Do I need to consider emergency planning in addition to self defense?

- Have I identified my critical assets?

- Do I need to purchase a handgun?

- Do I need to apply for a permit to carry? Note: statistically, it is much more likely you will lay your hands on someone using reasonable force than pointing a handgun at an adversary.

- Does this program addresses many of the issues outlined in this chapter or does it just focus on techniques?

This is not the world many of us grew up in. There are changing demographics, geopolitical circumstances and economics that should impact the methods we use to embrace personal safety. Be enlightened when it comes to choosing yours.

Self Defense Courses: How to Best Prepare For Real World Violence

Typically, most people that are interested in self defense will do one of two things. They either enroll in a martial arts course or attend some type of self defense seminar. Using the martial arts route, the amount of dollars spent on achieving a top designated rank is typically around $5000. This usually requires years of practice in which techniques that require gross, fine and complex motor skills are practiced repetitively. There are several basic concerns with martial arts training.

First, fine and complex motor skills, many of which are part of martial arts training, are not available to most people when under high stress. This is what most people experience when confronted by a potential assailant and is due to a reaction between the brain and the body that we have little control over.

The Sympathetic Nervous System is activated when the mind detects a potential threat to survive, and it reacts by mediating the involuntary responses to alarm by speeding the heart rate, raising the blood pressure, dilating the pupils of the eyes and a number of other responses. This system opposes and overrides the Parasympathetic Nervous System, which regulates many body functions. It does so in order to provide the body with the necessary capabilities to fight or flee from danger. In doing so, however, the body loses its fine and complex motor skills and increases its gross motor skills. These details are presented in Chapter 17.

One of the first things that deteriorate under high stress is your cognitive ability. This occurs at a time when decision-making is critical. This is another problem with most martial arts programs.

Many martial arts techniques are generally unrealistic in real world application. They teach techniques without putting them into the proper context. Additionally, the amount of legally accepted force required to overcome an assailant is not clearly defined. The solution to this is to learn self defense techniques within a clearly defined model — one in which rapid decision-making is a simple (not complex) cognitive process.

A decent self defense course should expose the most likely vulnerabilities people have. Then, it should equip an individual with no prior military, martial arts or self defense training to be proficient in defending themselves against the most likely threats they will encounter and do so on the basis of solid legal precedence of case law. Using a training model and curriculum that addresses these concerns will result in a realistic and scientific approach to self defense. This is rarely achieved by typical martial arts and self defense programs.

Holistic is defined as: "An all encompassing view based on the knowledge of the nature, functions, and properties of the components, their interactions, and their relationship to the whole." The program you choose to involve yourself in must mix the core principles and issues raised in this chapter in order to effectively equip you to deal with a wide range of threats and possibilities because personal safety goes far beyond proficiency with weapons and martial arts techniques.

The goal, presumably, is to build a protective perimeter around your personal and professional daily life. Just as border security is vital to a nation, so must organizations, individuals and communities be evermore more diligent to protect their own critical assets.

Undeniably, as we rapidly approach the end of the church age and now deeply entrenched in an era of terrorism and crime, the responsibility of security is falling on the private sector and creating a significant need for the privatization of services. Individuals and organizations are expected to be prepared. How can this be accomplished without sacrificing years of time and dedicating significant money towards training? The answer is choosing a proven, holistic system of self defense that is under-girded by a solid legal foundation and has real world application.

Individual Reflection or Group Discussion

There is a chance you will become a target, and you will need to think a different way in order to protect yourself. A good starting point is thinking about the communities and relationships you are currently part of.

1. Identify the communities that you belong to. These might include family, work, church, clubs and other organizations.

2. Identify the real risk (not perceived risk driven by outrage) in each community.

3. Make a list of things you think should be done to address those real risks.

Chapter 16
Civilian Use of Force in Self Defense

"There is no reason for anyone in this country, anyone except a police officer or a military person, to buy, to own, to have, to use a handgun. I used to think handguns could be controlled by laws about registration, by laws requiring waiting periods for purchasers, by laws making sellers check out the past of buyers. I now think the only way to control handgun use in this country is to prohibit the guns. And the only way to do that is to change the constitution."

Michael Gartner

"Studies indicate that firearms are used more than 2 million times a year for personal protection, and that the presence of a firearm, without a shot being fired, prevents crime in many instances. Shooting usually can be justified only where crime constitutes an immediate, imminent threat to life, limb or, in some cases, property."

NRA, July 2010

Wayne LaPierre said; "With respect to federal firearm laws covering felonious possession and use by a whole class of prohibited persons, NRA's position has been abundantly clear. It is a federal felony – a criminal act punishable by 10 years in prison –

for any convicted felon to possess any handgun, rifle or shotgun. It is a federal felony for anyone to possess a stolen firearm. It is a federal felony for anyone to give a firearm to a juvenile for the purpose of committing a crime. It is a federal felony for anyone to possess a firearm with the intention of committing a crime. It is a federal felony for anyone to use a firearm in the commission of a crime. It is a federal felony for anyone to cross state lines with the intention to unlawfully obtain a firearm or to commit a crime. If one were to add up all of the penalties for gun offenses by street criminals under existing federal law, total jail time with consecutive sentences could add up to literally hundreds of years in federal prison. (The media) should be questioning federal prosecutors on their refusal to use existing law to prosecute. With application of federal laws against violent criminals and firearms, the streets could be cleaned in a matter of months."

Lessons Learned

I am sprinting down an alley chasing a guy who has no shirt or shoes on and has just jumped an 8-foot wood fence surrounding a backyard and wishing I had running shoes on. This came about as a direct result of several police officers and my partner sneaking into the front door of a house in an attempt to arrest a fugitive who had an active warrant.

I had reluctantly allowed myself to be talked into private fugitive apprehension, otherwise known as bounty hunting, by my trusted partner at the time who was great at networking. He had networked himself into a relationship with a bail bond agency that was looking to beef up their apprehension capabilities.

Bounty hunting is nothing like you see on "Dog the Bounty Hunter". The people we went looking for were bad and dangerous. The work could be very exciting, although I found actual apprehensions to be fairly bloody. It can also be very boring. Collecting information and conducting investigations on individuals who had jumped bond was interesting, but ultimately we could spend many hours conducting these investigations along with days of surveillance only to find out the person we were looking for was in another country. In this line of work you do not get paid unless you produce a body. When we had the body it paid well.

This was a side job for both of us, and it was a perfect fit since we were both probation/parole officers who were part of a multi-agency task force that targeted the most dangerous offenders in the county. We also had created the JORP program, which stood for Juvenile Offender Recovery Program. The JORP program evolved out of a dirty little secret. That secret was there were hundreds of warrants that had been issued on juveniles who had violated their probation or parole terms and court orders - and those warrants were just collecting dust. I was advised that after a cursory visit by the Sheriff's Department Warrant Division to the last known address, the warrant was shelved for all practical purposes. We were the only two JORP officers who would go looking for the most dangerous juvenile offenders one evening per week.

We had tremendous success arresting these juvenile fugitives while working with a number of different agencies. We were so successful that I was instructed by the Juvenile Probation Department Chief Administrator to slow down because we were jamming up the juvenile criminal justice system. The juveniles we were apprehending had to be jailed, seen by a judge, and many of them were sent on to other facilities. Our success was putting too much financial and resource pressure on the system. My guess was that this was probably happening all over the country; criminals with warrants running amok with very few people looking for them.

So, although I did not need another thing on my plate of responsibility, I knew we were well situated and properly connected to conduct bounty hunting. I agreed to try if for a season. It lasted several years.

We would conduct all the interviews, complete the investigation and locate these fugitives through surveillance. All of these fugitives had active warrants, and once we located them we would request police assistance to make the apprehension. I always thought this was the smart way to work for a number of reasons. One of which, there would be less temptation for a fugitive to fight or run with the sight of uniformed police officers.

The guy who leaped over this fence must not have read the memo. He had a history of methamphetamine use, and the speed at which he came over that fence lead me to believe he must have been tweaked. The foot pursuit ended several blocks later amid the screeching of police car tires and the screaming of sirens coming to our aid. The fugitive had jumped behind another fence and into a back yard. I am quite sure he did not see me chugging along a block behind him. As I approached the yard I had seen him jump into, I motioned to another police officer to join me.

We entered the yard together and quickly discovered the fugitive. The police officer commanded him to the ground at gunpoint. Apparently the fugitive's response was not quick enough as I watched the officer's boot connect to the fugitive's face as he began to kneel on the ground. Blood seemed to explode from this guy's face. Another officer quickly joined us, and we began to attempt to handcuff the fugitive who was now prone and had his hands concealed under his chest. Fearing he might have a weapon, I took my kubaton (a stick-like control instrument) and placed it on a pressure point behind his ear directing him to bring his hands out from under him. His response was to growl at me. I then put the full force of my body weight into this pressure point and still got no response. Ah.....the wonder of drugs.

He was handcuffed and secured within 30 seconds as other officers joined us. The police originally wanted us to haul him away. We disagreed since it was their arrest, and they had split the guy's face open. Detention centers and jails often will not accept a prisoner like this because of the liability. A sergeant finally arrived to settle the dispute by asking who did the damage to this guy's face. They hauled him off to the hospital for stitches, and we got paid the next day.

We never had a problem with any of our bounty hunting activities but for some reason, this event came back to bite us. Several years later we were questioned as to whether we had inappropriately used our employer's resources to make this arrest. Although we had not, and were very careful about separating our roles, there was remarkable animosity toward us from one Corrections Administrator. Admittedly, there was a fine line that we respected between the resources we might use professionally at our government jobs and the work we did as private bounty hunters, but the main idea was to apprehend criminals and get them off the street. This same Administrator eventually tried to get us fired, although he never had the courage to confront us directly and tell us what his issues were. Weird, because we were both decorated officers with personnel files that were full of commendations and excellent annual performance reviews.

Lesson learned: Many good deeds will get punished in the natural. The good guys can be hindered in carrying out their work by a criminal justice system that is ill-prepared to deal with the statistical realities of criminals. Administrators are often driven by their own personal bias, agendas or politics. Every administrator has someone they answer to. They are required to submit to the desires of those decision-makers. Decision-makers are often completely out of touch with the reality and nature of criminal behavior. Ultimately, top decision-makers shape policy based on their own perception of how things should be – and this is driven by a lifetime of their own experiences, education, training and baggage.

Consider This

You have just finished buying groceries one evening and are on the way to your vehicle when you are confronted by a stranger who demands your money. You push him away in an attempt to escape. He trips and falls hitting his head against the ground. The police arrive and everything is sorted out. You are sent on your way, and the stranger is carted off to the hospital. You find out several days later the stranger died due to the traumatic brain injury he received when his head hit the ground. Several weeks later, you are served papers which indicate you are being sued by the stranger's family for wrongful death, due to your negligence. Is this possible?

The central idea behind a wrongful death lawsuit is that through negligence, carelessness or recklessness, someone died. These lawsuits, usually brought forth on behalf of the surviving family members, attempt to collect damages for expenses related to the death, pain and suffering experienced by the survivors and for future earnings of the deceased.

There is also the possibility of a personal injury lawsuit in which the injured party attempts to collect damages for their injuries based on negligence or intentional wrongdoing.

What rights do civilians have when using force to prevent injury to themselves or others? What are the legal limitations and implications on use of force by civilians? What legal thresholds will be examined by the courts? What specific type of force can be used in self defense?

To answer these questions, let's look at this from another perspective.

The Odds of Death

Consider the following odds of death as they relate to personal risk. These numbers vary to some degree depending on the annual totals. These odds are calculated by the National Safety Council on the most recently released data.

- Plane Crash: One-year odds are 1 in 400,000. Lifetime odds are 1 in 5,000. In this context, would the court consider it unusual or negligent for flight attendants to skip the safety instructions given to passengers?

- Accidental Drowning: One-year odds are 1 in 88,772. Lifetime odds are 1 in 1,140. In this context, would the Court consider it unusual or negligent for the owner of a pool to ignore reasonable efforts towards adult supervision while inviting young neighborhood children to use the pool anytime they wish?

- Falls: One year odds are 1 in 15,614. Lifetime odds are 1 in 200. In this context, would the court consider it unusual or negligent for the owner of a home to invite others over for a barbeque on the upper deck knowing the guard rails are loose and broken?

- Accidental poisoning: One-year odds are 1 in 14,107. Lifetime odds are 1 in 180. In this context, would the court consider it unusual or negligent for the owner of a business to have unidentified hazardous materials in the break room?

- Motor Vehicle Accident: One-year odds are 1 in 6,535. Lifetime odds are 1 in 84. In this context, would the court consider it unusual or negligent for automobile manufacturers to sell automobiles without safety restraints?

Using the same formula, I have crunched some numbers regarding crime.

- Assault: One-year odds are 1 in 25,263. Lifetime odds are 1 in 217. In this context, would the court consider it unusual or negligent for the intended victim to use force to escape or protect themselves?

- The odds of being a victim of any type of crime are approximately 8%. In this context, would the court consider it unusual or negligent for the intended victim to use force to escape or protect themselves?

- The odds of being a victim of violent crime, not necessarily involving death, are 1-2%. In this context, would the court consider it unusual or negligent for the intended victim to use force to escape or protect themselves?

What Does The Law Allow?

Almost all states within the United States allow civilians to use reasonable force in protection of their own or someone else's property or life. Check your own state statutes as they can vary considerably from state to state.

Most of these statutes do not define what reasonable force is. Using the example we opened with, is it reasonable to push someone down who is demanding your money but is not displaying, brandishing or threatening you with a weapon? This is where it gets tricky. Let's assume, for argument's sake, the stranger who died from the brain injury after you pushed him was found to have a concealed knife in his pocket? Does this make any difference?

Let's change the scenario. The same stranger produces a handgun and demands your money. You, being a legally licensed handgun permit holder, pull your handgun and shoot him. He dies. The police discover the handgun he pulled on you is really a BB gun or a toy gun. Does this change your liability?

The bottom line is that the courts will look at several factors:

- Do you have the legal (statutory) authority to use force and under what conditions?

- Were those conditions present at the time of the incident?

- Were you a reluctant participant? Did you create or exacerbate the problem?

- Did you consider retreating? Was it reasonable to consider retreating?

- Was the force you used reasonable given your perception of the events?

The problem most civilians confront when using force is that they do not understand what is reasonable. The legal definition of reasonable: "what is appropriate for a particular situation?" This definition is generally applied in the Law of Negligence. It is the standard of care that a reasonably prudent person would observe under a certain set of conditions. Someone who exercises such standards would not be negligent.

Let's go back to our example. Is it reasonable for the intended victim to push a stranger away who is demanding their money? Of course it is. We frequently hear about death and injuries that result from these types of crimes. If the civilian's perception is that they are about to be hurt or injured as a result of a crime, it is reasonable to use force to escape.

Was it reasonable for the civilian to shoot the stranger demanding money when the gun the stranger was using is a toy gun? Yes, it is. The civilian has no duty or obligation to ask the stranger if the gun he is holding in his hand is a toy gun or a BB gun. The civilian's perception at the time of the incident is that the stranger is holding a real gun with real bullets, and he might shoot.

Civilians vs. Cops

Civilians do not have the same *mission* as law enforcement officers have. Police are required by their mission and policy to respond to, and deal with, circumstances that may require use of force. Civilians are not required to get involved in any situation requiring the use of force. Civilians are not sent out to intervene in anything. Civilians can walk away from everything.

Civilians do, however, have almost the same *authority* as police officers when it comes to statutory authority governing the use of force. Civilians have the right to use "reasonable force", as do the police, if their perception is that an adversary is trying to hurt someone or unlawfully take property of another or, in some states, trespass on private property.

In most states, deadly force, or the taking of another's life, is justified if a civilian's perceptions of the activity taking place will likely result in great bodily harm or death. This is the same general rule for police officers. The difference is that in many states civilians must consider retreating. They must be a "reluctant participant", which means they had little choice with being caught up in the circumstances to begin with. Law enforcement personnel do not have these restrictions.

Another commonality between police and civilians is the ability to use reasonable force to detain someone during an arrest if a crime is committed in their presence. In many states civilians can make citizen's arrests under certain conditions. Check your state statutes for details.

Safe Communities

Many people are not aware of the thin statutory line between police officers and civilians. Statutorily, this allows civilians to form neighborhood patrols. Vigilante justice is never encouraged, but in an era in which law enforcement and governmental resources are spread thin, communities can take up a type of policing based on these statutes. Community safety patrols do not give civilians authority to enforce statutes and ordinances. It does, however, grant them the ability to protect their communities from threats towards life and property as well as civilian arrest authority and detention for a great number of crimes committed in their presence, and in some states, a suspect can be held by civilians if there is reasonable suspicion to believe they have committed a felony.

Examining Use of Force

Law enforcement professionals are held to a higher standard of training than civilians, which is why a Use of Force Model of some type is typically part of law enforcement training. The challenge for the civilian is to determine what is reasonable should they decide to use force. Reasonableness and timeliness are the two primary considerations a judge or jury will use to decide if the civilian's actions were acceptable in a use-of-force case.

Traditional martial arts and self-defense classes do not teach what is reasonable and timely. Most of these classes teach motor skills and techniques but do not provide the civilian a legal framework of force to work within.

Here's an example of the dilemma: A civilian comes upon an adversary who is standing several feet from another person, fists clenched, swearing, and threatening that other person. The adversary pushes that person hard, knocking them to the ground. Would it be reasonable for the civilian observing this, who has the right to use force, to intervene in the situation and to purposefully break the adversary's leg? Probably not. Unfortunately, this is a possible response for the civilian participating in traditional martial arts. Why? Many martial arts will teach you a number of techniques to deal with an adversary, several of which will break an adversary's leg.

Now, take the same situation and apply what you will learn from an appropriate Use of Force Model. The description above is one of an adversary whose actions are physically aggressive with no apparent weapons in hand. A good Use of Force Model will recommend appropriate techniques for this specific type of adversary. Impact pressure would be one of the appropriate techniques as would a striking technique. Impact pressure can be applied in various ways in which it is unlikely a leg will be broken and will likely be very effective. Strikes can also be very effective in a situation like this.

A good Use of Force Model does not teach civilians to break legs. It does, however, suggest impact pressure and striking specific areas of the body is appropriate. Let's assume the civilian performs a head strike or stun on the adversary, which momentarily affects the adversary's nervous system to the point they collapse and/or lose consciousness. See the difference? Momentary loss of consciousness is considered more reasonable than a broken leg in this situation.

Let's change this scenario one more time. The civilian uses a thigh stun or knee strike, which is an appropriate technique on this type of adversary. The civilian aims for the adversary's thigh with his knee, but the adversary turns at the last moment toward the civilian whose thigh stun ends up striking the adversary's knee breaking the knee joint.

In this instance, using either the traditional martial arts training or a Use of Force Model, the injury to the adversary is the same — a broken leg. But the context and framework is entirely different, and that will affect the considerations of timeliness and reasonableness from a legal perspective.

Self Defense for Teens - What Is Appropriate?

People often wonder if use of force has a different set of standards when juveniles are involved. The answer is no.

A man attending one of our courses shared that his 16-year old daughter was assaulted by an older female shortly after she got off her school bus. It was a lovely afternoon with no hint of danger. Shortly after the school bus left this particular stop, his daughter was grabbed from behind by the hair and pulled to the ground. Her female assailant jumped on top of her, slammed her head into the ground and then proceeded to break her nose.

A friend of the daughter tried to pull the assailant off of her, but these efforts were hampered by two males who were standing by watching the incident. They were presumably accompanying the assailant and pulled the daughter's friend off not allowing her to interfere any further.

Nearby, several other people watched and did nothing. A few people cheered the assailant on. One observer did call the police and got the license plate number of the car that left the scene with the assailant and her two male companions.

The fellow who attends our course reacted like any other concerned father – his daughter had been viciously attacked for apparently no reason. His anger was understandable. In the weeks following the incident, the police investigated the case and identified the assailant and her cohorts. The assailant, an adult, was already on probation. This case will grind its way through the criminal justice system, and we can only hope the end result will satisfy the victim and her parents.

As a result of this assault, the father asked me how his daughter should have protected herself. The answer to his question is that his daughter has the same right of self defense as any other civilian in the state. In the state of Minnesota, a person 16 years or older "may possess and use an authorized tear gas compound in the exercise of reasonable force in defense of the person or the person's property only if it is propelled from an aerosol container, labeled with or accompanied by clearly written instructions as to it's use, and dated to indicate its anticipated useful life." A person 18 years or older "may possess and use an electronic incapacitation device in the exercise of reasonable force in defense of the person or the person's property only if the electronic incapacitation device is labeled with or accompanied by clearly written instructions as to it's use and the dangers involved in its use."

And finally: "Reasonable force may be used upon or towards the person of another without the other's consent when the following circumstances exist or the actor reasonably believes them to exist........When used by any person in resisting or aiding another to resist an offense against the person."

Clearly, from a legal point of view she had the right to use reasonable force to protect herself. It would be reasonable for her to have used tear gas/pepper spray or an electronic incapacitation device on an assailant trying to smash her head into the ground.

The father's question poses an interesting dilemma. Minnesota State Statutes do not allow weapons on school grounds. It violates state law for his daughter to posses any weapon while on school property. The young woman attends a school that has a zero-tolerance policy in place for weapons of any kind. She had just completed her school day and gotten on a bus provided by the school district. The school district has some responsibility for the young woman's safety while she is attending school and until she steps off the bus. As soon as she steps off the bus, she is on her own. Now what?

This 16-year old student has the right to carry mace, pepper spray or a tear gas compound as soon as she steps off of the bus. But how would she access it if she has spent the whole day in settings in which it is either illegal or violates policy to possess such an item?

Most states in the United States have adopted laws similar to this statute from Minnesota: "whoever possesses, stores, or keeps a dangerous weapon or uses or brandishes a replica firearm or a BB gun while knowingly on school property is guilty of a felony and may be sentenced to imprisonment for not more than two years or to payment of a fine of not more than $5,000, or both." Most schools have written policies that reflect these laws. Several decades of mass public shootings (including schools) and gang violence have produced these laws and policies, most of which are directed toward thwarting violence and curbing liability. But by doing so, they have set up yet another problem.

In addition to the statutes cited above, most states also have laws similar to Minnesota's statute in terms of self defense. "Reasonable force may be used upon or towards the person of another without the other's consent when the following circumstances exist or the actor reasonably believes them to exist..........When used by any person in resisting or aiding another to resist an offense against the person......When used by a person in lawful possession of real or personal property, or by another assisting the person in lawful possession, in resisting a trespass upon or other unlawful interference with such property..."

Translation: you can use reasonable force against another without their permission if you believe they are trying to hurt you or someone else or you believe them to be attempting to take yours or someone else's property.

Let's get back to this man's 16-year old daughter. The situation she faced that day, with the existing laws in place, leaves her no room to defend herself except by weaponless defense using her hands (or legs and feet). Whatever she could do with her hands would be considered "reasonable" under the law as her only options.

The young lady did sustain a broken nose and required some surgery. Although restitution is an option in court, it is more often not collected. Let's take this a step further. What if she had died as a result of her head being slammed into the ground? Is there liability on anyone's part? I don't have the answer to that, but let's throw in a few more hypothetical factors to make it interesting.

The young woman had complained to school officials she was being regularly harassed by this woman at this particular bus stop. Her father had approached school officials and asked permission for his daughter to carry pepper spray due to the nature of the harassment.

School officials denied the request.

Now, what kind of case is there for liability? Negligence is defined as a party's failure to exercise the prudence and care that a reasonable person would exercise in similar circumstances to prevent injury to another party.

In a civil suit, generally the plaintiff in these cases must prove the following in order to be awarded restitution, compensation or reparations for their losses:

- That the defendant had a duty of care.
- That the defendant failed to uphold this duty.
- That this negligence led to the plaintiff's injury or death.
- That the actual damages that were caused by the injury.

Gross negligence is usually understood to involve an act or omission in reckless disregard of the consequences affecting the life or property of another.

This leaves us with quite a bit to think about. Should schools be offering self defense courses as part of their regular curriculums? Should parents take the responsibility of enrolling their kids in self defense courses? Have state laws and public school system policies gone too far in trying to protect students and mitigate violence?

These laws and policies are in place for a good reason. But in situations like this one, they also rob the victim of self defense options.

In a related matter, many schools also have a zero violence policy. I remember a number of years ago when my son intervened in a situation in which one of his acquaintances was taking a beating at school. My son stepped in and simply pushed the assailant away from his friend knocking the assailant to the ground. My son was given an in-school detention for several days along with his friend and the assailant. It mattered little to school officials who did what during the incident. They had a shotgun approach to these matters; everyone involved receives consequences.

I had an interesting chat with his guidance counselor and the vice-principal of the school several days later. I showed them the statutes regarding reasonable force and advised them they had no legal standing to take these statutory rights away from students. They conceded that was probably accurate and promised to have legal counsel look into it.

Here we have another dilemma. School policy seems to trump state statutes. Generally, a public or private entity such as a school, corporation, company or organization can restrict even further, through policy, what the statutes allow. For example, even though I am a legitimate handgun permit holder, which is allowed by state statute, my employer may ban weapons from their property. This is okay. However, when it comes to using reasonable force to protect yourself or another, they are treading on thin ice as there is case law that establishes the right to defend yourself – no matter where you are.

Primary Considerations

- Do your homework when choosing self defense training and defense weapons. Make sure that the techniques you learn are in the context of a Use of Force Model that has been tested by the courts and is appropriate for civilians. These programs are very difficult to find.

- No entity can take this basic right to self defense away. That is not to say those who exercise it will not suffer consequences for doing so, but be prepared to defend your actions from a legal basis.

Individual Reflection or Group Discussion

You need to begin to build some basic, foundational skills. If you think you will find yourself in the circumstances described in Chapter 9, part of your preparation should be a basic self defense course. You might find one locally. We encourage you to consider the Assault Prevention Course first, then optionally, the Personal Protection Course thereafter. These courses cover topics that will not be covered in a traditional martial arts course or self defense course. The physical techniques are easily practiced with a partner and are not age or gender specific.

Find a self defense course and commit to it. You might consider finding a local seminar you can take with your small group or a loved one. An alternate idea would be to order the Assault Prevention Course and work through the lessons together as a group.

These courses may be found at AssaultPrevention.Info

Chapter 17
High Stress Performance

"Safety is something that happens between your ears, not something you hold in your hand."

Jeff Cooper

"Your father knows what you need before you ask him. So do not worry, saying 'What shall we eat?' or 'What shall we wear?' For the pagans run after all these things, and your heavenly Father knows that you need them. But seek first his kingdom and his righteousness, and all these things will be given to you as well. Therefore do not worry about tomorrow, for tomorrow will worry about itself. Today's trouble is enough for today." Matthew 6:8b, 31-34

Lessons Learned

It is 1:00 am on a hot August overnight shift. Another officer and I are dispatched to a home where we are met by an elderly woman who reports that this is her daughter's residence and that her daughter has just been raped. I enter the living room where I find a 30 year-old woman who is whimpering like a scared animal. As gently as possible, I interview her and discover that she had taken her vehicle to a 7-11 store to buy some cigarettes just before midnight. She left the vehicle running and windows open as there were no other customers in the store, and she was going to be in the store for less than a minute.

She got back into her car and began to drive off when every horror film she had ever seen came to life with the guy who suddenly popped up in her back seat, held a knife against her throat, had her drive to a remote location and sexually assaulted her. He then had her drive him to back to the 7-11, and he walked off into the night. She drove home and called 911.

She was clearly in shock and unable to provide a good description of the perpetrator or the location she had been raped. Her husband had taken off looking for the guy based on his wife's weak description of him. Paramedics were called to the scene along with detectives to transport her to the hospital and collect evidence. The rest of us looked for the suspect and looked for further evidence in her car.

Lessons learned: People who have suffered trauma have very different reactions. The victim was unable to provide much information about the perpetrator or location despite the fact that she was obviously there and close to the perpetrator. Things I would have considered crazy seemed normal to victims, like the husband going to look for the suspect instead of staying with his wife. Things I might find normal seemed crazy to victims, like the victim driving home instead of calling the police from the 7-11 store. High stress reactions are varied and unpredictable.

High Stress Situations Defined

I listened to an interview with one of the victims of the I-35W bridge collapse, which is memorialized on the anniversary of the catastrophic bridge failure in Minneapolis, Minnesota. The victim, a female in her mid-20's, found herself in her vehicle at the bottom of the Mississippi river. She described pushing on all the windows in the car in an effort to escape without success. She was not able to describe how she eventually got out of the vehicle but remembers suddenly being in the water outside the vehicle and coming to the surface. Her actions in the vehicle and the loss of memory are a classic example of how the brain and body react under high stress.

Why do some people seem to be able to accomplish superhuman feats when they find themselves in seemingly impossible situations while others freeze, panic or are unable to defend themselves? Some survival capabilities are part of our genetic code. Part of our genetic heritage is the relationship our brains have with our bodies when placed under high stress. Most people will experience high stress if being attacked or assaulted.

High stress situations are defined as any situation that forces us to face our vulnerability and mortality. This would likely include an assault. High stress situations often include the following elements:

- The event is sudden and unexpected: Assailants and criminals do not advertise they are about to commit a crime or attack someone.

- The event will disrupt a person's sense of control: Most of us walk around with a sense of control over our actions and environment. An assault, by its nature, has the assailant making the rules, and the victim frantically trying to counter those actions being presented to them.

- The event may disrupt a person's beliefs, values and very basic assumptions about how the world works. In a nation where there is an 8% chance of being a victim of any crime and a 1-2% chance of being a victim of violent crime, most of us walk around feeling generally secure. Being a victim of a violent crime has a strong tendency to disrupt one's sense of how the world is supposed to work, which includes not being the victim of violent crime.

- The event includes an element of loss — control, ego and self-esteem. If you have been the victim of a violent crime, you already know this to be true. In the aftermath there are lingering effects that may subside or last a lifetime. One of these effects is a sense that you could have or should have prevented the incident or performed better during it. These thoughts can seriously affect ego and self-esteem.

- High stress situations come in all varieties. Examples include a car accident, a personal emotional trauma, a missing child, an assault, a shooting, an attack or threat.

Reactions to high stress come in all varieties. Reactions are dependent on several elements:

- What is the intended victim's cognitive ability? This is the intellectual ability or thinking process which includes planning, tactics and decision-making.

- What are the intended victim's affective skills — their ability to control psychological reaction under stress?

- What are the intended victim's motor skills? Have they been trained in the use of appropriate force, tactics, techniques and weapons?

All three of these skill sets are called into play during a high stress situation, and deeply affect the outcome.

Elements of an Assault

There is good research available from the investigation of law enforcement officer involved assaults and deaths that have parallel principles to a civilian assault. Civilians, of course, do not have the mission that law enforcement officers have. But presumably, the traits exhibited by the violent people law enforcement officers deal with are the same traits exhibited by the adversary to perpetrate violent crime on civilians. This research has the following applications to a violent crime being perpetrated on a civilian.

- The incident is usually spontaneous.
- The incident is life threatening.
- The incident occurs at very close range — 75% are less than 10 feet.
- The adversary has the initiative and the intended victim reacts to the threat.
- There is no time to think of a response.
- The intended victim experiences extreme life threatening stress.
- There may be more than one adversary.
- The adversary may not be the original target of the intended victim's attention, so the intended victim is caught off guard.
- There may be a physical altercation involved.
- The adversary will be younger than the intended victim and in better shape.
- The adversary will anticipate the intended victim's actions and responses.
- The intended victim will not anticipate the adver-

sary's actions and responses.

- The intended victim may hesitate to evaluate the situation because they do not know what to do. They have no skills or training to deal with it.

- The adversary decides to use force and acts: the intended victim must react, but cannot respond in time.

The chances of the intended victim winning under these conditions and in these situations are poor, and survival usually depends on luck! The dilemma the intended victim faces when confronted with spontaneous violence is the need to evaluate the level of force available to overcome the resistance and to react in time to win. The first part calls for a cognitive decision; the second for an immediate acceptable motor response.

When placed under life-threatening stress, our performance as human beings has a tendency to collapse. There are many factors that work against our ability to successfully counter an assault. There are also a number of factors that work in our favor, in order to survive. The challenge is learning how to manipulate and manage these factors.

The Relationship between the Body & Brain

There is a relationship between performance and stress. Most of us are already "wired" in such a manner that we rise up and perform better when it is required. This relationship is often referred to as the Yerkes-Dodson Curve. It works something like this. When there is:

- No stress, there is no performance. Imagine sitting on the sofa surfing through television channels. No great stress, no great performance. Just hit the button on the remote. Life is good.

- Great stress, there is great performance. You walk in to work and your supervisor advises a colleague is sick, and you will be covering their work as well as your own. Or perhaps you are at home, and one of your children is sick in addition to a very busy schedule. Generally speaking, performance improves greatly when it is needed. People rise up and figure out a way to handle these unexpected difficulties. Life can be stressful.

- Huge stress, there is a marked decrease in performance, unreliable performance, or terrible performance. As in the example used above, now imagine that your supervisor tells you the whole department is out sick, and you have to handle all the work. Impossible. You want to go home and crawl into bed assuming the fetal position. This is the type of thing that happens when we are attacked, feel threatened or are in danger. Our performance is lost.

If that is not bad enough, let's consider what the nervous system does to the body during these high stress incidents.

The sympathetic nervous system is activated when the mind detects a potential threat to survive. It reacts by mediating the involuntary responses to alarm by speeding the heart rate, raising the blood pressure and dilating the pupils of the eyes. This system opposes and overrides the parasympathetic nervous system, which regulates many body functions. It does this in order to provide the body with the necessary capabilities to fight or flee from danger. This is commonly referred to as the "Fight or Flight Syndrome". However, in doing so, the body loses its fine and complex motor skills and increases its gross motor skills. Some of the effects we have little control over as a result of the sympathetic nervous system overriding the parasympathetic nervous system, which include:

- Increased heart rate and blood pressure.
- Dilation of blood vessels in major muscle groups.
- Loss of fine and complex motor skills.
- Constriction of blood vessels to the brain.
- Loss of peripheral vision.
- Increased visual dependency.
- Pupil dilation.
- Focus on visual stimulus and a tendency to exclude other senses.
- Hyper-vigilance, panic or brain stall.
- Constriction of surface level blood vessels.
- Decreased sensory perception to pain.
- Mental confusion following the incident.
- Adrenaline release.
- Glycogenolysis: The splitting up of glycogen in the liver yielding glucose.
- Crouching: A natural tendency to begin to stoop towards the ground.

While this process is taking place, the heart begins to beat rapidly. At 115 beats per minute, the body starts to lose cognitive ability and fine motor skills. At 145 beats per minute, the body loses complex motor skills. At 175 beats per minute, the body is in condition to employ its gross motor skills to fight or flee – and survive.

Motor Skills Affected in High Stress Situations

- Gross Motor Skills are the movement and action of large and / or major muscle groups. Gross motor skills are considered cognitively simple and require very little decision-making. Examples include walking, running, pushing a car or pulling a rope. These skills are readily available, exemplified and primed for action under high stress.

- Fine Motor Skills are skills that use small muscle mass groups such as hands and fingers and frequently involve eye-hand coordination. An example might be picking up a pen between your thumb and forefinger. Fine motor skills require more cognitive processing. Depending on the tactical method, retrieving a handgun and shooting it might be considered a fine motor skill. These skills deteriorate rapidly under high stress.

- Complex Motor Skills are movements that involve a series of muscle groups requiring eye-hand coordination, precision, tracking and timing. An example would be for you to walk over to a desk and pick up a pen between your thumb and forefinger, rotate the pen clockwise 180 degrees, then set it back down — all within 15 seconds. Other examples include martial arts techniques using multiple movements. These skills deteriorate rapidly under high stress.

In simple terms, if you sense threat, this is the interaction that begins to take place between your brain and the body. Many of the things listed would not be high on my list of reactions I want to experience if someone is trying to hurt me. Under high stress, one of the first things to deteriorate is the cognitive ability to make decisions! That's not good.

Thus far we have painted a grim picture of the odds when dealing with a violent adversary. But we can alter the odds.

Required Survival Skills

As complex as all this might sound, there is a simple solution. To begin to bring all these negative effects back into a more reasonable arena, breathe deeply. Research reveals after three deep breaths many of these negative effects begin to dissipate. This will enhance your ability to respond to danger.

In order to alter the odds before an incident, training is required in the observation of environmental and behavioral clues, preparedness, motor skills practice (self defense), tactics and simulations. The appropriate type of training will include practical psychomotor skills training that includes techniques and tactics placed in context with an appropriate legal framework. In simulations, a perceived threat might be presented to a student activating the sympathetic nervous system and thus limiting the survival response that is available. This prepares the civilian for real-life circumstances.

Additionally, survival gross motor skills are typically push-pull type movements with arms and legs that include strikes and kicks with arms, legs, elbows, knees, and impact instruments; even drawing and aiming your handgun, should be part of this type of training.

During the incident, the only thing that will effectively alter the odds in the civilian's favor is their capabilities based on prior experience and training. Once the incident commences, only training and the will to survive can assist the intended victim.

Our Genetic Heritage

Have you ever watched one of those television programs that examine the world of animals? Some animals are loners, and some travel in groups. Many animals will mark their territory. If that territory is violated by an outsider, there is a good chance a fight will ensue. Human beings, when threatened, will exhibit some of the same behaviors animals do. These behaviors are genetic. Properly understood they can be harnessed and applied in threatening situations giving intended victims an advantage over the potential adversary.

Animals mark their territories to entice mates and establish dominance. For example, some animals use scents while others might use sounds. Some may scratch or rub against trees. Others urinate or use their dung to establish territory. Fish use smells and body coloring. Lizards use coloring. Suffice it to say, there are a number of methods animals use when marking territory. When a marked territory is violated by an outsider, usually a fight ensues. The outcome of these violent encounters depends on a number of factors including species, size and power. But, it is within these encounters much can be learned about aggression and how it relates to the interaction between humans and threatening situations.

Personal safety is primarily about the choices you make. The primary safety tool any human being possesses is cognitive function — the ability to think under stress. There are several aspects of cognitive function that need to be considered in personal safety. One of those is what we are all born with — our genetic heritage. The other is how we perform when we are under stress.

Evolutionary Combative Behavior

The term itself may turn some people off as it has a rather harsh sound and conjures up images of warfare. Let's put some perspective to the term. To what lengths would you intervene to protect your child or a loved one? If you found yourself in circumstances in which you believed you were about to lose your life, to what lengths would you go in order to survive?

Combative behavior is part of our genetic heritage and can be developed through training. Human behavior and body movements are closely linked. For example, humans are wired to react defensively to a "looming" threat. The brain is hard-wired in a way that reacts strongly to the visual threat of assault. Typically if someone is assaulted, their hands go up to ward off the attack while flinching away at the same time. This is genetic; it is instinctive and requires very little thought or cognitive functioning. It is a natural reaction within us to survive threat. It is the same response you might have if someone suddenly threw something at your head. We can utilize these naturally based behaviors as tools to dominate and control potential violence and truly violent confrontations.

Ideally, your goals when it comes to personal safety are: To present a professional and confident presence in routine situations and to use appropriate techniques in potentially violent circumstances and emergency situations with the intent of escape.

The American Heritage Dictionary of the English Language defines aggression as: "the act of initiating hostilities or invasion; the practice or habit of launching attacks; hostile or destructive behavior or actions."

There are several types of aggression.

- Affective aggression is displayed towards fellow members of one's group or species aimed at intimidating and establishing dominance over the opponent. It is typified by high emotional arousal and some kind of aggressive emotional display. This is often typical macho, bravado or "tough guy" behavior. It is displayed because it is unnatural to use lethal dominance against one's own group. In simple terms, it is an emotional display of anger or fear with the main goal of causing injury or harm in order to maintain dominance or control.

The effectiveness of this type of aggression as it relates to personal safety is poor. This behavior is ineffective and usually exacerbates situations. In one study of police officer related assaults, 75% of officers added to the problem, contributed mostly by body language and words. Example: A potential adversary approaches. You get in his face using a sumo-wrestler stance and start calling him names. Is this type of behavior likely to calm the situation or escalate it? Certainly, it would not be considered professional behavior that would increase your probability of escape.

- The second type of aggression is predatory. Predatory aggression is exhibited between members of different species. There is little or no emotional arousal and little emotional display. Typically, the animal assumes a "stalking" posture. In humans, it is often how the hunter will stalk prey. The hunter's functional posture — stalking — is used in order to be in position for an instant transition to an explosive and lethal attack.

The effectiveness of this type of aggression as it relates to personal safety is poor. It is not appropriate to stalk, hunt down and kill others. Example: A potential adversary approaches. You get into a crouched position and begin to circle him slowly from a distance. If the goal is to present a professional and confident presence with the intent of escape, is this type of behavior likely to calm the situation or escalate it?

- Finally, there is pseudo-predatory aggression. This aggression has evolved in humans to suit those situations in which neither purely affective nor purely

> predatory behavior were appropriate. It is aimed at achieving dominance with as little risk as possible, utilizing behavioral and performance traits from predatory rather than affective, although affective aspects can be part of the confrontation.

The effectiveness of this type of aggression as it relates to personal safety and attack management is very good. This type of aggression does not assume a fighting stance. It assumes a semi-stalking posture. This will elicit efficiency of movement, no great arousal, no great emotional display, and minimal communication with the potential Adversary. Example: a potential adversary approaches. You assume a ready stance, which consists of:

- Your feet are shoulder width apart.
- Your strong side is ½ step back.
- Knees are slightly bent.
- Hands are above the waist.
- You maintain two-arm lengths distance from the adversary.
- Your body is at a 45-degree angle to the adversary.
- You are, to the best of your ability, positioned to adversary's side.
- You look directly at the adversary and communicate very little except to advise them you do not want any trouble and to leave you alone.

If the goal is to present a professional and confident presence with the intent of escape, is this type of behavior likely to calm the situation or escalate it? What message are you sending to the potential adversary?

To find this ready stance position, stand up. Take a half-step back with your strong side. Your body and brain should intuitively know which side of your body that is. Keep your hands above your waist in a natural position. Now bend your knees slightly. In a high stress situation with an adversary, you would assume this position and keep at least two-arm lengths away from them. You say very little while maintaining eye contact. If they move, you also move - keeping the distance. If you look like a sumo wrestler at this point you are crouched way too low.

Keeping two-arm lengths away ensures the adversary will be unable to grab, stab, hit or kick you. The arms above the waist allow for a quick counter response against the Adversary if needed. Maintaining eye contact is a sign of strength. Whatever does come out of your mouth should be measured, direct and natural. This position and demeanor exudes confidence. Practice this stance until it becomes natural as it is not a natural movement. However, elements of it are instinctive and genetic. These elements need to be harnessed and focused in a manner that allows us to take advantage of what we are already hard-wired with to survive threat.

High Stress Performance & Killing

Lt. Colonel Dave Grossman in his book On Killing sets forth valuable data and research that has a direct link to how the body, the brain and the psyche interact under the high stress that comes with lethal force decision-making.

Essentially, his findings are in agreement with the notion that man is not naturally a predatory killer who routinely engages in predatory aggression. He cites study after study that all come to similar conclusions — "the vast majority of combatants throughout history, at the moment of truth when they could and should kill the enemy, have found themselves to be conscientious objectors."

At the roots of this reluctance to take the life of another are two things; distance and desensitization.

Distance has a significant effect on the ability of one person to take another's life. By distance, he is referring to cultural, moral, social or mechanical distance, although I would add to that any type of physical, geographical, emotional, spiritual or psychological distance. The greater the distance, the easier it is psychologically to take another's life.

Desensitization is acquired through training, which is an effective method of breaking down the reluctance of a man or woman to kill another. I remember the first time I was exposed to a large amount of blood from another person. I became physically uneasy to the point of almost being ill and was unable to take any decisive action. Contrast that to later in my career standing with another officer over a man who was half decapitated from a roll-over accident in which he was partially thrown through the windshield of his vehicle. After completing the accident investigation and while waiting for the coroner to arrive, we had a casual conversation about our families and where we might catch dinner later that evening. In between those experiences were a lot of others involving my exposure to mass trauma to the human body. I had been effectively desensitized through the exposure to the blood and guts of others.

We know that to effectively survive or control an assault, three things must work together in order to survive:

- One of those is cognitive ability – your ability to make decisions under stress. This can be accomplished through learning — typically in a classroom setting, independent study or both.

- Motor skills are the next component – the ability to make purposeful body and muscle movements that are necessary to complete a task. This would be things like drawing and shooting a gun, applying a wrist lock or successfully blocking a punch.

- Finally, a person's effective skills – the ability to control psychological reactions under high stress. From an instructional viewpoint, this is where desensitization comes into play. I know, as an instructor, I can successfully program a student to react automatically with very little thinking to an observed behavior.

Grossman demonstrates this through his research culled from the Vietnam War in which the willingness to kill was almost the inverse of that it was in previous wars. He credits this, in part, to the training that Vietnam vets received.

An interesting side note: Police used to miss about 90% of the time when involved in police-related shootings despite the fact that most of these confrontations took place at less than 21 feet. The reason? Poor training. Officers used to be trained to pull their weapon under specific circumstances and bring the firearm with their strong hand up to their strong eye and look at the rear sight of the handgun – through to the front sight – and to the target.

This method of shooting is actually a fine and sometimes complex motor skill. Most of this instruction took place in the classroom, and most practice was on the range. Additionally, many officers involved in shootings suffered PTSD (Post Traumatic Stress Disorder) in the aftermath.

Today, police hit their target about 90% of the time and suffer little PTSD. Why? The training changed. Modern police firearm training incorporates instinct shooting, which is much closer to a gross motor skill, visualization and simulations which approximate real-life circumstances and environments. The simulations alone accomplish a great deal of desensitization. Combine this with the incessant onslaught of media depicting violence and violent acts along with a video game culture, and you have a person that is desensitized to the act of killing.

Perception Is Everything

A quick primer on perception. It is an extremely important principle of personal safety. Perception is most people's reality. Someone's perception may be far removed from reality, but perception is the basis of thoughts, impulses and behavior. Therefore, we act out based on our perceptions.

The brain is a big computer. It is constantly receiving, evaluating and processing information. You are constantly sending information out to others by virtue of your body language, tone of voice, posture and language. These behaviors are forming the image of who you are in other people's minds. In this context, your behaviors are forming the adversary's perception of who you are. If the potential adversary's perception is that you are professional and well trained, they are less likely to resort to violence. Contrast this to an adversary's perception that you pose no obstacle to them reaching their goals.

Perception is everything! Read your adversary. They are reading you. How do they perceive you? How do they perceive the circumstances?

- Verbal content is 7-10% of true intent. People lie and are deceptive to varying degrees. We all do this every day. How many times has someone asked you, "How are you doing?" Your answer is usually, "Fine." But is it? Almost everyone is dealing with something that is challenging in their personal lives, yet we tell people all the time we are doing well.

- Voice: Listen to the pace, pitch, tone and modulation. This will reveal 33-40% of true intent. Example: a person who is very excited, under stress or about to explode will often speak in a rushed manner.

- Non-verbal body language: Body motion, posture, distance, body movements, stance and hand placement will reveal 50-60% of true intent. Example: people who are nervous tend to be fidgety. Body language is something we do unconsciously and something we process unconsciously.

If body language is the primary source of the message we send out to other people's perception and that perception will affect their behavior, we should consciously shape our body language in order to send the appropriate message. This applies to aggression because of some of the natural, hard-wired body language we automatically and unconsciously rely on in threatening situations.

Conclusion

There is great value in understanding the principles involved with high stress and aggression; greater than the value of achieving a black belt or some other type of mastery in traditional martial arts or handguns. If I am about to face an imposing adversary and I had my choice of choosing a black belt martial artist, a handgun shooting expert or someone who has studied and incorporated the principles outlined here, I will choose the latter every time.

Individual Reflection or Group Discussion

If you experience the things listed in Chapter 14, you will likely experience high stress. God made us human, with deep emotional reactions. Some of these things may trigger high stress reactions.

Think of several instances when you were under high stress. This can be anything that might have been traumatic on a personal level.

Refer to the "Relationship Between the Body and the Brain" section of this chapter.

1. Did you experience any of the things listed there?

2. Did you regain more recall and details of the event several days later?

3. Did you second guess what you could have or should have done to avoid it?

4. Had you been better trained, prepared or had more experience, would the outcome have been different?

5. Apply these questions to both the natural world - like a car accident or assault - and the spiritual world where you may have experienced personal failure or attack.

Chapter 18
Choosing A Firearm

"The framers gave us the Second Amendment not so we could go deer or duck hunting but to give us a modicum of protection against congressional tyranny."

Walter E. Williams

"Be strong and courageous; do not be frightened or dismayed, for the Lord your God is with you wherever you go." Joshua 1:9

"Then Jesus asked them, 'When I sent you without purse, bag or sandals, did you lack anything?' 'Nothing,' they answered. He said to them, 'But now if you have a purse take it, and also a bag; and if you don't have a sword, sell your cloak and buy one. It is written: 'And he was numbered with transgressors'; and I tell you that this must be fulfilled in me. Yes, what is written about me is reaching its fulfillment.' The disciples said, 'See, Lord, here are two swords.' 'That is enough,' he replied." Luke 22:35-38

Lessons Learned

Another summer; another hot August night. I am assigned to work at a local carnival providing security. I am with an officer from another department. As things begin to wind down for the evening, we begin to listen to a pursuit on the police radio. When it was all over, we eventually discovered a juvenile male had stolen his father's pickup truck in another state. He stopped at a truck stop just off of the interstate in our jurisdiction and drove off without paying for his gas. This was reported to law enforcement officials, and an officer spotted him on the interstate. Other officers joined the chase and this kid exited the interstate into a small town where the local police joined the chase. He then attempted to run several police officers down with the truck. They were attempting to put spike strips down in the roadway to puncture his tires. He jumped back onto the interstate and headed our direction.

There were now many officers in pursuit from a number of jurisdictions. We headed off to the interstate as we listened to the pursuing officers reporting they were at speeds in excess of 100 miles per hour. As I discussed strategy with my fellow officer, we agreed that there was potential for catastrophe as the chase would be approaching a construction area in which the two-lane interstate would narrow to one lane. Additionally, this interstate carries a lot of vacation traffic in the summer. We agreed we needed to try to end this before the pursuit reached that area. As we approached the interstate, we could see the pursuit stretched before us for several miles on a straightaway. We were also about two miles from the area where the interstate would bottle-neck for construction. I decided to try and get out in front of the stolen truck and try to match its speed while I zigzagged across the interstate in front of him. I asked the other officer to have his gun out and in a shooting position in case whoever was driving the truck was armed and shot at us. After all, he had already tried to run over several police officers and had been running from officers for more than 30 minutes. I timed things the best I could from the shoulder of the interstate.

I pressed the accelerator pedal to the floor and was projected out onto the interstate where the engine promptly stalled – for just a few precious seconds – then picked back up into full acceleration. Those few seconds cost us a lot. I began to weave back and forth while trying to push the gas pedal through the bottom of the car. I glanced in the rear view mirror to see the speeding truck begin to take aim to go around us on the right side. I swerved to the right. Suddenly, there was an explosion of glass and smoke inside our car. The truck had rear-ended us at over 100 miles per hour. My car careened for about 50 yards then came to rest on the right shoulder of the interstate — dead. I looked in the rear view mirror and observed the truck which had flipped and was now partway down an embankment. Around the truck were several squad cars, lights flashing and sirens blaring. The other officer with me started to jump out of the car, and I grabbed him telling him it was over. We began to examine ourselves to see if we had sustained any injuries. I immediately noticed the trunk of my car was now in my back seat. The pursuing officers later reported the truck had opportunity to get around us but chose to ram us. It looked intentional from their view. This kid was 16 years old and had tried to kill several officers. He sustained very few injuries himself. He was charged with multiple counts.

The next day, I went to the jail to talk to him. He was brought to a book-in area. I noticed several other officers had joined me as well as a few of the jail personnel. Odd. Later I discovered they all thought I was going to beat this kid for what he had done. If I had, I'm not sure if they would have intervened or cheered me on. All I wanted to do was to make the actions of this kid real to him. I showed him pictures of my family and some pictures of other officers. I told him heartfelt stories about some of the officers he had tried to run over and the bravery of others. I told him about some of the officers I knew who had been injured — who had sacrificed their bodies on behalf of public safety. He never said a word. All he did was stare at me.

Lesson learned: There are people who could care less about the lives of others. They are mean-spirited, self absorbed and narcissistic. There are people willing to kill me in order to reach their goals, however twisted those goals may be. These people do not share the same basic values that many of us do.

Firearm Facts

In 2000, *Time* magazine published this:

"The top 10 guns used in crimes in the U.S. in 2000, according to an unpublished study by U.S. Bureau of Alcohol, Tobacco and Firearms and obtained exclusively by Time magazine:

1. Smith and Wesson .38 revolver.
2. Ruger 9 mm semiautomatic.
3. Lorcin Engineering .380 semiautomatic.
4. Raven Arms .25 semiautomatic.
5. Mossberg 12 gauge shotgun.
6. Smith and Wesson 9mm semiautomatic.
7. Smith and Wesson .357 revolver.
8. Bryco Arms 9mm semiautomatic.
9. Bryco Arms .380 semiautomatic.
10. Davis Industries .380 semiautomatic.

The list is derived from the center's investigations of 88,570 guns recovered from crime scenes in 46 cities in 2000. Street criminals are interested almost exclusively in semiautomatics, preferring their superior firepower. Gun traffickers like to peddle cheap semiautomatics to teenagers because they can tack on a hefty mark-up and still offer a weapon that costs less than an upscale gun like a Ruger or Smith and Wesson semiautomatic. That's why inexpensive semiautomatics dominate the top ten list."

Is this important? Only from the standpoint that you know what you are most likely to encounter from an armed assailant. If you know what you are going to have to deal with, you know how to prepare for it. Times have not changed much. Cheap semi-autos are still the favorite criminal weapon.

But Aren't Firearms Dangerous?

This is the time-honored, hotly debated political football that seems to always be part of the news cycle whenever there is some type of high-profile shooting.

If you simply look at the question logically, there is a simple answer. No tables are necessary. No convincing statistics are needed. No great revelations will be exposed.

People kill. Guns do not. Guns are inanimate objects. I could kill someone with a car, a knife, a paperclip or a spatula. Objects don't kill people. People kill people. A paperclip can be used to hold together pieces of paper or to thrust into an eyeball, a jugular vein or a femoral artery.

Additionally, being shot or shooting someone does not guarantee death. Here are a few handgun defense facts:

- 40% of those shot in the heart will survive.
- If shot in the heart, a person may still fight for over one minute.
- If you are shot in the chest with a handgun, your chances of dying is 14%.
- If you are shot twice, your chances of dying are 70%.
- If shot in the chest with an AK-47, the odds of death are 17%.
- If shot in the chest with a shotgun, the odds of death are 64%.
- Somewhere around 80% of people shot with a handgun survive.

This reveals several things. Shooting an adversary does not

necessarily stop them, although it probably will get their attention and cause enough damage for you to escape. Conversely, if you get shot, death is not imminent. You can survive.

Why Do I Need A Firearm?

If you have any inclination that you might experience anything mentioned in Chapter 14, a firearm would be a prudent thing to own.

Additionally according to crime statistics in the United States, with a population of approximately 320 million, there is about an 8% chance of being a victim of any crime. Your chances of being a victim of violent crime are about 1-2%. Within the category of violent crime, a weapon was used 24% of the time. Therefore, unless you are employed in a high-risk profession, the chances of facing an armed adversary in which lethal force is a viable option is approximately 0.25 – 0.5%. This is not to say that you could not use lethal force on an adversary that was not armed, but justifying that would require some type of disparity of force between you and them such as multiple attackers or a physical condition which leaves you at a severe disadvantage.

So, the first decision you should make in determining whether you should own a handgun is whether you think you need one or not.

According to the FBI, a justifiable homicide is defined as:

- The killing of a felon by a peace officer in the line of duty.

- The killing of a felon during the commission of a felony by a private citizen.

In 2007 there were 391 killings by police that were ruled justifiable and 254 killings by private individuals found to be self-defense. I would guess the great majority of those 254 had no foreknowledge they would need to shoot someone.

There is a very small chance statistically you will find yourself in a situation in which the use of a handgun is appropriate and legally justified. It is much more likely from a statistical standpoint you will find yourself in a situation in which you will use less-than-lethal force. For most people this means defending themselves with pepper spray, an impact weapon, control instruments, an electronic incapacitation device or their hands.

Having said that, can you predict whether you will ever be the intended victim of a lethal adversary? And, if you experience the things listed in Chapter 14, it is almost a safe assumption that whatever restraint there is in the world right now will be gone, thereby leaving us with unchecked violent and predatory behavior. Since most people cannot foresee the future, many like to be prepared for the worst case scenario, hence the decision to own a handgun.

How To Choose A Firearm

The committed devotion some handgun owners have for a particular make and model of gun is no different than the personal preference a person might have for a good fitting pair of shoes, a favorite meal or their shampoo. I get that. The emotional attachment many of them have for a particular caliber is another matter entirely and rarely based on objective data. This I don't get.

As a Master Firearms Instructor, I am frequently asked what type of firearm and what caliber would be best for self defense. People ask me this because they either don't know what to purchase or have the perception that as a firearm instructor, I am a technical expert with firearms. I am not a technical expert with firearms – I am a practical one. I could not explain one alloy from another, production details of any particular model or match grade barrels and scopes. I can, however, teach you how to use one in self defense. I can do this with great certainty that what I share with you is grounded in a firm, legal foundation based on real-life experience backed by extensive research into real-world lethal force encounters.

So, here it is.

The best self defense handgun in the world is the one that fits your hand perfectly, like a custom-made glove. It is one that you can control and shoot accurately under a variety of conditions. It is one that is within your reach when you actually need it. It is one that does not jam frequently. This is probably not the answer you expected, but it is true.

A Little More Detail, Please?

Get the right tools for the right job. What does this mean? Have you ever heard the saying, "Don't take a knife to a gun fight"? If you are concerned about lethal threat, buy a handgun.

Handguns are made of metals, alloys and plastics. Although some handgun aficionados might disagree, there is not a lot of garbage out there when it comes to firearms. Generally, most manufacturers put forth a good effort at making quality weapons.

Semi-automatics will give you more firepower but fail more often than revolvers. The primary reason for failure is using hand-loads. The next most popular reason for semi-automatic failure is using non-factory magazines followed by the shooter not operating the gun properly. Most failures had nothing to do with the actual gun.

If you are considering a semi-auto, understand the following:

- The slide must go backward and forward.
- Shooting a semi-auto requires counter-pressure with your hand.
- The magazine must be seated properly.
- The slide must go back to get a round into the chamber from a new magazine.

- You must decide if you want to carry the gun with a bullet in the chamber and the safety, if it has one, on or off.

If you are considering a revolver, understand revolvers are more reliable than semi-autos. Revolvers have no external safety – all are internal. In the next chapter you will discover that even though revolvers are more reliable than semi-autos, a revolver is more easily used by an adversary against you.

If the handgun you purchase does not have rubber grips, go buy some and replace the originals. You will have more control when shooting.

In any case, always master the function of your gun and understand its limits.

Shotguns are better lethal adversary-stoppers than any handgun. If you desire a shotgun for self defense, buy a 20 gauge or 12 gauge — Mossberg or Remington. Load it with 00 buckshot staggered with a rifled slug.

Rifles are not a great self defense option. Most sniper encounters occur within 100 yards. One of the best choices will be a .223 caliber such as the Ruger Mini-14 or the AR-15.

Bigger Is Not Always Better

The bigger, the better - right? In theory that is true.

Let's take a closer look at caliber. Presumably, the reason you own a self defense firearm is to neutralize a lethal threat and escape. Have you ever been hit with a bullet? It hurts – regardless of caliber. For the great majority of assailants, any caliber bullet that strikes their body is going to get their attention and be a healthy deterrent to further abhorrent behavior. From this standpoint, a .22 caliber is better than nothing. This caliber is easy to conceal and easy to control. But, there are other factors which affect a person's reaction to being hit with a bullet.

High stress physiology and the masking of pain that alcohol, drugs or certain mental health issues bring must be considered as evidenced by the fact that almost 50% of criminal offenders report being under the influence at the time of their offense.

It turns out that for most street encounters, the real determinant is the manufacture of the bullet and not the caliber. There are lots of makes and models out there. How do you weed through them all? I would start by considering what these experts have to say.

Evan Marshall: "In my opinion, it doesn't make much difference whether you select a 9mm, .40 caliber, a .357 caliber, or a .45 caliber as long as you use the proper ammunition. Any weapon of these calibers is adequate for law enforcement use. My advice is to select a weapon that you can fire most accurately given the different size, weights, and recoil of each weapon."

Chuck Hawks: "Well designed bullets, which include most of the JHP pistol bullets now on the market, expand very reliably at their intended impact velocity. How do you imagine the 115 grain JHP 9x19 +P load, 125 grain JHP .357 load, 155 grain JHP .40 S&W load, and 230 grain JHP .45 ACP loads earned those outstanding 90%+ one shot stop records in the real world? In a sentence: due to the consistent performance of their JHP bullets. The famous 125 grain .357 JHP bullet is the most effective one shot stopper of all handgun loads, penetrates 13.25" in ordinance gelatin and produces a football shaped stretch cavity. This is how the very best bullets perform. And bullet performance has a great effect on stopping power."

The ammunition you decide to use depends on the situation. Do you want to penetrate walls? Full metal jacket bullets are likely to penetrate deeper. Hollow-points deform on impact, making them less likely to go through walls or through the adversary and into the person standing behind the adversary. If you're trying to defend yourself against attack, your goal is to neutralize the adversary.

Even a fatal wound might leave the attacker mobile long enough for him to kill you, either with his own gun or with some other weapon if he doesn't have a gun. Shooting an adversary with a hollow-point is much likelier to knock him down. It is also likelier to kill him, but that's a side effect not the goal. The goal is to neutralize the lethal threat.

Some Additional Tips

As a self-defense firearm instructor, I am often asked the same questions about self defense shootings and handguns. Here, without lengthy explanations, are the answers to the most commonly asked questions.

- Buy and use American ammunition.

- Avoid ammunition that makes exorbitant claims.

- Never use reloads as your duty or carry ammo. It is the biggest reason for jams and misfires. Use factory loads only.

- For self defense, use hollow points. It has better stopping power than full metal jacket.

- Plus P or +P ammunition means the pressure in the bullet is greater than the standard .38 ammo. Plus P loads should be fired in steel frame revolvers – not aluminum frame.

- 9mm is the most widely used pistol in the world, and the primary load that law enforcement uses worldwide. For self defense, use hollow points only and never heavier than 125 grain. It comes in standard and +P loads. Plus P loads should be used in newer models only – post 1985.

- For .357, the most reliable round on the market is arguably the Federal .357 Magnum 125 grain jacketed hollow-point. This round just might be the most effective round on the market in terms of stopping power — period. If you don't like the recoil, use .38 +P rounds in it.

- .40 caliber has established a great street record. Use any .40 S&W ammunition.

- Any caliber above this is going to have significant recoil for the average self defense shooter.

Final Note

If you go to the cop who lives down the street or the neighbor who is an avid hunter or the cousin who is a competitive shooter and ask their opinions regarding the best choice of handgun for personal defense, you may get varying opinions leaving you confused. Do not let others confuse you.

If you take what is presented here at face value, you would go buy a .357 revolver and use Federal .357 Magnum 125 grain jacketed hollow-point bullets. If you are worried about not having enough firepower with a revolver, you should know the average shots fired per lethal self defense encounter is less than six. Then, go purchase a Remington or Mossberg 12 or 20 gauge. Get some rifled slugs and 00 buckshot to go with it. Next, if you want to cover the whole range of lethal self defense, look for a Ruger Mini 14 or an AR-15 type weapon.

Opinions and feelings about firearms can change by the minute. Facts don't. Choosing a handgun and cartridge for personal defense is something that should be considered with care, but it is not complicated.

Individual Reflection or Group Discussion

This can be a great group exercise that stretches out over several weeks or months.

1. Find your state statutes that govern lethal or deadly force. Read them.

2. Find your state statutes that govern your ability to possess and carry a handgun. Read them.

3. Buy a handgun that fits your hand well. Go to your local gun range where handguns are available to rent. Try some different models until you find one that you are comfortable with.

4. Consider who has access to it. Do children? Decide how you will store your handgun.

5. Take a handgun course from a reliable source. Start by checking with your local gun shop. They will either offer a class or can direct you to someone who is authorized to do so.

6. Practice shooting, and keep your handgun clean.

Chapter 19
Handgun Conceal and Carry Options

"It is, therefore, a fact of law and of practical necessity that individuals are responsible for their own personal safety, and that of their loved ones. Police protection must be recognized for what it is: only an auxiliary general deterrent."

Peter Alan Kasler

"From that day on, half of my men did the work, while the other half were equipped with spears, shields, bows and armor. The officers posted themselves behind all the people of Judah who were building the wall. Those who carried materials did their work with one hand and held a weapon in the other, and each of the builders wore his sword at his side as he worked." Nehemiah 4: 16-18

Lessons Learned

I carried a Ruger .357 magnum for a while and then switched to a Smith and Wesson 9mm semi-automatic. My duty shotgun was the tried and true Remington 870. I also carried a Ruger Mini-14 rifle. My partner and I constantly practiced drills when our shift was slow. We would go through abandoned buildings and practice room entry and clearing. We would go to the outdoor range at night and practice low-light and no-light shooting, with or without obstacles, noise and flashing lights as distractions. We took officer safety very seriously.

One night I was directed to respond to a "man with a gun" call. These are potentially very dangerous calls. In fact, officers and firemen used to debate who was crazier — the officer racing to a "man with a gun" call or a fireman racing to go into a burning building.

Another officer and I arrived about the same time and parked several houses away from the residence in question. As I cleared my car door and began to walk towards the house, a man came flying out the front door with a gun in his hand. I instinctively reached for my weapon, which was in my snappy new retention holster, while moving backwards looking for cover. I had practiced drawing my weapon from it repeatedly with great success. It required me to release the thumb break and then push down and forward on the handgun simultaneously. The holster was marketed as a great retention holster. However, under high stress and dual tasking, I could not get the handgun out. I ended up almost ripping it out of the holster that night.

Lesson learned: Under high stress, things that seem simple become complex. Additionally, the best type of practice is that which significantly replicates real life. This is called simulation training.

How To Carry A Weapon

Many states have implemented some type of personal protection legislation that allows a citizen who does not have a criminal record and passes certified training to carry a handgun for personal protection. While statistics show the chances of actually using a handgun for self defense remain incredibly low, many people find carrying one allows them to feel more secure. Inevitably, handgun permit holders must decide the best method to carry a handgun for defensive purposes. In order to determine this, let's examine the dynamics that surround self defense shootings.

Traditional carry systems for civilians are designed primarily to *hold* a handgun, not *secure* them from others. At the same time it is imperative people have the ability to quickly retrieve any defensive weapon they need for any given situation, particularly under high stress. These principles have direct application to off-duty and plainclothes criminal justice professionals as well as civilians.

The holsters, fanny packs, briefcases, backpacks and clothing on the market today that are specifically designed and marketed for conceal carry purposes have several major drawbacks.

For fanny packs, briefcases and backpacks: why not use all that empty space to organize other items I might need? Lethal force is usually not the appropriate option in a confrontation with a potential assailant, yet that is what most of these carry systems concentrate on — the gun. They all have some type of method to secure a handgun. But where are the holders for pepper spray, a flashlight, extendible baton, stun-gun, handcuffs or a kubaton?

In the case of fanny packs, a perception existed that someone with a fanny pack was likely carrying a concealed weapon. Although fanny packs are no longer chic in terms of fashion and popularity, the stereotypical thinking was, "Why would someone have a fanny pack except to carry a concealed weapon?"

In the case of belt systems and holsters, we need to recognize that under high stress the body loses many of its fine and complex motor skills. Locating, un-holstering, aiming and firing a handgun require fine and sometimes complex motor skills. Many of today's holsters (and holders for other items like pepper spray) require the owner to unzip, tear away, unsnap, rotate, push down or use some other combination of movements to retrieve their handgun or other defensive weapons.

For these reasons the traditional method of carrying a handgun needs to be measured against some other factors.

Lesson in Physics and Body Design

The body works best in forward motion, not to the rear or sideways. The closer to the center of the body, the stronger your movements are going to be. The center of the body is where the wrists intersect when standing straight and letting the arms hang down in front of the body, crossing the wrists over each other. Your center will be just below or near the abdomen. This area, your center, is vital in employing self defense tactics.

Holding and striking power is most effective when the center of the body is brought into play. For purposes of this discussion, we will concentrate on holding power. This principle is best demonstrated by holding a 10-pound weight or a chair in your hand at arm's length with your arm fully outstretched. Chances are good that your arm will grow weary very rapidly. Now, bring the weight or the chair closer to your center. It is much easier and more balanced holding the weight near your center or waistline. Ergonomically then, it makes sense to involve the strongest part of the body, the center, for tasks involving carrying and holding. Additionally, carrying weapons in the waistline area allows quick location and retrieval of the weapon as opposed to pants pockets, a purse or bag, or the ankle area. This is one good reason that uniformed law enforcement personnel use waist belt systems to carry their duty gear.

In theory, the risk of having your handgun or other defensive weapons taken from you drop significantly by carrying these items near the center of your body for one primary reason. If an adversary tried to grab your handgun from its holster on your waistline, you would naturally grab it in an attempt to hang on to it. You are better suited doing this by using your center as part of this defense.

However, these waistline belt systems can get hung up or snagged on things when moving around or running. Additionally, a quick visual study of most waistline belt systems reveals something interesting to a discerning eye. With a little practice, it is fairly easy for an adversary to remove a handgun from a holster or take pepper spray from its holder. All the adversary needs is an understanding of how these holders work. In fact, just about all handcuffs, mace or pepper spray, batons, flashlights and the like are universally held in holders that either have an open-top, snap-top or Velcro-top. Although carrying weapons in this manner allows the owner quick weapon acquisition, they also allow the adversary quick removal of the same items.

We are faced with a double-edged sword here. Carrying a handgun or other defensive weapons using "waistline retention" allows for a stronger defense, yet you remain vulnerable to these same items being removed quickly by an adversary. We need to look a little deeper.

Statistically, over 70% of physical altercations end up on the ground. Although speed will prevail with an adversary while standing, speed does not prevail on the ground — size does. On the ground a bigger and more powerful adversary has the outcome in their favor. Now picture this. You are on the ground fighting with an adversary while attempting to protect your handgun from the adversary's grasp. Using waistline retention for a handgun may add an additional risk in this scenario.

Waistline retention is good for quick weapon acquisition and defensive strength but presents great opportunity for an adversary to take the weapon away.

Lesson in High Stress

Most people being confronted with lethal force decision-making will experience high stress. Also known as the Fight or Flight Syndrome, high-stress situations trigger an incredible reaction between the brain, the body and emotions. This relationship is detailed in Chapter 17. Suffice it to say that there is a relationship between performance and stress. When there is no stress, there is no great performance. When there is great stress, there is great performance. When there is huge *distress* there is a marked decrease in performance, which becomes unreliable.

Typically under high stress, the first thing to deteriorate is cognitive function — the ability to make decisions. This has implications in reference to the method a handgun is carried.

The sympathetic nervous system is activated when the mind detects a potential threat to survive. It reacts by mediating the involuntary responses to alarm by speeding the heart rate, raising the blood pressure and dilating the pupils of the eyes among many other things. This system opposes and overrides the parasympathetic nervous system, which regulates many body functions, in order to provide the body with the necessary capabilities to fight or flee in the presence of danger. In doing so, however, the body loses its fine and complex motor skills. These skills require complex cognitive processes and small muscle mass groups including hands and fingers. Eye-hand coordination, precision, tracking and timing are affected. However, the gross motor skills are increased — a cognitively simple process requiring very little decision making. Gross motor skills are typified by push and pull movements with the arms and legs.

The question now becomes under high stress, is it wise to carry a handgun or other defensive weapon in a manner that requires complex decision-making and fine or complex motor skills in order to acquire them? Locating and drawing a handgun or retrieving other defensive weapons depends on the holster or holder and method of carrying these items. Some holsters and holders require the owner to unsnap, push down and then twist the item or some other combination of movements. These are fine, complex motor skills. Attempting to accomplish these movements under high stress is very difficult because fine and complex motor skills are greatly diminished or have disappeared altogether.

Imagine the decision-making process and fine or complex motor skills that are involved in retrieving your handgun from your waistline, then locating the pepper spray in your jacket pocket, and finally grabbing the kubaton from your front pants pocket. Locating these items in *one* area is a much simpler cognitive process that requires fewer fine and complex motor skills. As stated earlier, herein lays one of the advantages of carrying these weapons using waistline retention. Your handgun is in a snap holster on your belt. Your pepper spray is sitting in a holder with a Velcro cover on your belt. Your kubaton is tucked into the pants at the waistline. There is not a lot of complicated cognitive decision-making going on if you decide to grab one of these. Acquiring these weapons under high stress will primarily require gross motor skills, using the arm and hand to locate the item, then pull it out and employ it. Again, it depends on the complexity of the holster or holder.

Clearly, the method chosen for carrying defensive weapons, including handguns, should be such that in order to retrieve them requires very little cognitive function (decision-making) and utilizes gross motor skills.

Lesson in Weapon Retention

Research regarding law enforcement officers killed reveals that between 8% and 19% are killed with their own handguns by an adversary. The percentage varies depending on the block of years studied. One thing that is consistent is that most officers killed in this fashion are overwhelmingly killed with revolvers, not semi-automatics. The theory is that a revolver in the hands of an adversary requires only that the trigger is pulled, where as a semi-automatic that is locked and cocked is more challenging for the adversary to shoot. In experiments using civilians, it took an average of less than 2 seconds for them shoot a revolver and about 16 seconds for them to figure out the safety on the semi-auto. Richard F. Cipriano authored a good paper on this issue. There is a direct correlation to civilian carry methods.

Many holsters are marketed as having exceptional retention capabilities. These holsters are designed to make it difficult for an adversary to take a gun away from you. However, for the adversary, it takes just a bit of practice with many of these retention holsters to become proficient at removing the handgun from the holster. For other items on a belt system (baton, radio, handcuffs, pepper spray) the adversary simply needs to unsnap a latch or flip a Velcro tab and pull the item out.

I have viewed video and read stories regarding a number of law enforcement personnel having their own handgun taken from their holsters by an adversary. If 8-19% of officer deaths result in an adversary using the officer's handgun to kill them and most officers use waistline retention consisting of belt systems and belt holsters, either the carry system is less than desirable or training in weapon retention is substandard.

Lesson in Self Defense Shootings

Most self defense shootings occur at 10 feet or less. Some studies report up to 90% of civilian shootings are at 2 feet or less. If we accept most self defense shootings occur at 10 feet or less, a large frame gun, although it may be a personal preference, is not required nor will it improve accuracy from a practical standpoint. Smaller frame guns are more easily concealed.

Additionally, if an adversary unexpectedly pulls a weapon out and threatens you from a distance of 10 feet or less, you should be thinking about using your hands for defense because you will never be able to retrieve an appropriate weapon in time and employ it. This principle simply implies that the adversary's action is always going to be quicker than your ability to process the unfolding scenario and react appropriately. There is significant research regarding this phenomenon.

Even if you are carrying a handgun or other weapons, will you have time to get them out and use them against an adversary?

Criminals do not usually advertise from 50 yards away their intention to harm you.

Another Lesson in Self Defense Shootings

Lethal force situations require assessing the situation and determining what force is appropriate. The brain then interacts with the body in order to get the body to retrieve the appropriate weapon. For many, this may require fine and complex motor skills as the hands locate and un-holster the gun, then bring it to a shooting position. The traditional shooting method for many people is to bring the handgun to eye level, aligning the rear sights of the gun with the front sight to the target using their dominant eye. There is mounting evidence this traditional shooting style does not mesh well with how the brain and body react under high stress.

As a Master Firearms Instructor, I train my students and clients as follows:

- Locate the handgun, and pull it out.
- Point the handgun at the adversary extending the arms from the sternum area.
- Squeeze the trigger.

Also known as instinct shooting, you will notice this technique primarily relies upon gross motor skills — pull and push movements with arms. This technique is based on physics, body design and high stress principles. Our client's accuracy is in excess of 90% at 21 feet or less.

As few steps as possible should be required to retrieve a handgun or other weapon, and gross motor skills should be utilized. Fine and complex motor skills should be eliminated. Note: we do recognize that placing the finger on the trigger and squeezing it is considered a fine motor skill, which is impossible to eliminate.

Let's summarize the main issues presented thus far:

- Lethal force is not always the appropriate option. Statistically, it is much more likely you will use less-than-lethal force with an adversary. Where should you carry your pepper spray, flashlight, impact instrument, stun-gun, handcuffs or kubaton?

- Fanny-packs are a signal to others you may be carrying a concealed weapon.

- Waistline retention of weapons is good for quick weapon acquisition and defensive strength but presents risk for those weapons to be taken away.

- 70% of physical confrontations end up on the ground.

- If 8-19% of officer deaths result in an adversary using the officer's handgun to kill them, and most officers use waistline retention, either the carry system is less than desirable or training in weapon retention is deficient.

- Statistically, you are better off owning a semi-automatic than a revolver.

- If you are carrying a handgun or other weapons, will you have time to get them out and use them against an adversary?

- Under high stress the cognitive process begins to deteriorate rapidly and the body loses many of its fine and complex motor skills. Many weapon retention systems actually require these skills in order to retrieve the weapon.

- Smaller frame guns are more easily concealed.

- As few steps as possible should be required to retrieve a handgun or other weapon, and gross motor skills should be utilized. Fine and complex motor skills should be eliminated.

- The method chosen for carrying defensive weapons, including handguns, should be such that in order to retrieve them requires very little cognitive function.

- Consider using instinct shooting instead of traditional shooting methods.

Based on these considerations, what is the best method of carrying?

If you are like most people who have the legal authority to carry a handgun, you will likely carry your handgun using some type of waistline retention method. If you are a woman, you will likely carry it in your purse. Does your jacket cover the handgun? Where is your pepper spray, kubaton or impact weapon? Are they in your car? Are they in the pockets of your jacket? Are they loose in the purse? Let's consider one more variable.

The Wild Card

Here's the wild card. What about the weather and your environment? If it is 90 degrees outside, a jacket will become very uncomfortable. Additionally, wearing a jacket or long shirt on a hot day may actually draw attention to you because it is not normal. Does your schedule require you to be in and out of meetings and buildings all day long? Do you have to stop at the bank or pick up groceries? Do you have a doctor appointment? These three elements — weather, environment and schedule — will have impact on your carry method.

The question most often asked by those who are considering carrying a handgun is: What is the best way to carry it? This is the wrong question. The questions you should be asking are:

- What is the likelihood I will be involved in circumstances in which a favorable outcome for me will depend on my ability to retrieve my handgun or other weapon within several seconds? In other words, should I carry my handgun using a waistline retention method?

- If I choose a waistline retention method, how confident am I that I can successfully defend myself from an adversary trying to remove these weapons?

- What if I end up on the ground?

- Does the weather, my environment or my schedule today have any impact on my carrying method?

On a typical day, I may attend several meetings at different locations with people ranging from CEOs to civilians. I might have a doctor appointment or need to stop at the grocery store. It is impractical and uncomfortable for me wear a jacket all day long. When I do take it off, I am wondering if my handgun is being viewed by others. Knowing that lethal force is statistically unlikely, I also carry some less-than-lethal weapons. If I need these items, I do not want to be fumbling around under high stress trying to locate and retrieve them.

As I began to ponder this dilemma, I searched for a retention system that would allow me to carry my handgun, extra ammunition, pepper spray, extendible baton, kubaton, handcuffs and flashlight in an organized manner. I could not find one. This made no sense to me, so I designed one myself considering all the factors outlined in this article.

It looks like a book cover or small business portfolio with several zippers. Inside, I have several pockets sewn in with Velcro tabs to secure my handgun and other less-than-lethal weapons. I have taken this into virtually every environment from the bar to the boardroom without raising any suspicion or concern. Everything I need is within arm's reach by unzipping one zipper; it is all in front of me. I am not reaching into my pocket or behind my back fumbling with some type of retention holster.

The downside is that it may take an extra second or two for me to retrieve the appropriate weapon. Also, if the adversary manages to remove this pack from my possession, he will have all my weapons.

Conclusion

The purpose of this chapter is to present the variables involved in carrying weapons. There is no perfect method of carrying your handgun or other less-than-lethal weapons. If you have the legal ability to carry a handgun, please consider these principles carefully before you decide upon a carry method.

Individual Reflection or Group Discussion

1. Think about and list the activities you are involved in on an average day.

2. If you have a firearm, how will you carry it?

Chapter 20
Developing a Model of Personal Safety

"The only fence against the world is a thorough knowledge of it."

John Locke

"A wise man is strong, yes, a man of knowledge increases strength; for by wise counsel you will wage your own war, and in a multitude of counselors there is safety." Proverbs 24:5

Lessons Learned

The long haired, mustached welder was a large blue collar worker who probably stood to be about 6′-4″ and weighed 250 pounds with no fat on him. His arms were huge from years of working with them. He had an intimidating presence. I met him one night at his residence as I had been sent to his home on a disturbance call. Upon arrival I discovered the welder in the street outside the home of the person who had called 911 with a baseball bat in his hand screaming at the occupants. With some strong encouragement, I convinced the welder to put the bat down and talk to me. He told me his young son had been molested by this neighbor whom he often let look after his boy. His son had described some inappropriate touching after a visit to this neighbor's house. The welder had gone to confront the neighbor and threatened him while doing so. The neighbor immediately called for law enforcement. I proceeded to gather as much information as I could, which I soon turned over to a detective for follow-up investigation. As I listened to the Welder share what he believed to have happened to his son at the neighbor's home, I watched him struggle between tears and anger. This was a man who loved his son and had a clear view of how things should be handled. Someone had violated his son's innocence, and he was going to exact some revenge. This was perfectly justifiable in his mind, as it would be in many people's.

After a lengthy conversation, I convinced this man to let the criminal justice system work, and if he was not satisfied with the results, he could do what he felt a father needed to do. He agreed, although it was a real struggle for him.

Fast forward. A temporary court order is put into place in which the suspect is to have no contact with the child victim and the welder. As this case worked its way through the criminal justice system, I ran into this man several times, and we began to develop a bond and friendship. The suspect neighbor had admitted to inappropriately touching the young boy in interviews with detectives. Ultimately, the court ordered the perpetrator to leave the state and never return, placing him on some type of probation.

The welder, who has been adhering to the deal he made with me, was understandably upset. We talked after the perpetrator was sentenced.

Him: Well, I did what you asked me to do. I let the system deal with it. Do you think that is a fair sentence for someone who has admitted to molesting my son?

Me: Do what you have to do.

Several days after the sentencing he picked up that baseball bat, bashed the now guilty neighbor's door in and proceeded to break out some windows in the home. The welder also whacked the neighbor several times before he managed to escape and call the police. The welder was arrested, and I spoke to him in jail several days later. He was more than willing to face the consequences for his actions. He was satisfied the man who had admitted to molesting his son had now been justifiably beaten. In his mind, the sentence given the perpetrator did not come close to justice. He wanted this man to suffer because he was smart enough to know that at some point in the future, the act perpetrated on his son had great potential to screw up his son's life. Ultimately, the welder admitted to an assault and was sentenced to a short stay in the county jail. The offending neighbor had left the neighborhood and the state by the time the welder was released.

Fast forward again. About four months later, I have a dozen Banditos pulled over on the interstate, and I am alone. It is very uncomfortable to be a lone law enforcement officer amongst this many outlaw motorcycle gang members. We had been directed to identify motorcycle gang members coming through our jurisdiction, which is a major thoroughfare for drugs. These guys are giving me a hard time as I try to collect identification from them. Suddenly, I sense a presence coming up behind me. It is the welder with a pipe in his hand. He walks up next to me and just stands there staring at the bikers.

Him: Hi Terry. Is there any problem here?

There was immediate cooperation from the bikers. The welder stood by until I had collected the information I needed. The bikers went on their way. Before the welder left, I thanked him. He told me that because I had treated him fairly and had explained each step of the legal process to him regarding the case with his son, he would watch my back whenever he had the chance.

Lessons learned: Sometimes there is little justice in the criminal justice system. Knowing the reality of the world I was walking in was a critical foundation to any future success and effectiveness I would have in confronting violence and empathizing with victims. People remember their dealings with the criminal justice system. People remember their dealings with me. Treat people fairly, and they will do the same to you. There is strength in numbers.

From the neighborhood to the nation, crime statistics are published frequently and are readily available to the public. Most often these statistics are used by lawmakers to shape public policy and by criminal justice system administrators to develop strategic crime deterrent programs. But what, if any, value do these statistics hold for the average citizen?

If you get all of your relevant news information from most major media outlets, whether it be through newspapers, magazines, television or internet, you will likely have a skewed perception of crime in the United States. Why? Because most media outlets have a formula they use in choosing which stories they will cover.

James Hamilton is a professor of Public Policy, Economics, and Political Science at Duke University. In his excellent book, All the News That's Fit to Sell: How the Market Transforms Information into News, he makes several powerful observations.

His book examines how economic forces shape the media. Professor Hamilton discovered if the demand for hard news is not present, media outlets will focus on other subjects.

"As the demand for hard news coverage decreases, profit-driven broadcasters and news media will not want to invest their money in these types of stories. Network evening news is extremely market driven, and networks usually focus on attracting marginal viewers, which make up about 40 percent of the market. So even if the average loyal network news viewer enjoys having hard news coverage, networks are not focused in keeping them, but instead working diligently to capture those casual viewers."

The old adage "you are what you eat", is applicable. Although there are a number of influences which drive news coverage, suffice it to say that most Americans being fed information by major media outlets will not always get accurate and detailed knowledge regarding the subjects that are covered. This is not to say that all Americans are uninformed, but those who are well informed frequently use sources from several media outlets or conduct some limited research on their own.

Perception is most people's reality, and that perception may not actually be reality. Let's examine one example of this.

Many people in the United States perceive gang members to be very dangerous and potentially a great risk to their personal safety. Since most people do not have personal experience with gang members to draw from, they assume the sensational stories regarding gang-related homicides and violence presented by the media is widespread.

The reality, according to the Bureau of Justice Statistics National Crime Victimization Survey, is that in the 1970's, nineteen states (201 American cities) reported gang problems. By the 1990's, all states (1,487 communities) reported gang problems. This represents a 640% increase in about 25 years. This startling increase in gang activity provides a reason for the sensationalized media coverage.

However, although gangs have grown, various studies show that victims perceived their perpetrators to be gang members in about 6% of violent victimizations. This has fallen from the peak in 1996, when gang members where perceived to be responsible for 10% of all violent crime.

The net result is the public walking around in fear of gang members, when there is a far greater chance they will be assaulted by someone who is not a gang member.

Let's assume for a moment that these figures are actually true and not just the victim's reported perception. If gang members are responsible for 6% of violent crime, who is responsible for the remaining 94%? Logic dictates the public should have a keen interest in who represents the greatest percentile of threat in violent crime, and the natural expectation is that media outlets would have an interest as well. But logic, or common sense for that matter, does not fit the formula many media outlets use in choosing what they cover. I have several friends that have spent many years in media who have confirmed this notion.

Let's take a look at the realities of some crime statistics. The benefit of doing so is that if we know how violence usually manifests itself in people, we know how to prepare for it. If you adhere to the prophetic proclamations of Jesus, John and others in the Bible, one of the things you can expect is more violence and perhaps widespread civil chaos and confusion. In this type of environment, violence usually increases.

Violent Crime

There are several categories of crime. The category of violent crime is defined as murder, rape and sexual assault, robbery, and assault. The statistics related to Violent Crime generally take several years to get collected and analyzed. The information presented here is from the Bureau of Justice Statistics National Crime Victimization Survey. Consider the following, and check these realities against your perceptions. The statistics are from the source indicated above. The conclusions are mine, and some of them would not be easy to implement.

In one year, U.S. residents age 12 or older experienced approximately 23 million crimes.

- Property crimes: 77%
- Crimes of violence: 22%
- Personal theft: 1%
- Conclusion: You are far more likely to be the victim of a property crime than a crime of violence.

In 2005 for every 1,000 persons age 12 or older there occurred:

- 1 rape or sexual assault.
- 1 assault with injury.
- 3 robberies.
- Conclusions: You are far more likely to be the victim of a robbery than an assault with injury or sexual assault. However, robberies have violent characteristics.

Murders were the least frequent violent victimization with about 6 murder victims per 100,000 persons.

- Conclusions: There is a .006% risk of being a murder victim.

Since 1994, violent crime rates have declined, but they do fluctuate year to year.

- Conclusion: You are probably far safer than you have been led to believe.

Males were more likely to be violently victimized by a stranger than a non-stranger, and females were more likely to be victimized by a friend, an acquaintance, or an intimate. Males experienced higher victimization rates than females for all types of violent crime except rape/sexual assault.

- Conclusion: Males should be wary of strangers. Females should be careful of their choice in friends, acquaintances, and intimate relationships.

Fifty-three percent of violent crime occurred during the day between 6 a.m. and 6 p.m.

- Conclusion: This is a useless statistic, except it may challenge perceptions that the majority of crime occurs in the evening.

The location of about a quarter of incidents of violent crime was at or near the victim's home. Among common locales for violent crimes were on streets other than those near the victim's home (19%), at school (12%), or at a commercial establishment (8%).

- Conclusion: If you stay away from home, school and commercial establishments, you can avoid significant risk. This, of course, is unlikely.

For violent crime, about half occurred within a mile from home and 76% within five miles. Only 4% of victims of violent crime reported that the crime took place more than fifty miles from their home.

- Conclusion: You are safer away from home – far away. How often are you that far away from home?

Of the victims of violent crime, 22% were involved in some form of leisure activity away from home at the time of their victimization, 22% said they were at home, and another 20% mentioned they were at work or traveling to or from work when the crime occurred.

- Conclusion: Avoiding leisure activity, home and work will reduce risk by 64%. This, of course, is also unrealistic.

Six urban residents, four suburban residents and four rural residents per 1,000 were victims of an aggravated assault.

- Conclusion: Move to the suburbs or rural areas.

In 24% of the incidents of violent crime, a weapon was present.

- Conclusion: Clearly, a weapon is not always present. Therefore, a handgun is not always the solution.

Teens and young adults experience the highest rates of violent crime. Beginning with the 25-34 age categories, the rate at which persons were victims declined significantly as the age category increased.

- Conclusion: The older you get, the safer you become.

Per every 1,000 persons in that racial group, 27 blacks, 20 whites and 14 persons of other races sustained a violent crime.

- Conclusion: Race is a factor, but when all the racial data is reviewed, it is insignificant in relation to how people might prepare for the risk of violence.

Don't believe everything you see or hear from media outlets. You may end up with a perception that is far removed from reality. Within crime statistics, there is valuable information that can be applied to personal choices that will directly affect you or your loved ones. Use them to begin to build your own model of personal safety.

What's The Point?

You should have a basic understanding of the nature of violence. Crime statistics are worthy of discussion. The greater understanding you have of the subject, the more informed you will be when making decisions that may affect your personal safety. The purpose of evaluating relevant information regarding violence is not to frighten you or create paranoia. It is to raise awareness and examine prevention strategies, thereby giving people the ability to develop their own Model of Personal Safety. This process begins by defining the problem.

Violent confrontations are unexpected, unplanned and unpredictable. You can get into situations from which you cannot escape. If this were not true, there would be very few accidental deaths, car accidents, or violent crime victims.

I agree with those who feel that many problems can be avoided by simply paying attention to your environment. I also endorse the application of appropriate interpersonal communications in situations that present personal risk.

BUT.....there are still situations that evolve in which we cannot observe our way out of, talk our way out of, or escape from. Now what?

My roommate in law enforcement academy was a world-ranked karate black-belt. He was also a police officer. I had seen him compete internationally on television before I personally met him. He shared the following story with me.

As a police officer, he had arrested an individual for driving under the influence. Months later, he was off-duty and grocery shopping one evening. The individual he had arrested was in the store with several friends. They began to follow him around the store and make veiled threats. The officer thought it in his best interest to leave the store.

Once in the dimly lit parking lot, the officer was confronted by two of the people who had been following him around the store. He did his best to avoid a confrontation and advised them that he did not want any trouble. One of them produced a bat and began to attack him. He used his significant martial arts skills to ward off the attack now coming from both individuals. What he did not know, or see, was a third companion of this group approaching him from behind. The rear-side attacker hit him so hard he was knocked unconscious and fell to the ground.

This group of attackers failed to recognize a Good Samaritan who had been observing the confrontation. The Good Samaritan also happened to be a sword collector who had several of his swords in his trunk. The Good Samaritan quickly retrieved one of his swords and confronted the group of attackers while he stood over the fallen officer. The officer believes this saved his life.

My brother-in-law owns an investment firm. One of his female employees, who is a senior citizen, was attacked while Christmas shopping in broad daylight. After buying some gifts at a suburban mall, she began to make her way to her car in the parking lot. She noticed an individual coming towards her. She was suddenly hit from behind and knocked to the ground. Her purse was taken, and the assailants fled.

Here are two real-life examples you did not read about in the newspaper in which these individuals found themselves in circumstances they could not escape from.

Below, are some arguable statistics about crime in the United States. They are arguable due to the estimated percentage of unreported and under-reported crime. For example, it is estimated that up to 55% of sexual assaults go unreported. Additionally, these statistics change from year to year.

Violence in America

- One burglary every 11 seconds.
- One motor vehicle theft every 20 seconds.
- One aggravated assault every 28 seconds.
- One robbery every 47 seconds.
- One rape every 5 minutes.
- One murder every 22 minutes.

You might be thinking, "With almost 320 million people in the United States, what are the chances that I will be a victim of violent crime?" If you evaluate your personal safety by asking this question, you are asking the wrong question.

The appropriate question is, "If I do find myself in an unexpected, violent situation from which I cannot escape, what am I going to do?"

There is good research that comes from interviews with criminals. Below, is what some of this research reveals:

Offenders and Weapons

- 60% carried a weapon while traveling.
- 50% carried a weapon while socializing.
- 63% are usually armed at work.
- 83% of juvenile detention center inmates reported owning a gun.
- 35% of juvenile detention inmates and 10% of high school students said it is "OK to shoot a person if that is what it takes to get something you want."

The Impact of Drugs

Statistically, we know that drug and alcohol use increase the risk of violence.

Forty nine percent of all state prison inmates reported that they were under the influence of drugs or alcohol or both at the time they committed the offense for which they were currently sentenced.

The US Department of Health and Human Services, Office of Applied Studies, reports:

- An estimated 20.4 million Americans aged 12 or older were current (past month) illicit drug users, meaning they had used an illicit drug during the month prior to the survey interview. This estimate represents 8.3 percent of the population aged 12 years old or older.
- The estimated number of persons aged 12 or older

needing treatment for an illicit drug problem was over 7 million.

- The estimated number of persons aged 12 or older needing treatment for an alcohol problem was over 18 million.

From a June 2006 U.S. prison study by the bipartisan Commission on Safety and Abuse in America's Prisons: Within three years of their release, 67% of former prisoners are rearrested and 52% are re-incarcerated. This recidivism rate calls into question the effectiveness of America's corrections system, which costs taxpayers $60 billion a year.

What Can We Learn From These Statistics?

The Criminal Justice System in the United States does not work. It is broken. That, however, is a subject for another book.

Presumably, the greatest risk for personal violence comes from those who are candidates for incarceration, and there is close to an even chance they will be under the influence at the time of their offense.

With a population of approximately 320 million, your chances of being a victim of violent crime are about 1-2%. We know from solid research how to alter the odds in your favor should you find yourself in that 1-2% category.

Before an incident, the following are proven elements that alter the outcome of a violent encounter:

- Appropriate observation of the environment and behavioral clues.

- Preparedness for unexpected violence.

- Appropriate motor skills practice. In this context, a motor skill is the term used when referring to martial arts, defensive shooting and other self-defense techniques.

- Tactical training. Self-defense techniques alone are not sufficient to significantly reduce personal risk in violent confrontations. They must be learned in the proper context of the realistic aspects of violence.

Practicing technique and tactics through simulations that replicate real-life encounters is very helpful and is something most martial arts courses and self defense seminars do not accomplish.

- Simulations approximate real life by posing a problematic situation requiring a trainee to decide how to respond and to apply the response correctly.

- Simulations provide opportunities to decide and act and to make mistakes.

- Simulations provide opportunities to practice applying a skill in the face of real life distractions and complications.

- Simulations will test performance in those conditions or find out how parts of a team or a system work together without suffering real life consequences.

- Simulations approximate real life in that they are in real environments with real people and preferably with realistic "tools"–the things the people in the simulation might normally be carrying or have access to. For safety reasons, no live weapons are ever allowed.

- A story is taking place. The people in the Simulation are given the pretext of the story. The role players are given specific directions as to what role they are to play.

- The trainee has choices of action.

- The trainee must make decisions which will affect outcome.

- Someone or something's actions are unpredictable to some degree so the trainee is not sure what will happen. While the role players are given the whole story, the trainees are given only part of the story.

- The outcome of the simulation depends on the combination of the events and the trainee's reaction to them.

Unfortunately, the great majority of self-defense and martial arts programs miss the mark completely when considering these elements.

During the incident, your capabilities based on experience and training will affect the outcome. Once the incident commences, only training and the will to survive can assist you. Do you see the common thread here? It is appropriate training.

Having conducted considerable research into the characteristics of real-life violence and having been involved in a lot of violence professionally, I find that most people who acknowledge these characteristics are able to begin to put them to constructive use in building a model of personal safety.

I have just described the elements that are critical in surviving the outcome if you are involved in a physical confrontation. These elements should be considered in determining how you begin to assemble your model of personal safety.

Most people begin by conducting a personal risk/needs assessment. This is best accomplished by considering your personal circumstances.

Individual Reflection or Group Discussion

- What are my usual daily patterns, and what environments do they expose me to?
- Within those environments, what is the nature of reported crime?
- What personal observations have I made in those environments?
- Is my home safe from theft, burglary, flood and fire?
- If someone does attempt to break into my home, do I have an alarm or a plan?
- In the event I do find myself in a situation from which I cannot escape, what are my alternatives?
- Do those alternatives require any special preparation, training, equipment or self-defense devices? Should I carry a handgun, pepper spray, impact weapons, stun device or other types of self-defense devices?
- Where can I get appropriate information and training should I decide that self-defense is an appropriate part of my response?
- What type of self-defense training should I seek?

These answers should lead you to action.

Be realistic about your chances of being a victim of violent crime, both today and in the future. In doing so, determine if training is a good investment in your personal safety. Next, be selective about the training you choose to become involved with. Whoever you choose should be well-versed in these principles.

Chapter 21
Emergency Planning

"The solution to violence in America is not more laws, more guns, more police, or more prisons. The solution to violence is acceptance of reality. From there, you can hear the messages of intuition. From there, you can evaluate risk and organize defenses. Reality is the highest ground you can find – and the safest – because from there you can see what's coming."

Gavin De Becker

"Commit to the Lord whatever you do, and your plans will succeed." Proverbs 16:1

Lessons Learned

The early morning of my daughter's birth started with my pregnant wife waking me and telling me her back was hurting. Within a short period of time, her water broke, and off we went to the hospital. Several hours later, we met our daughter who was born with no complications. Mom and child were both in good shape. It was one of the most powerful experiences I had been through. The day rolled into afternoon, and I was beginning to drag from the long day and all the well-wishers who had stopped by the hospital. I went home to get some sleep and returned that evening. As I walked into the hospital through the emergency room, I was met with a rushed greeting from one of the emergency room staff. Law enforcement officers generally frequent hospitals due to the nature of their work and develop relationships with hospital staff. As this nurse sped by me, she indicated they were buried in bodies and short-staffed. She immediately enlisted me to help in one of the trauma areas. A team of medical professionals were furiously working to save a man's life that had been in a car accident. They were pumping fluids into him at an accelerated rate. I was asked to take several fluid bags and press them against the wall to increase the flow of these fluids into the victim's body. As I did this, the team was shocking the man's heart, again and again and again, without success. The attending physician decided to massage the heart in a last ditch attempt to save his life. This would not be the last time I would observe a procedure like this as the physician cut deep into the victim's chest cavity. As soon as he penetrated the chest wall, blood went squirting across the room as if it was being projected from a small hose. This was from the blood and pressure that had built up in the victim's chest. The doctor continued to work and rammed his hand into the man's chest – massaging the heart. It was not successful. After what seemed to be several minutes, the doctor called the time of death.

Lesson learned: I was thanked for my assistance and then numbly proceeded to the nursery to see my daughter. I asked to hold her. As I held her, I had tears running down my face – thinking about all the things I could never protect her from and what a miracle she was – and what a miracle life really is. Within the scope of 16 hours, I had watched my daughter enter into life and watched a stranger's exit from it. Life is a precious gift. It is worth fighting for.

What is Emergency Planning?

Emergency planning has to do with your survival in the event of an unexpected disaster, catastrophe or event. Take your pick from any number of the catastrophes listed in Chapter 14. Unless there is direct supernatural intervention from God, Christians along with all other people will have to figure out how to live through it. Remember the earthquake in Japan? Or Katrina? Or any of the other recent natural disasters? In every instance, there were Christians living in these places and affected by the events.

There are several good sources for data on the increase in natural disasters. Generally, these events include drought, earthquake, famine, extreme temperatures, flood, insect infestation, slides, volcanic eruptions, wave and storm surge, wild fires, cyclones, tornados and wind storms. There has been a steady increase in these events since 1900 but a distinct rise in the last several decades. Some people wonder if these events have to do with global warming. Maybe they do. The cause matters very little since God can use anything to initiate these events. The real point is that there seems to be an increase in birth pains as discussed in Chapters 6 and 7.

As I write this chapter in May of 2011, there has been a rash of unexplained mass animal deaths over the last six months. A multitude of birds suddenly falling from the sky in one location and an estimated million fish dead in one small harbor in California are among several stories circulating.

What is most fascinating to me is the apparent lack of interest that media outlets have in these phenomena. Watching a recent news report about one of these events, I was somewhat amused by the quick natural explanations provided by reporters and experts on the subject. Consistently, the explanation is a natural one. There is no serious attempt to link these events with prophecy. The reluctance to call it what it is, is actually proof these events are connected to the prophetic words of Jesus, since he said there would be great deceit.

If one of Satan's primary tools is deception and there is to be more of it as we approach the end of this age along with false teaching, shouldn't we expect a significant amount of denial concerning these events?

Government Will Save Me

Do not be lulled into complacent thinking that government will save you in such an instance. They will do what they can. Government officials and agencies are well-intended, but these types of events can quickly overwhelm government resources. Your survival and your loved-ones survival, is your personal responsibility.

Let's look at one example. There are things that happen that we have no control over such as a hurricane. The outcome, however, is something we have a great deal of control over through emergency planning. The Hurricane Katrina disaster was due to several factors. The nature of the event was catastrophic, and no one had any control over that. But in the aftermath we all discovered poor planning throughout the years and observed terrible coordination between agencies. Katrina serves to reinforce the misguided belief of safety through government.

Now imagine for a moment that there was appropriate emergency planning for New Orleans being under water in the event those levees broke down and flooded for any reason. It should have looked something like this:

- If the levees did break, vehicles would be inoperable, and people would be stranded. This leaves boats and helicopters as the rationale alternatives to distribute emergency supplies and to provide rescue efforts.

- An emergency shelter (the dome) is designated as such, with food and water stockpiles within quick logistical reach.

- Emergency personnel are given response stations and locations.

- Police, fire, EMS and state resources are coordinated

with several types of contingency plans using many scenarios.

- Coordination with federal officials is an unknown factor for any state; take it if you can get it but don't count on it.

With Katrina everyone was quick to point the finger at the federal government. Granted, the response was terribly uncoordinated, but what had the state and local government done to plan for what seemed to be inevitable? How about the individual residents who live there? Had individual residents considered taking any personal steps to protect their families with something as simple as an inflatable raft or some extra food and water?

What Constitutes An Emergency?

For our purposes of emergency planning, a disaster or catastrophe is defined as a natural or man-made hazard that negatively affects you. Not every natural event fits this definition. For instance, a super-tornado in an unpopulated region is unlikely to have much impact on you. However, a major drought in the most productive food-belt region of any country may have a global impact on a lot of people. The following list provides examples that meet this definition. This is not a complete list.

- Accident
- Criminal Acts
- Fire
- Explosion
- Chemical Leak or Spill

- Terrorism
- Earthquake
- Tsunami
- Flood
- Volcanic Eruption
- Earthquake
- Economic Collapse
- Engineering Disaster (i.e. bridge collapse)
- Riot
- War
- Landslide or Mudslide
- Wildfire
- Weather: Heat, Cold, Thunderstorm, Hail, Hurricane, Tornado, Snow
- Pandemic & Infectious Disease
- Avalanche
- Drought
- Famine
- Impact Event (meteor)

- Sink Hole

- Solar Flare (present danger to satellites, communication systems, power grid systems through electromagnetic radiation)

- Storm Surge

What Commonalities Do These Emergencies Share?

Look again at the list above. There are a myriad of possibilities, combinations and consequences that might result from these types of emergencies. When it comes down to basic survival you can live:

- 3 minutes without air.

- 3 days without water or liquids.

- 3 weeks without food.

What About Air?

If you are entrapped – get out as quickly as possible. Examples might include your car under water or thick smoke in the house. Contaminated air caused by fire, chemicals or nuclear fallout might be other examples.

Leave the entire area immediately if possible. If not, find shelter upwind from the contaminated area.

In the unlikely event that chemical or radiological hazards cause officials to advise people in a specific area to "shelter-in-place" in a sealed room, households should have a room selected for this purpose. If appropriate and practical, cover shelter openings such as windows, doors and vents. A roll of duct tape and scissors with plastic sheeting will allow you to accomplish this.

Ten square feet of floor space per person will provide sufficient air to prevent carbon dioxide buildup for up to five hours.

Beware of public shelters. As people continue to enter public shelters, the effectiveness of such sheltering diminishes with time as the contaminated outside air gradually seeps into the shelter.

Always keep a shut-off valve wrench near the gas and water shut-off valves in your home. Many of these valves have their own shut-off handles.

What about Water & Liquids?

In an emergency, having a supply of clean water for drinking, food preparation, and hygiene is a top priority. A normally active person needs to drink at least 2 quarts (a half gallon) of water each day. You will also need water for food preparation and hygiene. For this, store at least an additional half-gallon per person, per day. The general rule of thumb: each person will need a gallon a day.

Store at least a 3-day supply and consider storing a two-week supply of water for each person. If you are unable to store this much, store as much as you can. You can reduce the amount of water your body needs by reducing activity and staying cool. If supplies run low, don't ration water; drink the amount you need today and look for more tomorrow. Don't risk dehydration.

How and Where To Store Water

Learn where the water intake valve to your home is. If you hear reports of broken water or sewage lines or if local officials recommend doing so, you would need to shut off water to your house at the incoming water valve to stop contaminated water from entering your home.

If possible, store water in a cool, dark place in your home, each vehicle, and your workplace. Preferably in store-bought, factory-sealed water containers. If these are not available you may use food-grade-quality containers made for storing water. These are available from sporting goods and surplus stores and other retailers. These containers must be thoroughly washed, sanitized, and rinsed. If the water you store in them is from your tap, you may need to treat it before being stored.

Safe Use Of Water Containers

Wash containers with dishwashing soap and rinse with water. Sanitize by swishing a solution of 1 teaspoon of liquid household chlorine bleach to a quart of water on all interior surfaces of the container. Rinse thoroughly with clean water before use.

Avoid using store-bought water past the expiration or "use by" date on the container. Change stored water every six months.

Alternate Emergency Water Sources Inside Your Home

Inside - if a disaster catches you without a stored supply of clean water, you can use the water in your hot-water tank, pipes and faucets or ice cubes. If your tap water is safe to drink, so is the water in your pipes and hot-water tank even if the idea seems unappealing. If you don't drink tap water, the water in your pipes and hot-water tank may still be useful for sanitation.

To use the water in your hot-water tank, be sure the electricity or gas is off, and then open the drain at the bottom of the tank. Start the water flowing by turning off the water intake valve at the tank and turning on a hot-water faucet. Refill the tank before turning the gas or electricity back on.

To use the water in your pipes, identify and turn on the highest faucet in your home to let air into the plumbing. You then can get water from the lowest faucet.

Alternate Emergency Water Sources Outside Your Home

Outside - if you need to find water outside your home try rainwater, streams, rivers, ponds, lakes, natural springs and other moving bodies of water. Take steps to make water from any of these sources safer before drinking it. You should not drink flood water. Avoid water with floating material, an odor, or dark color. You can use saltwater but you must distill it first.

Ways To Make Outdoor Water Safer

Note: These instructions are not for treating water to be stored, only for emergencies when no other water is available.

Untreated water can make you very sick. Besides having a bad odor and taste, it can contain toxic chemicals, heavy metals and germs that cause such diseases as dysentery, typhoid and hepatitis. Before drinking outdoor water, using it in food preparation or for hygiene, make it safer to use by:

- Straining it. Pour the water through paper towels, a clean cloth, or a coffee filter to remove any suspended particles.

- Boiling it. In a large pot or kettle, bring water to a rolling boil for 1 full minute. Cool it, and pour it back and forth between two clean containers to improve its taste before drinking it. This oxygenates the water.

- Chlorinating it. Using household liquid bleach that contains 5.25 to 6.0 percent sodium hypochlorite (listed on the label) as its only active ingredient, add 16 drops (1/8 teaspoon) per gallon to water in a large pot or kettle. Stir and let stand for 30 minutes. If the water does not have a slight bleach odor, repeat the dosage and let stand another 15 minutes. If it still does not smell of chlorine, find another source of water and start over.

- Distilling it. Fill a pot halfway with water. Tie a cup to the handle on the pot's lid so that the cup will hang right-side-up inside the pot when the lid is upside-down without dangling into the water. Boil the water for 20 minutes. The water that drips from the lid into the cup is distilled.

None of these methods is perfect. The best solution is to use all of them. Boiling and chlorination will kill most microbes but will not remove other contaminants, such as heavy metals, salts and most other chemicals. Distillation will kill or remove most of any remaining contaminates.

Keeping it simple: The simplest method of water storage is to buy a good supply of bottled water and rotate the supply if you feel you need to. The FDA claims water will store indefinitely as long as the containers have remained sealed. After long-term storage, the bottled water's appearance, smell or taste may change somewhat, but the water will still be safe to consume. The expiration dates are meant to be indicators of quality not safety.

What about Food?

You may not need to go out and buy foods to prepare an emergency food supply. You can use the canned goods, dry mixes, and other staples on your cupboard shelves.

Consider storing foods that you eat regularly. The best foods for storage are those that require no refrigeration, no preparation, or no cooking. Include vitamin, mineral, and protein supplements to ensure adequate nutrition.

Store enough food for two weeks. It is better to have extra you can share than to run out. Individuals with special diets and allergies will need particular attention, as will babies, toddlers, ill and elderly people. Nursing mothers may need liquid formula, in case they are unable to nurse. Canned dietetic foods, juices, and soups may be helpful for ill or elderly people. Make sure you have a manual can opener and disposable utensils.

During and after a disaster, eat at least one well-balanced meal each day — more if you are working hard. If activity is reduced, healthy people can survive on half their usual food intake for an extended period and without any food for many days. Food, unlike water, may be rationed safely except for children and pregnant women.

For emergency cooking, you can use a fireplace or a charcoal grill or camp stove outdoors. Use only approved devices—like candle warmers, chafing dishes, and fondue pots—for warming food. If you heat food in its can, be sure to open it and remove the label before heating. Never leave open flames unattended.

How and Where to Store Food

Keep food in a dry, cool spot and out of the sun if possible. Wrap perishable foods, such as cookies and crackers, in plastic bags and keep them in sealed containers.

Empty opened packages of sugar, dried fruits and nuts into screw-top jars or airtight cans to keep them fresh and unspoiled. Avoid canned goods that have become swollen, dented or corroded. Avoid fatty, high-protein or salty foods when your water supply is low.

Keep your hands clean — it's one of the best ways to keep from getting sick. If soap and running water are not available, use alcohol-based hand gels or wipes to clean hands. Germs on your hands can transfer to food during handling.

Inspect all food for signs of spoilage before use. Throw out perishable foods, such as meat and poultry that have been left out at room temperature for more than 2 hours.

Eat salt-free crackers, whole grain cereals and canned foods with high liquid content if your water supplies are low.

If there's a power outage, eat food in the refrigerator first, the freezer next, and finally from your stored supplies. In a well-filled, well-insulated freezer, foods will usually still have ice crystals in their centers, meaning foods are safe to eat for at least two days.

Replace your stored food on a regular basis.

Within six months, use:

- Boxed potatoes
- Dried fruit
- Dry, crisp crackers
- Powdered milk

Within one year, use:

- Canned, condensed meat and vegetable soups
- Canned fruits, fruit juices and vegetables
- Hard candy and canned nuts
- Jelly
- Peanut butter
- Ready-to-eat cereals and uncooked instant cereals
- Vitamins

In proper containers and conditions, the following can be stored indefinitely:

- Baking powder
- Bouillon products
- Dried corn
- Dry pasta
- Instant coffee, tea and cocoa

- Soft drinks
- Vegetable oils
- Salt
- Soybeans
- Wheat (for bread making)
- White rice

Keeping it simple: I acknowledge that for most families, a good variety of foods is important. However, great variety will also require greater storage space and costlier turnover when you replace expired foods. If you want to keep it simple:

- Quick Oats: Combine the quick oats, protein powder and super foods with water to make a smoothie. This is a nutritional powerhouse.
- Protein Powder
- Super Foods Supreme or similar. This is a powdered fruit/vegetable mix.
- Beef Jerky or other similar items
- Granola Bars
- Candy
- Instant Pasta
- Dried Soup Mixes

There are now a number of companies that produce or distribute pre-assembled food kits.

What Is "Shelter-In-Place"?

If you are told to "shelter-in-place," act quickly. Follow the instructions of local authorities. In general:

- Bring children and pets indoors immediately. If your children are at school, do not try to bring them home unless told to do so. The school will shelter them.

- Close and lock all outside doors and windows. Locking may provide a tighter seal.

- If you are told there is danger of explosion, close the window shades, blinds, or curtains.

- Turn off the heating, ventilation, or air conditioning system. Turn off all fans including bathroom fans operated by the light switch.

- Close the fireplace or woodstove damper. Become familiar with proper operation of flues and dampers ahead of time.

- Get your disaster supplies kit, and make sure the radio is working.

The room should have 10 square feet of floor space per person in order to provide sufficient air to prevent carbon dioxide buildup for 5 hours. In this room, you should store scissors, plastic sheeting pre-cut to fit over any windows or vents and rolls of duct tape to secure the plastic. Access to a water supply is desirable as is a working hard-wired telephone. Don't rely on cell phones because cellular telephone circuits may be overwhelmed or damaged during an emergency. Also, a power failure will render most cordless phones inoperable.

If you are instructed to seal the room, use duct tape and plastic sheeting such as heavy-duty plastic garbage bags to seal all cracks around the door into the room. Tape plastic over any windows. Tape over any vents and seal electrical outlets and other openings. As much as possible, reduce the flow of air into the room.

Keep listening to your radio or television until you are told all is safe or you are told to evacuate. Do not evacuate unless instructed to do so.

When you are told that the emergency is over, open windows and doors, turn on ventilation systems, and go outside until the building's air has been exchanged with the now clean outdoor air. Follow any special instructions given by emergency authorities to avoid chemical or radiological contaminants outdoors.

What If I Am In My Vehicle?

Admittedly, taking shelter in a vehicle may be an uncomfortable experience particularly in very hot or very cold weather. Still, such discomfort is safer than possibly exposing yourself to chemical or radiological contaminants in the outside air. Having a portable disaster supply kit in your vehicle could make the experience less unpleasant.

The appropriate steps depend on the emergency situation. If you hear a warning signal, listen to local radio or television stations for further information. You will be told what to do including where to find the nearest shelter if you are away from your "shelter-in-place" location.

If you are very close to home, your workplace or a public building, go there immediately and go inside. Follow the "shelter-in-place" recommendations for that location.

If you are unable to get indoors quickly and safely, pull over to the side of the road. Stop your vehicle in the safest place possible. If it is sunny outside, it is preferable to stop under a bridge or in a shady spot to avoid being overheated. Turn off the engine. Close windows and vents. If possible, seal the heating, ventilating, and air conditioning vents with duct tape or anything else you may have available.

Listen to the radio periodically for updated advice and instructions. Modern car radios consume very little battery power and should not affect your ability to start your car later. Stay where you are until you are told it is safe to get back on the road. Be aware that some roads may be closed or traffic detoured.

Supplies for your vehicle could include:

- Bottled water and non-perishable foods such as granola bars.

- Seasonal supplies: Winter blanket, hat, mittens, shovel, sand, tire chains, windshield scraper, a florescent distress flag, sunscreen lotion and a shade item such as an umbrella or wide brimmed hat.

- Flashlight, extra batteries, and maps.

- First aid kit and manual.

- White distress flag.

- Tire repair kit, booster/jumper cables, pump, and flares.

What Should A Workplace Emergency Plan Look Like?

Check with your workplace to learn their plans for dealing with an emergency that would require sheltering-in-place. Those plans should include the following.

- Employers should close the office making any customers, clients or visitors in the building aware that they need to stay until the emergency is over.

- Close and lock all windows, exterior doors and any other openings to the outside.

- Avoid overcrowding by pre-selecting several interior rooms with the fewest number of windows or vents. The appropriate location depends entirely on the emergency situation. If a chemical has been released, you should take shelter in a room above ground level because some chemicals are heavier than air and may seep below ground. On the other hand, if there are radioactive particles in the air, you should choose a centrally located room or basement.

- Knowing what to do under specific circumstances is an important part of being prepared. The rooms should have adequate space for everyone to be able to sit including an estimated number of visitors. Large storage closets, utility rooms, pantries, break rooms and copy and conference rooms without exterior windows would work well.

- Access to bathrooms is a plus. It is ideal to have hard-wired telephones in the rooms you select.

- The rooms should be equipped with a disaster supply kits.

- A knowledgeable person should use the building's mechanical systems to turn off all heating, ventilating and air conditioning systems. The systems that automatically provide for exchange of inside air with outside air, in particular, need to be turned off, sealed or disabled.

- Unless there is an imminent threat, employers should

ask employees, customers, clients and visitors to call their emergency contacts to let them know where they are and that they are safe.

- If time permits and it is not possible for a person to monitor the telephone, turn on call-forwarding or alternative telephone answering systems or services. If the business has voicemail or an automated attendant, it should be switched to a recording that indicates that the business is closed and that staff and visitors are remaining in the building until authorities advise it is safe to leave.

- If you are told there is danger of explosion, close any window shades, blinds or curtains near your workspace.

- Take your workplace disaster supply kits and go to your pre-determined sheltering room and, when everyone is in, shut and lock the doors. There should be a radio or a TV in the rooms.

- Turn on the radios or TVs. If instructed to do so by officials, use duct tape and plastic sheeting such as heavy-duty plastic garbage bags to seal all cracks around the doors and any vents into the room. Seal any windows and/or vents with sheets of plastic and duct tape. As much as possible, reduce the flow of air into the room.

- Businesses should assign one or two people to collect information on who is in the building when an emergency happens so that first responders will know everyone is accounted for if necessary.

- One person per room should write down the names of everyone in the room. Call your business-designated emergency contact to report who is in the room with you and their affiliation with your business.

- Keep listening to the radio or watching TV for updates until you are told all is safe or you are told to evacuate.

- When you are told that all is safe, open windows and doors, turn on heating, ventilating and air conditioning systems and go outside until the building's air has been exchanged with the now-clean outdoor air. Follow any special instructions given by emergency authorities to avoid chemical or radiological contaminants outdoors.

What Should A School Emergency Plan Look Like?

The appropriate steps depend on the emergency situation. If you hear a warning signal, listen to local radio or television stations for further information. You will be told what to do, including where to find the nearest shelter if you are away from your "shelter-in-place" location. Check with the school or day-care center to learn their plans for dealing with this type of emergency. Their "shelter-in-place" plans should include the following:

- Close the school. Activate the school's emergency plan. Follow reverse evacuation procedures to bring students, faculty and staff indoors.

- If visitors are in the building, provide for their safety by asking them to stay.

- Ideally, have access to the school-wide public address system in the room where the top school official takes shelter.

- Have at least one telephone line under the school's listed telephone number in one of the shelter rooms available for a designated person to answer the calls of concerned parents. If time permits and it is not possible for a person to monitor the telephone and the school has voicemail or an automated attendant, change the recording to indicate that the school is closed and that students and staff are remaining in the building until authorities say it is safe to leave.

- Classrooms may be used if there are no windows or the windows are sealed and cannot be opened. Large storage closets, utility rooms, or meeting rooms could be used. A gymnasium without exterior windows would also work well. Access to bathrooms is a plus.

- Have all children, staff and visitors take shelter in preselected rooms that have phone access and stored disaster supply kits and, preferably, access to a bathroom. Shut the doors.

- Have all shelter rooms closed. Lock all windows, exterior doors and any other openings to the outside.

- If told there is danger of explosion, make sure window shades, blinds or curtains are closed.

- Turn off heating, ventilating and air conditioning systems. Systems that automatically provide for exchange of inside air with outside air must be turned off, sealed or disabled.

- If instructed by officials, use duct tape and plastic sheeting to seal all cracks around the doors, windows and vents into the room. As much as possible, reduce the flow of air into the room.

- If children have cell phones, allow them to try to use them to call a parent or guardian to let them know that they have been asked to remain in school until further notice and that they are safe. This may reduce the potential number of incoming calls.

- Schools should assign one or two people to collect information on who is in the building when an emergency happens so that first responders can know everyone is accounted for if necessary.

- One teacher or staff member in each room should write down the names of everyone in the room and call the school's designated emergency contact to report who is in that room.

- Everyone should stay in the room until school officials, via the public address system, announce that all is safe or say everyone must evacuate.

- Once the word has been given that all is safe, everyone should go outside when the building's ventilation systems are turned back on. Follow any special instructions given by emergency authorities to avoid chemical and radiological contaminants outdoors.

What Does An Emergency Supply Kit Look Like?

A disaster supply kit is a collection of basic items that could be needed in the event of a disaster. Use your discretion based on whether the kit will be in your home, car, or work location. Typically, here are the items you would be considering:

- Water – a minimum of one gallon per day for each person.

- Items for infants including formula, diapers, bottles, pacifiers, powdered milk and medications not requiring refrigeration.

- Items for seniors, disabled persons or anyone with serious allergies including special foods, denture items, extra eyeglasses, hearing aid batteries, prescription and non-prescription medications that are regularly used, inhalers and other essential equipment.

- Kitchen accessories - a manual can opener; mess kits or disposable cups, plates and utensils; utility knife; sugar and salt; aluminum foil and plastic wrap; re-sealable plastic bags; several mixing jars.

- Small propane cook stove and propane.

- A portable, battery-powered, hand-crank or solar radio or television.

- Several flashlights and extra, fresh batteries. Candles, matches and a lighter.

- Basic First Aid Kit.

- One complete change of clothing and footwear for each person - including sturdy work shoes or boots, raingear and other items adjusted for the season, such as hats and gloves, thermal underwear, sunglasses, dust masks.

- Blankets or a sleeping bag for each person.

- Sanitation and hygiene items - shampoo, deodorant, toothpaste, toothbrushes, comb and brush, lip balm, sunscreen, contact lenses supplies and any medications regularly used, toilet paper, towelettes, soap, hand sanitizer, liquid detergent, feminine supplies, heavy duty plastic garbage bags and ties, medium-sized plastic bucket with tight lid, disinfectant, and household chlorine bleach.

- Other essential items - paper, pencil, needles, thread, small ABC type fire extinguisher, medicine dropper, whistle, emergency preparedness manual.

- Entertainment - including games and books, favorite dolls and stuffed animals for small children.

- A map of the area marked with places you could go and applicable telephone numbers.

- An extra set of keys and identification - including keys for cars and any properties owned and copies of driver's licenses, passports and work identification badges.

- Cash, coins and copies of credit cards.

- Required medications and copies of medical prescriptions.

- Copies of important documents. Your actual Passport, Visa and credit cards.

- A small tent, compass and shovel.

- Food - a three-day supply. You may want to consider stocking a two-week supply of food and water in your home. Your food supply may be simple or complex.

How you go about assembling your emergency kit depends on the level of comfort you wish to experience during the emergency.

Pack the items in easy-to-carry containers, label the containers clearly and store them where they would be easily accessible. Duffle bags, backpacks, and covered trash receptacles are good candidates for containers. In a disaster situation, you may need access to your disaster supply kit quickly depending on whether you are sheltering at home or evacuating. Following a disaster, having the right supplies can help your household endure home confinement or evacuation.

Make sure the needs of everyone who would use the kit are covered, including infants, seniors and pets. It's good to involve whoever is going to use the kit, including children, in assembling it. Don't forget to take your pets and service animals into account.

There are now a number of companies that produce or distribute pre-assembled food kits and emergency supplies. A quick Internet search should provide you a healthy list.

Keeping it simple: Make a basic emergency supply kit using several duffel bags or backpacks. Put it in your vehicle. Presumably, you are usually with your vehicle whether at home, work or play. Then your emergency supplies will always be within close proximity when you need them.

Maintaining a Healthy State of Mind

These types of events can cause fear and confusion amongst the masses. If you remember the Rodney King situation, there was civil unrest, riot, assaults and looting that occurred within several hours. And these actions were not controlled by police due to the sheer numbers.

The aftermath of Katrina gave us insight into less than stellar behavior from the police department, city officials, state officials and the federal government.

Everyone has their own ways of dealing with stressful situations. Being caught off-guard often leads to panic and confusion. Having a plan will diffuse most of the anxiety that comes with a catastrophic event. The bottom line is that the more you prepare for the unexpected, the better you will manage those situations.

Individual Reflection or Group Discussion

As you develop your emergency plan, keep the following in mind. When it comes down to basic survival, you can live:

- 3 minutes without air.
- 3 days without water or liquids.
- 3 weeks without food.

Consider or discuss what types of emergencies are most likely to happen in your world. Some places are more prone geographically to certain natural events. Also, consider the list from Chapter 14. Determine what could happen to you should you be in the midst of one of these circumstances.

1. Develop an emergency plan. A good emergency plan will cover a multitude of events and catastrophes.

2. If need be, consider the disaster plans at your workplace, your children's school or daycare center, and other places where your family or significant others spend time.

3. Build an action checklist and complete it. Your checklist should include how you will communicate with others, emergency supplies and an evacuation plan. Your evacuation plan should include two places to meet. One is outside your home in the case of a fire or carbon monoxide. The other is outside of your neighborhood or even your city in case you cannot return home. Everyone must know the location's address and phone number if one exists.

4. Develop different methods for communicating during emergency situations. Cell phones may not work and

the Internet, which most of us have come to rely upon, may not be available.

- Ask an out-of-state friend to be your "family contact". After a disaster, it's often easier to call long distance. Other family members should call this person and tell them where they are. Everyone must know your contact's phone number.

- Phone contact with a designated family member or friend who is unlikely to be affected by the same disaster.

- Email notification via a distribution list.

5. Share plans beforehand with significant others. Meet with them and discuss the plan. Plan to share responsibilities and work together as a team.

6. Practice your plan. Work out any problems that might be exposed.

Chapter 22
Terrorism

"When I say that terrorism is war against civilization, I may be met by the objection that terrorists are often idealists pursuing worthy ultimate aims - national or regional independence, and so forth. I do not accept this argument. I cannot agree that a terrorist can ever be an idealist, or that the objects sought can ever justify terrorism. The impact of terrorism, not merely on individual nations, but on humanity as a whole, is intrinsically evil, necessarily evil and wholly evil."

Benjamin Netanyahu

"There are six things the LORD hates, seven that are detestable to him: haughty eyes, a lying tongue, hands that shed innocent blood, a heart that devises wicked schemes, feet that are quick to rush into evil, a false witness who pours out lies and a person who stirs up conflict in the community." Proverbs 6:16-19

Lessons Learned

Several years ago I was involved in a case in which a jilted husband, separated from his wife, suspected her of being unfaithful to him. In fact, his wife had a boyfriend and was attempting to keep it a secret.

The jilted husband hand-delivered a pipe bomb, in a toolbox, to his estranged wife's residence in the wee hours of the morning. She discovered it later that day on her front doorstep. In an interview I conducted with her several days later from her hospital bed, she advised me:

- She thought the package looked odd due to it being wrapped in a reversed grocery paper bag and having a return address on it she did not recognize.

- She called her boyfriend, who was at work, and advised him of the discovery.

- The boyfriend advised her to move the package to the back porch. This action indicated to me they both thought something was suspicious about the package.

- The boyfriend advised her to carefully remove the outer wrapping on the package. She did so and found a new red toolbox.

- Next, she attempted to open it but reported the latches on the toolbox seemed tight.

- With the boyfriend still on the phone, they joked about it being a bomb from her estranged husband but agreed he was not THAT crazy.

- Finally, they agreed she should use a rake handle to open the latch while the toolbox was left on the porch, and she hid behind a portion of the back door – reaching out towards the toolbox.

- She managed to unlatch the tool box which was spring-loaded. BOOM! She lost several fingers, was full of shrapnel, and the residence started on fire.

This is a perfect example of how justification, rationalization and denial got in the way of intuition. We found evidence of pipe bomb materials at the estranged husband's home and identified the store where he bought the toolbox. A warrant was issued. We tracked him to somewhere in Mexico.

Lesson learned: Pay attention to your intuition. It is trying to tell you something.

I debated inserting a chapter on terrorism because there is an overwhelming amount of information available from multiple sources including FEMA, Homeland Security, the FBI and others. But to do so would be like ignoring the elephant in the room. The fact is that we have been involved in a global war on terror for almost a decade. It has put a huge strain on the deficit in the US, and lives have been sacrificed fighting it. There has been a dramatic increase in terroristic acts in the last decade. Radical Muslims have overtly expressed their hatred of Jews and Israel who are among the prominent players in Middle East events as we near the end of the church age. Other nations are not particularly enthusiastic about Israel either. Additionally, there are now an alarming number of domestic terrorists springing up. It is a fact of life.

Defined

Terrorism is a type of violent struggle that makes deliberate use of violence against civilians to achieve political aims. This is a struggle that is intended to harm public morale, in which the terrorist organizations use all means available to them to carry out fatal attacks that will spread fear among a much wider population than those experiencing the attack, influence the public agenda and attract political and international attention to their ideological demands.

By definition, terrorists want the biggest bang for their buck. They usually use IED's, suicide bombings or mass hostage taking in public gathering places to get someone's attention about something. Terrorists have been known, however, to make targeted attacks against corporations and entities that do not share their values. Additionally, although kidnappings are rather rare in the United States, they do still happen – and more so overseas. For these reasons you should have a basic, functioning knowledge of terrorism.

Terrorism is an international issue without borders. Different countries and movements around the world have found terrorism to be an effective means of advancing their political objectives. There are approximately 1.3 billion Muslims (people who practice Islam). Muslim birth rates are huge and the Islam faith is expected to overtake Christianity at some point, which sits at 2.3 billion.

The Islamist terrorists are responsible for 98% of terrorism. Not everyone who practices Islam is a terrorist. Some Muslims believe in a complete separation of church and state. Others want expression through the established political system. There are Muslims who believe the world should operate through God's laws; not man's. It is a very small group of Muslims willing to use violence in order to achieve this. In the faith of Islam, a defensive war justifies any and all violence – even against women, children and other Muslims. Radical Muslims believe they are under attack from western values.

Jihad has several meanings:

- Personal: It is the internal struggle to be a better Muslim.

- Military: It is the external fight for Islam.

- Radical: There is no greater spiritual status than to die for this.

Young people are often recruited by radicals for the following reasons:

- Young people often push the envelope and are looking for thrills.

- They are easily influenced.

- They are looking for a sense of belonging and family.

The Executive Summary from American Jihadist Terrorism: Combating a Complex Threat, produced by the Congressional Research Service:

> "Between May 2009 and November 2010, arrests were made for 22 'homegrown', jihadist inspired terrorist plots by American citizens or legal permanent residents of the United States. By comparison, in more than seven years from the September 11, 2001 terrorist strikes through May 2009, there were 21 such plots. Two resulted in attacks, and no more than six plots occurred in a single year (2006). The apparent spike in such activity after May 2009 suggests that at least some Americans, even if a tiny minority, continue to be susceptible to ideologies supporting a violent form of jihad. This report describes homegrown violent jihadists and the plots and attacks that have occurred since 9/11. 'Homegrown' and 'domestic' are terms that describe terrorist activity or plots perpetrated within the United States or abroad by American citizens, legal permanent residents, or visitors radicalized largely within the United States. The term 'jihadist' describes radicalized individuals using Islam as an ideological and/or religious justification for their belief in the establishment of a global caliphate, or jurisdiction governed by a Muslim civil and religious leader known as a caliph. The term "violent jihadist" characterizes jihadists who have made the jump to illegally supporting, plotting, or directly engaging in violent terrorist activity."

In 2008-2009 there was a significant increase in activity within the United Sates. Many people have questioned why the US has not had serious attacks since 9/11. A large part of that is due to governmental and law enforcement efforts to stop it. Over 22 plots have been thwarted in the US since 9/11 — over 60 in the United Kingdom.

Terrorist sleeper cells have probably been in the US for years. It is probable and likely they have already studied and "cased" many soft targets. Making explosives is as simple as getting a recipe off of the Internet and then visiting your local hardware store. Why, then, have there not been suicide bombers and Improvised Explosive Devices exploding in the US? One of the primary reasons is the radical leadership behind terrorism is not stupid. They have not given sleeper cells the "green light". The US is a great place for foreigners to receive an excellent education, make good money to send back home, and operate freely in a republic. Why screw up a good thing?

Methods of Terrorism

This section is a very general outline of terrorism and terrorist tactics. If you have more than a general interest in knowing what to look for and how to prepare, please visit the Homeland Security or FEMA website.

As you read through this chapter, the overwhelming suggestion is that if you observe something that gets your attention, or speaks to your intuition, or causes a second look, or seems out of place or strange – something is probably not right, and you need to pay attention to it. What you do with that is entirely up to you, but do not ignore it.

A Quick Lesson with Intuition

Intuition is a hard-wired, genetic part of who we are. It is the "sixth sense", gut feeling, "funny" feeling or instinct. Call it what you will, but it should not be ignored or rationalized away. It is there for a reason. It is always working even when you are asleep. It is a survival gift.

The biggest enemies of intuition are justification, rationalization and denial. Example: I wake at 3 am and hear noise in my basement. My justification, rationalization or denial says: "It must be the furnace making noise", when really it is a burglar rummaging through the house.

Victims, in post-crime interviews, often refer to a moment when their intuition was trying to tell them something, and they justified it, rationalized it or denied it away.

Conventional Terrorism

The Improvised Explosive Device is still the #1 weapon of choice for terrorists accounting for over 50% of all attacks.

Suspicious Object (Explosive Charge): A suspicious object is one that is unfamiliar and arouses suspicion due to its location because it has been placed there for the purpose of sabotage. If you come across a suspicious object, keep other people away from it and immediately inform authorities. One or more adults should watch over the suspicious object to make sure no one comes near making sure they themselves are at a safe distance and if possible, behind a protective barrier.

Suspicious Person (Suicide Attack): A suicide attack is an "operational method in which the very act of the attack is dependent upon the death of the perpetrator." The terrorist is fully aware that if he does not kill himself, the planned attack will not be implemented. The attack is carried out by activating explosives worn or carried by the terrorist in the form of a portable explosive charge or planted in a vehicle he is driving. If you identify a suspicious person, keep him in sight and inform authorities. Try to prevent the suspect from approaching and/or entering the building.

From Terrorist Threat Indicators by Richard Marquis

- Are unknown or suspicious people conducting boundary probing? They are checking to see how close they can get to the target.

- Wear heavy clothing to hide explosives regardless of the season, although there are now undergarments specifically made to hide explosive on the suicide bomber.

- Display a robotic gait or nervously look around.

- Show signs of tunnel vision and are not responsive to commands.

- Give the appearance of being drugged.

- Wear too much cologne or have other unusual smells.

- Carry a large backpack.

- Have wires protruding from sleeves or hands in pockets for detonation.

- Have a fresh shave or make other attempts to "blend in".

- Shows signs of emotion and irritation, or perspire excessively.

- Shows signs of being in clandestine collaboration and contact with other people directing signals and movements towards them.

- Appearance is unusual, does not suit their personality, or their clothes are not appropriate to the season.

- The suspect gives the impression that they may be concealing a weapon in his clothing.

Suspicious Vehicle (Booby-Trapped Car): If you discover a suspicious vehicle and none of the signs can be ruled out, it should be treated as if it is a weapon. Do not touch it or try to open the doors. Keep people away from the vehicle and close off access to the road. At the same time, inform the authorities about the vehicle and explain what has aroused your suspicion. A suspicious vehicle is one displaying one or more of the following signs:

- Suspicious or extra electric wires connected to the car.

- Additional electrical switches which appear suspicious.

- A safety catch / catches in or near the vehicle.

- Torn pieces of insulating tape.

- A wrist watch, alarm clock or timer.

- Extraneous wires.

- Non-identical license plates.

- Absence of license plates.

- Signs of break-in indicating a stolen vehicle.

- Items or containers of flammable material inside the vehicle.

- A car parked in an unlikely and suspicious manner.
- A vehicle that appears to be low due to excessive weight.

Non-Conventional Terrorism

These tactics involve the use of a non-conventional component (atomic, biological or chemical) and is therefore likely to cause more serious damage to the surrounding area, affecting water or food, or causing disease in people, animals or plants. The use of conventional terrorism can sometimes lead to a non-conventional incident such as rockets fired at a plant containing hazardous materials. This then becomes a hazardous materials incident.

Suspicious Packages and Letters: Be wary of suspicious packages and letters. They may contain explosives, chemical or biological agents. Be particularly cautious at your place of employment. Some typical characteristics postal inspectors have detected over the years which ought to trigger suspicion include parcels that:

- Are unexpected or from someone unfamiliar to you.
- Have no return address, or have one that can't be verified as legitimate.
- Have protruding wires or aluminum foil, strange odors, or stains.
- Show a city or state in the postmark that doesn't match the return address.
- Are of unusual weight given their size, or are lopsided or oddly shaped.
- Are marked with threatening language.

- Have inappropriate or unusual labeling.

- Have excessive postage or packaging material such as masking tape and string.

- Have misspellings of common words.

- Are addressed to someone no longer with your organization or are otherwise outdated.

- Have incorrect titles or titles without a name.

- Are not addressed to a specific person.

- Have hand-written or poorly typed addresses.

With suspicious envelopes and packages other than those that might contain explosives, take these additional steps against possible biological and chemical agents.

- Refrain from eating or drinking in a designated mail handling area.

- Place suspicious envelopes or packages in a plastic bag or some other type of container to prevent leakage of contents. Never sniff or smell suspect mail.

- If you do not have a container, then cover the envelope or package with anything available (e.g., clothing, paper, trash can, etc.) and do not remove the cover.

- Leave the room and close the door, or section off the area to prevent others from entering.

- Wash your hands with soap and water to prevent spreading any substance to your face.

- If you are at work, report the incident to your building security official or supervisor who should notify police and other authorities without delay.

- List all people who were in the room or area when this suspicious letter or package was recognized. Give a copy of this list to both the local public health authorities and law enforcement officials for follow-up investigations and advice.

- If you are at home, report the incident to local police.

Biological agents are organisms or toxins that can kill or incapacitate people, livestock, and crops. The three basic groups of biological agents that would likely be used as weapons are bacteria, viruses, and toxins. Most biological agents are difficult to grow and maintain. Many break down quickly when exposed to sunlight and other environmental factors, while others, such as anthrax spores, are very long lived. Biological agents can be dispersed by spraying them into the air, by infecting animals that will carry the disease to humans and by contaminating food and water.

Chemical agents are poisonous vapors, aerosols, liquids, and solids that have toxic effects on people, animals, or plants. They can be released by bombs or sprayed from aircraft, boats, and vehicles. They can be used as a liquid to create a hazard to people and the environment. Some chemical agents may be odorless and tasteless. They can have an immediate effect (a few seconds to a few minutes) or a delayed effect (2 to 48 hours). While potentially lethal, chemical agents are difficult to deliver in lethal concentrations. Outdoors, the agents often dissipate rapidly. Chemical agents also are difficult to produce. A chemical attack could come without warning. Signs of a chemical release include people having difficulty breathing; experiencing eye irritation; losing coordination; becoming nauseated; or having a burning sensation in the nose, throat, and lungs. Also, the presence of many dead insects or birds may indicate a chemical agent release.

A nuclear blast is an explosion with intense light and heat, a damaging pressure wave, and widespread radioactive material that can contaminate the air, water, and ground surfaces for miles around. A nuclear device can range from a weapon carried by an intercontinental missile launched by a hostile nation or terrorist organization to a small portable nuclear device transported by an individual. All nuclear devices cause deadly effects when they explode including blinding light, intense heat, nuclear radiation, blast effects, fires started by the heat pulse and secondary fires caused by the destruction.

The extent, nature, and arrival time of these hazards are difficult to predict. Geographical dispersion of hazard effects will be defined by the size of the device, the height at detonation, the nature of the surface beneath the explosion and existing meteorological conditions. Even if individuals are not close enough to the nuclear blast to be affected by the direct impacts, they may be affected by radioactive fallout. Any nuclear blast results in some fallout. Blasts that occur near the earth's surface create much greater amounts of fallout than blasts that occur at higher altitudes. This is because the tremendous heat produced from a nuclear blast causes an up-draft of air that forms the familiar mushroom cloud. When a blast occurs near the earth's surface, millions of vaporized dirt particles also are drawn into the cloud. As the heat diminishes, radioactive materials that have vaporized condense on the particles and fall back to Earth. The phenomenon is called radioactive fallout. This fallout material decays over a long period of time and is the main source of residual nuclear radiation.

In addition to other effects, a nuclear weapon detonated in or above the earth's atmosphere can create an electromagnetic pulse

(EMP) — a high-density electrical field. An EMP acts like a stroke of lightning but is stronger, faster, and shorter. An EMP can seriously damage electronic devices connected to power sources or antennas. This includes communication systems, computers, electrical appliances, and automobile or aircraft ignition systems. The damage could range from a minor interruption to actual burnout of components. Most electronic equipment within 1,000 miles of a high-altitude nuclear detonation could be affected. Battery-powered radios with short antennas generally would not be affected. Although an EMP is unlikely to harm most people, it could harm those with pacemakers or other implanted electronic devices.

In general, potential targets for these weapons include:

- Strategic missile sites and military bases.
- Centers of government such as Washington, DC and state capitals.
- Important transportation and communication centers.
- Manufacturing, industrial, technology, and financial centers.
- Petroleum refineries, electrical power plants, and chemical plants.
- Major ports and airfields.

A Radiological Dispersion Device (RDD), often called "dirty nuke" or "dirty bomb", is considered far more likely than use of a nuclear explosive device. An RDD combines a conventional explosive device—such as a bomb—with radioactive material. It is designed to scatter dangerous and sub-lethal amounts of radioactive material over a general area. Such RDDs appeal to terrorists because they require limited technical knowledge to build and deploy compared to a nuclear device. Also, the radioactive materials in RDDs are widely used in medicine, agriculture, industry, and research and are easier to obtain than weapons grade uranium or plutonium. The primary purpose of terrorist use of an RDD is to cause psychological fear and economic disruption. Some devices could cause fatalities from exposure to radioactive materials. Depending on the speed at which the area of the RDD detonation was evacuated or how successful people were at sheltering-in-place, the number of deaths and injuries from an RDD might not be substantially greater than from a conventional bomb explosion. The size of the affected area and the level of destruction caused by an RDD would depend on the sophistication and size of the conventional bomb, the type of radioactive material used, the quality and quantity of the radioactive material, and the local meteorological conditions—primarily wind and precipitation. The area affected could be placed off-limits to the public for several months during cleanup efforts.

What Can Be Done to Fight Suicide Terrorism?

Individuals and organizations that are concerned about being a target of terror should be conducting protective intelligence, practicing operational counter-terrorist measures and protective anti-terrorist measures. Psychological measures should be employed to whatever degree is possible.

- Operational (counter-terrorist) measures are efforts towards putting pressure on those elements involved in the overall planning and implementation of attacks.

- Security Measures (anti-terrorist measures) should be taken in order to prevent the Adversary from reaching his target or getting inside the target.

- Psychological Measures has to do with countering the moral damage of these attacks. Of foremost importance

> is the task of supporting and strengthening the civilian population in dealing with suicide terrorism. Civilians are the main victims of terrorism and it is they who are on the front line in the fight against terrorism.

There is, almost always, a precursor, or "tell" before a terror attack. Much like Mass Shooters, the terrorist leaves a trail of things that are often missed by officials and the public.

- Parking or loitering in the same area over a period of days, with no apparent reason.

- Cameras or video cameras with special magnification lenses or night vision devices.

- Photos, maps, sketches, or blueprints of potential targets.

- Computer access to information about sensitive sites, such as nuclear plants.

- Unusual false alarms requiring law enforcement or emergency response.

- Evidence of coded communication.

- Books and pamphlets promoting Jihad.

- Bomb-making manuals.

- Flight manuals.

- Logs or records detailing the activities or movements of law enforcement or security personnel.

- Thefts at military surplus stores.

- Rental of storage units for suspicious items.

- Modification of vehicles, including trucks and limousines, to accommodate heavy loads.

- Access to emergency vehicles.

- Signs of training and testing.

- Possession or attempts to acquire: ammonium nitrate fertilizer, body armor, propane bottles and tanks, uniforms, identification, license plates, service vehicles, weapons, ammunition, chemicals, identification documents, prepaid cell phones, and ATM cards.

- Funding sources include: counterfeit designer clothing, drugs, money laundering, smuggling, stolen property, sales of publications and fraud.

Domestic Terror warning signs include: radical bumper stickers, homemade or missing license plates, fraudulent driver's license or registrations, message-tattoos, video surveillance on property, weapons, ammunition or explosives, possession of radical literature, etc.

The average terrorist does not look like one. They look like all of us. Therefore, profiling based on race, gender and looks is futile. Profiling should be done, and it should be based on the behavioral indicators already mentioned.

Additionally, if you are ever caught up in a terror event, you have two choices and must make them quickly. Flee immediately if you can. If not, you must fight and do it quickly. Case study after case study reveals the longer you wait to respond, the worse things are going to get. A terroristic act needs to be met with a violent counterattack immediately.

Individual Reflection or Group Discussion

The Department of Homeland Security launched a public awareness campaign in July 2010. "If You See Something, Say Something™" was intended to be a "simple and effective program to raise public awareness of indicators of terrorism and violent crime, and to emphasize the importance of reporting suspicious activity to the proper state and local law enforcement authorities."

1. In regard to what you have read in this chapter, list or discuss three specific traits that you might observe which would cause you to actually report your observations to law enforcement authorities.

2. There have been a number of terror incidents both in the United States and abroad in which innocent civilians have found themselves in situations from which they could not escape. These include school shootings, mall shootings, mass transit attacks, workplace violence and hostage-taking. Think about them and discuss what immediate actions you would take in these various situations.

3. Most companies in the United States have no emergency plans in place for such events. Does your workplace have one?

Are your children and family members versed in what actions they should take should they find themselves in the midst of an event like this?

CHAPTER 23
LAST CALL –
THE FINAL OPPORTUNITY

"Intuition is knowing without knowing why, knowing when you can't see the evidence. Denial is choosing not to know something even when the evidence is obvious."

Gavin De Becker

"Unless commitment is made, there are only promises and hopes; but no plans."

Peter F. Drucker

"Once the notion of eternity drops from your head into your heart, it changes everything."

Terry Hipp

"Whoever acknowledges me before others, I will also acknowledge before my Father in heaven. But whoever disowns me before others, I will disown before my Father in heaven." Matthew 10: 32-33

Lessons Learned

As a detective, I am informed by some fellow officers one morning that a baby has been killed by the family dog at a local residence. They went on to inform me that they killed the dog, and both the dog and the baby were with the coroner. I was to investigate this death. My partner was out sick for a few days so the complete investigation would fall on me. For several days I sat through autopsies of the infant and the dog by the medical examiner collecting evidence. I went to the scene and took pictures. I interviewed neighbors, the former dog's owner and the parents of the deceased infant. This is what I had pieced together.

The dog, a Doberman, had been purchased by the father of this infant from a person who had informed the father that the Doberman was a former police dog who had been flushed out of police work due to its unreliable, inconsistent and sometimes explosive behavior. This was confirmed through my interviews with the prior owner of the dog and the police department who had the dog before that.

My guess was that the father thought it would be cool to have a "tough" dog. Why would anyone want a dog like this? The neighbors were afraid of it when it was outside and had complained about the dog's demeanor. The dog was generally left outside, and when it was inside the home, it was kept on a leash which was attached to what can only be described as a metal clothesline in the living room — admittedly because of the dog's explosive behavior. The mother, who was the only one home with the infant on that fateful day, said she was in the back bedroom folding laundry. The infant was in another bedroom sleeping in a crib. The dog, for some reason, was in the residence but not attached to the metal clothesline. According to the mother, the Doberman had gone into the bedroom, jumped up into the crib and taken the infant out of the crib and into the living room. She heard some commotion in the living room and came out to investigate finding the dog with the baby in the grip of its teeth. She had to beat the dog with an object to get it to let go of the baby, then chased the dog outside. She promptly called the police.

There were several problems with her story. I found no blood in the crib or the room of the infant, and head wounds have a tendency to bleed profusely. I did, however, find blood along with bits of skull and brain matter in the living room where the dog had shook the infant like a rag doll while its teeth were imbedded in the baby's head. In the backroom where the mother was reportedly folding clothes, I found an ashtray with a partial joint in it. There were some clothes on the bed, but I always wondered if she was in the back bedroom getting high.

There were no charges brought against the parents. In the meeting I had with the prosecutor, we discussed the value and appropriateness of a "child neglect" type of prosecution. We decided that no matter what the outcome, there would be no sentence that could match the living hell these parents would have to go through — all brought on by their own ignorance or negligence.

Lesson learned: Despite the evidence available, people make incredibly self-absorbed and ill-informed decisions that carry horrendous consequences. What seems remarkably obvious to me is not necessarily obvious to others.

The infant would grow up in heaven.

This incident bothered me for a long, long time. I had nightmares in which this 6-month old infant would rise from the autopsy table, look at me and ask, "Why didn't you do something to defend me?"

Lesson learned: There are weaker ones who need the stronger ones to defend them.

Men and Women of Valor

God is our ultimate defender, and he empowers us to do that which we might normally think impossible.

Jeremiah was a priest and a prophet. Called by God, Jeremiah saw his nation disintegrate both morally and militarily. He continually warned Judah of God's approaching judgment. For the most part, Jeremiah's audience could have cared less about what he had to say. He was whipped, beaten, put in stocks and imprisoned. Yet, he endured. Jeremiah understood obedience. He was a man of valor.

Ruth, Esther, Deborah and Rahab are but a few of the courageous women who grace the pages of the Bible. They took great risks or endured great sacrifice in order to do the next right thing.

1 Chronicles 11:10-25 describes some of David's mighty warriors. They include:

- Jashobeam, who killed three hundred men in one encounter with a spear.

- Eleazar, who is described as joining David in a great victory.

- Abishai, who also killed three hundred men with a spear.

- Benaiah, who is described as a valiant fighter who performed great exploits which include striking down Moab's two mightiest warriors, going into a pit on a snowy day and killing a lion, and striking down an Egyptian who was five cubits tall – that is about 8-9 feet tall.

> 1 Chronicles 12:21-22 "They helped David against raiding bands, for all of them were brave warriors, and they were commanders in his army. Day after day men came to help David, until he had a great army, like the army of God."

These guys were not super-human immortals. They were men who understood their mission and stood on it. And you'll notice that God did not automatically wipe out the enemy for them. He empowered these warriors to fight supernaturally. God had His hand on them.

All of these people had several things in common:

1. They knew God and were empowered by Him.

2. They stood on principle against great odds.

3. They confronted - each in their own way - those things that were rooted in evil.

Story after story; life after life; person after person; promise after promise.

- Why do you think there are so many examples in the Bible of people who overcame great odds? Because that is the way the Christian is supposed to live.

- Why all the graphic imagery about spiritual warfare and Satan wanting to kill? Because we are living in a battlefield, and it is a war.

- Why all the promises about moving mountains, healing the sick and trampling on snakes? Because that is what the Christian should be doing.

> John 14:12-14 "Very truly I tell you, whoever believes in me will do the works I have been doing, and they will do even greater things than these, because I am going to the Father. And I will do whatever you ask in my name, so that the Father may be glorified in the Son. You may ask me for anything in my name, and I will do it."

Jesus lives inside you. He and the Father are one. He does what He sees the Father doing. He sits at the right-hand side of the Father interceding on your behalf. All you have to do is believe and embrace this by giving Him permission to work in your life. Look at how Jesus prayed to God for his disciples, then all believers:

John 17:6-26 "I have revealed you to those whom you gave me out of the world. They were yours; you gave them to me and they have obeyed your word. Now they know that everything you have given me comes from you. For I gave them the words you gave me and they accepted them. They knew with certainty that I came from you, and they believed that you sent me. I pray for them. I am not praying for the world, but for those you have given me, for they are yours. All I have is yours, and all you have is mine. And glory has come to me through them. I will remain in the world no longer, but they are still in the world, and I am coming to you. Holy Father, protect them by the power of your name, the name you gave me, so that they may be one as we are one. While I was with them, I protected them and kept them safe by that name you gave me. None has been lost except the one doomed to destruction so that Scripture would be fulfilled. I am coming to you now, but I say these things while I am still in the world, so that they may have the full measure of my joy within them. I have given them your word and the world has hated them, for they are not of the world any more than I am of the world. My prayer is not that you take them out of the world but that you protect them from the evil one. They are not of the world, even as I am not of it. Sanctify them by the truth; your word is truth. As you sent me into the world, I have sent them into the world. For them I sanctify myself, that they too may be truly sanctified. My prayer is not for them alone. I pray also for those who will believe in me through their message, that all of them may be one, Father, just as you are in me and I am in you. May they also be in us so that the world may believe that you have sent me. I have given them the glory that you gave me, that they may be one as

> we are one - I in them and you in me - so that they may be brought to complete unity. Then the world will know that you sent me and have loved them even as you have loved me. Father, I want those you have given me to be with me where I am, and to see my glory, the glory you have given me because you loved me before the creation of the world. Righteous Father, though the world does not know you, I know you, and they know that you have sent me. I have made you known to them, and will continue to make you known in order that the love you have for me may be in them and that I myself may be in them."

Jesus is on your side.

> Hebrews 11 "Now faith is confidence in what we hope for and assurance about what we do not see. This is what the ancients were commended for. By faith we understand that the universe was formed at God's command, so that what is seen was not made out of what was visible. By faith Abel brought God a better offering than Cain did. By faith he was commended as righteous, when God spoke well of his offerings. And by faith Abel still speaks, even though he is dead. By faith Enoch was taken from this life, so that he did not experience death: "He could not be found, because God had taken him away." For before he was taken, he was commended as one who pleased God. And without faith it is impossible to please God, because anyone who comes to him must believe that he exists and that he rewards those who earnestly seek him. By faith Noah, when warned about things not yet seen, in holy fear built an ark to save his family. By his faith he condemned the world and became heir of the righteousness that is in keeping with faith. By faith Abraham, when called to go to a place he would later receive as his

inheritance, obeyed and went, even though he did not know where he was going. By faith he made his home in the promised land like a stranger in a foreign country; he lived in tents, as did Isaac and Jacob, who were heirs with him of the same promise. For he was looking forward to the city with foundations, whose architect and builder is God. And by faith even Sarah, who was past childbearing age, was enabled to bear children because she considered him faithful who had made the promise. And so from this one man, and he as good as dead, came descendants as numerous as the stars in the sky and as countless as the sand on the seashore. All these people were still living by faith when they died. They did not receive the things promised; they only saw them and welcomed them from a distance, admitting that they were foreigners and strangers on earth. People who say such things show that they are looking for a country of their own. If they had been thinking of the country they had left, they would have had opportunity to return. Instead, they were longing for a better country—a heavenly one. Therefore God is not ashamed to be called their God, for he has prepared a city for them. By faith Abraham, when God tested him, offered Isaac as a sacrifice. He who had embraced the promises was about to sacrifice his one and only son, even though God had said to him, "It is through Isaac that your offspring will be reckoned." Abraham reasoned that God could even raise the dead, and so in a manner of speaking he did receive Isaac back from death. By faith Isaac blessed Jacob and Esau in regard to their future. By faith Jacob, when he was dying, blessed each of Joseph's sons, and worshiped as he leaned on the top of his staff. By faith Joseph, when his end was near, spoke about the exodus of the Israelites from Egypt and gave instructions concerning the burial of his bones. By faith Moses' parents hid him for three months after he was born, because they saw he was no ordinary child, and they were not afraid of the king's edict. By faith Moses, when he had grown up, refused to be known as the son of Pharaoh's daughter. He chose to be mistreated along with the people of God rather than to enjoy the fleeting pleasures of sin. He regarded disgrace for the sake of Christ as of greater value than the treasures of Egypt, because he was looking ahead to his reward. By faith he left Egypt, not fearing the king's anger; he persevered because he saw him who is invisible. By faith he kept the Passover and the application of blood, so that the destroyer of the firstborn would not touch the firstborn of Israel. By faith the people passed through the Red Sea as on dry land; but when the Egyptians tried to do so, they were drowned. By faith the walls of Jericho fell, after the army had marched around them for seven days. By faith the prostitute Rahab, because she welcomed the spies, was not killed with those who were disobedient. And what more shall I say? I do not have time to tell about Gideon, Barak, Samson and Jephthah, about David and Samuel and the prophets, who through faith conquered kingdoms, administered justice, and gained what was promised; who shut the mouths of lions, quenched the fury of the flames, and escaped the edge of the sword; whose weakness was turned to strength; and who became powerful in battle and routed foreign armies. Women received back their dead, raised to life again. There were others who were tortured, refusing to be released so that they might gain an even better resurrection. Some faced jeers and flogging, and even chains and imprisonment. They were put to death by stoning; they were sawed in two; they were

> killed by the sword. They went about in sheepskins and goatskins, destitute, persecuted and mistreated— the world was not worthy of them. They wandered in deserts and mountains, living in caves and in holes in the ground. These were all commended for their faith, yet none of them received what had been promised, since God had planned something better for us so that only together with us would they be made perfect."

All of them are living demonstrations of faith in action.

Satan is Good at What He Does

I am best able to write without the distractions that come with being in my daily work environment. As I left town in the spring of 2011 and headed towards our cabin to complete this book, here is what I experienced:

- My father was hospitalized for several days with a potentially life-threatening condition.

- Because I was in a remote area, one of my brothers got in his vehicle to come and inform me of this.

- That brother became sick on the way to our cabin.

- When he arrived we established contact with the rest of the family and vacillated for several days as to whether we needed to head home. For me that meant a 16-hour drive.

- I ended up contracting my brother's illness; a horrific sinus infection and bronchitis – eventually requiring urgent care, antibiotics and relocation to a more secure environment.

- While I was gone, a good friend of my wife's died.

- Because of these events, I had to make several unplanned trips. In the course of 21 days, I packed and unpacked ten times. I opened and closed our cabin twice — no small feat and time-consuming since it is off the grid.

- The cabin sits on a ridge, and for the few days I was alone at the cabin the spring winds were gusting at 50-60 mph making for a noisy solitude.

- Eventually, my father was stabilized, treated and released.

- Through this, I managed to get everything completed except the last chapter.

- Within two days upon my return home as I began work on the last chapter, I was overcome with a spirit of oppression I have rarely felt. I had thoughts I can only describe as defeatist and hopeless — clearly from Satan and not part of my nature, nor part of God's nature.

These events caught me off guard. Satan prowls around seeking to devour. I should have expected that if this book was going to impact even one life toward the kingdom of God that Satan would turn up the heat. As I worked through these events, I was frequently citing scripture out loud.

> Matthew 16:18-19 "And I say also unto thee, That thou art Peter, and upon this rock I will build my church; and the gates of hell shall not prevail against it. And I will give unto thee the keys of the kingdom of heaven: and whatsoever thou shalt bind on earth shall be bound in heaven:

> and whatsoever thou shalt loose on earth shall be loosed in heaven."
>
> James 4:7-8 "Therefore submit to God. Resist the devil and he will flee from you. Draw near to God and He will draw near to you."
>
> Philippians 4:13 "I can do all things through Christ which strengtheneth me."
>
> Romans 8:28 "And we know that in all things God works for the good of those who love him, who have been called according to his purpose."
>
> Romans 8:38-39 "For I am convinced that neither death nor life, neither angels nor demons, neither the present nor the future, nor any powers, neither height nor depth, nor anything else in all creation, will be able to separate us from the love of God that is in Christ Jesus our Lord."

This was a spiritual attack, so I used spiritual weapons. The only offensive weapon is scripture. After several days, the attacks finally ceased.

Standing Strong

Nowhere in the Bible is striving for excellence discouraged. The bible condones prudent, wise planning and preparation under God's guidance. The Bible makes clear, as Christians, we are to come against evil wherever we see it.

> Romans 12:9-21 "Love must be sincere. Hate what is evil; cling to what is good."
>
> Proverbs 8:13 "To fear the LORD is to hate evil."

> Psalm 97:10 "Let those who love the LORD hate evil, for he guards the lives of his faithful ones and delivers them from the hand of the wicked."

John Piper said: "I don't disagree that we should hate the horrific evil that is in the world. We should hate Satan's designs to destroy people, even though God could snatch Satan out of this world in a minute. He could take him away. He is clearly willing that there should be a Satan, otherwise he would destroy him in a minute. Therefore the fact that Satan is there by God's permission and design does not reduce my hatred of Satan, because God ordains that I hate Satan. In fact, one of the reasons he leaves Satan marauding in the world is precisely so that there would be an occasion for me to declare myself to be morally against evil. If there were no evil here then that kind of dynamic wouldn't even happen."

Love and hate are both Biblical, both are parts of God's design: both are part of God's nature. There is Biblical direction to hate evil and to come against it. Today the silence against evil is deafening, and the few who do stand up to it are often ignored, written off as crazily out of touch, drowned out, ostracized, attacked, imprisoned or killed.

Hate the sin. Love the sinner. God hated sin and loved the sinner. "For God so loved the world that he gave his one and only Son, that whoever believes in him shall not perish but have eternal life."

Our apparent comfort with evil did not evolve overnight. It happens through the slow, systematic decline and desensitization of every moral value the Bible promotes. It happens through the sleazy nonsense the world puts on a pedestal. It happens through the deceptive disguise of political correctness. It happens through the subtle academic indoctrination of our children into a fantasy world of education where mankind is engaged in a lifelong group hug singing "Kumbaya". It happens through the veil of terrorism by relinquishing freedom for security. It happens through the constant bombardment of biased and skewed information promoted by media around the world. It happens through every movie, television show and mouse click that slides us a little closer to Sodom and Gomorrah. It happens through the sea of deceit and lies wrapped up in a mirage of truth, spin, smoke and mirrors.

The truth about evil is closer to the Wizard of Oz. We see one thing, but it is another behind it.

I Can Hold Off For A While, Can't I?

Connecting the dots between the world we live in today and what Jesus forecast many years ago is not difficult. Through the years, many people have forecast "end of the world" dates unsuccessfully. I'm not quite sure why they would try.

> Matthew 24:36 "But about that day or hour no one knows, not even the angels in heaven, nor the Son, but only the Father."

This is not some cryptic verse. It is what it is. The prognostications about the end of the world have done nothing but add to the jaded view secular people have of Christians in general. The Bible would define these people as false prophets and false teachers.

Much like there is valid disagreement on the timing of the rapture, there is disagreement on whether unsaved people will get the opportunity of coming to Christ during the tribulation or after the rapture.

Is it possible that some unsaved people hedge their bets by thinking that they can wait until things get real bad, and then come to Christ? And, in the meantime, they can live as they please?

This following passage of scripture is talking about the antichrist. It has also been used controversially to "prove" whether people will have the opportunity to be saved during the tribulation. Many good people believe no one will get a chance to come to Christ during the tribulation.

2 Thessalonians 2 "Concerning the coming of our Lord Jesus Christ and our being gathered to him, we ask you, brothers and sisters, not to become easily unsettled or alarmed by the teaching allegedly from us—whether by a prophecy or by word of mouth or by letter—asserting that the day of the Lord has already come. Don't let anyone deceive you in any way, for that day will not come until the rebellion occurs and the man of lawlessness is revealed, the man doomed to destruction. He will oppose and will exalt himself over everything that is called God or is worshiped, so that he sets himself up in God's temple, proclaiming himself to be God. Don't you remember that when I was with you I used to tell you these things? And now you know what is holding him back, so that he may be revealed at the proper time. For the secret power of lawlessness is already at work; but the one who now holds it back will continue to do so till he is taken out of the way. And then the lawless one will be revealed, whom the Lord Jesus will overthrow with the breath of his mouth and destroy by the splendor of his coming. The coming of the lawless one will be in accordance with how Satan works. He will use all sorts of displays of power through signs and wonders that serve the lie, and all the ways that wickedness deceives those who are perishing. They perish because they refused to love the truth and so be saved. For this reason God sends them a powerful delusion so that they will believe the lie and so that all will be condemned who have not believed the truth but have delighted in wickedness. But we ought always to thank God for you, brothers and sisters loved by the Lord, because God chose you as firstfruits to be saved through the sanctifying work

> of the Spirit and through belief in the truth. He called you to this through our gospel, that you might share in the glory of our Lord Jesus Christ. So then, brothers and sisters, stand firm and hold fast to the teachings we passed on to you, whether by word of mouth or by letter. May our Lord Jesus Christ himself and God our Father, who loved us and by his grace gave us eternal encouragement and good hope, encourage your hearts and strengthen you in every good deed and word."

What seems reasonable in the context of "what if?" is this: These verses are clearly talking about the tribulation when the antichrist is being established and coming to power. It is in that context that this is being described: "He will use all sorts of displays of power through signs and wonders that serve the lie, and all the ways that wickedness deceives those who are perishing. They perish because they refused to love the truth and so be saved. For this reason God sends them a powerful delusion so that they will believe the lie and so that all will be condemned who have not believed the truth but have delighted in wickedness."

Remember, God did not make His word so complex that only a theologian was going to be able to understand and interpret it. He made it to be understood by the common man and woman. Some people have a tendency to read way too much into scripture. God is not a God of confusion. Common sense seems to indicate from reading this passage that about halfway through the tribulation there is a cutoff — a tipping point where the opportunity to come to Christ is cut off by God himself. Up to that point, God is a God of second, third and fourth chances, as evidenced by a simple look at our own lives.

But, why would anyone want to gamble their eternity on whether there will be a chance during the tribulation to come to Christ? What if there isn't?

Living Through It

You can't make this stuff up. In Katrina we saw police disarming law-abiding civilians who needed protection. I finish this chapter on the heels of what is the second worst tornado outbreak in history. The TSA is now groping civilians in the name of security. Animals are falling out the sky and fishes are washing up on the shores. Children kill their parents, and parents chain their kids to beds or make them live in closets. The world economy sits on the brink. The US is embroiled in two wars – in the name of a global war against terrorism. The whole Middle East seems to be discontent. Food prices are rapidly increasing, and gas is around $4.00 a gallon in the US. It might get better in the short term, but ultimately it is going to get worse.

Here is what I find particularly disturbing. If you look at the things forecast in Chapter 14, it is hard to imagine many of them taking place without some widespread, massive coercion by governmental forces. Somehow, these things will get enforced. For example, when the Bible says the antichrist will demand worship, that doesn't sound voluntary.

Clearly, at a minimum, the stage is being set for the end of this age. The description of America below is not some revelatory vision I have seen. Instead, I just went back to look at Chapter 14 and pieced together this partial picture. I don't know that life will look like this for the Christian. But, what if it does?

America, the most powerful nation on earth, has become a third world nation because of its insolvency. Stores have been looted. Food is scarce. There is civil war. Not a day goes by without a tsunami, earthquake, mega-storm or some other large natural disaster. The seas and skies are completely unpredictable. No one can conduct any commerce unless they take the mark of the beast. The government you have known has turned against nearly every belief you have ever held close. There is unprecedented violence and hatred. People from around the world are dropping like flies from famine and disease. Wild animals are attacking people for no apparent reason. There is political and economic mayhem.

It's coming. You cannot stop it. The only wild card is the timing.

You are living in the midst of this. Now what?

Are you prepared to live through it?

Your Quick Start Guide

How can you practically prepare for what is sure to come?

- Secure your eternity. Accept Christ as your Lord and Savior. Without Christ, your eternity will be very, very hot and uncomfortable; you will be full of torment, gnashing your teeth and in constant anguish.

- Get to know God, Jesus and the Holy Spirit. Read the Bible and pray. Prayer is a conversation with God. Get plugged into a local church and the body of Christ. Embrace the promises of the Bible.

- Learn, understand and practice the principles of spiritual warfare. Know your enemy. Use the defensive weapons of truth, righteousness, the gospel of peace, faith, the helmet of salvation and prayer. Use the offensive sword of the Spirit, which is the word of God.

- Begin to examine the world around you and the relationships you are in. Begin to recognize that which is ungodly or unscriptural. This is critical. If you cannot see that which is wrong, you have no ability to defend against it.

- Discover (or re-discover) the heart of righteous anger. Prayerfully consider your options and responses to those things. In your own way, you must take a stand against evil.

- Put into the context of Biblical prophecy that which is going on around you and in the world at large. Beware of false teachings and false prophets.

- Pay down your debt. The gap between the rich and poor is rapidly widening. You are a slave to the lender.

- Conduct some basic emergency planning.

- Put together a disaster/emergency kit.

- Take a self defense course that is grounded in your legal authority.

- Purchase a firearm and become proficient with it. Consider other weapons (stun gun, taser, rifle, shotgun, pepper spray, extendible baton, etc.) as well.

- Develop your own model of personal safety. Once you have accomplished this, you will view the world differently.

- Answer the call of Jude. Pick up the sword and fight for the kingdom of God.

Psalm 27:1-3 "The LORD is my light and my salvation—whom shall I fear? The LORD is the stronghold of my life—of whom shall I be afraid? When evil men advance against me to devour my flesh, when my enemies and my foes attack me, they will stumble and fall. Though an army besiege me, my heart will not fear; though war break out against me, even then will I be confident."

Individual Reflection or Group Discussion

1. What will you do next?

2. Are there people in your life that you strongly desire to see in eternity? Who are they?

3. As a result of what you have read in this book, what will change for you?

4. If you do nothing, which is an option, how do you justify it?

Waiver & Biography

Jesus told his disciples that He was sending them out into the world as sheep amongst wolves, and they should be shrewd as serpents but innocent as doves.

The Bible tells me that Satan and his horde are prowling around looking for ways to steal from me, devour me or kill me.

When I consider that this book might possibly impact a few people toward the kingdom of God and move some people toward Jesus, I should expect some type of backlash or attempt from Satan to discredit me and the words in it.

In respect to the "shrewd as serpents" instruction, I am going to preempt one of the tactics of the enemy, which would be to discredit me. I will do it myself.

Career

I am always a bit uncomfortable sharing my career accomplishments. The greatest leaders I have met are humble, and I want to exemplify that trait. I understand that I need to establish credibility with you, dear reader. I think I can offer a unique perspective of the Big Picture.

There are some very skilled colleagues of mine in martial arts, but they have never been involved in a serious physical confrontation. Their entire experience of violence has been practicing their craft under tightly controlled conditions. Real-life violence has no controls. I know some soldiers who have had excellent training but never been involved in a real mission outside of training. Real missions are not like training, although training is the best preparation for a real mission. I know of executive protection schools that are led by some talented instructors who may have protected some celebrities but have never had any real threat come against the person they are protecting. They have gotten to where they are based on charisma, luck, networking, manipulation, clever marketing and sometimes even deceit. I have a gifted attorney friend who has helped craft gun laws but to my knowledge has never faced any real-life violence.... and so on. Many of my contemporaries have specialized expertise but do not have the depth of experience or the education that came with the roles I have served in.

What do I have to offer you? I have the very unique perspective of serving in all three facets of the criminal justice: Law Enforcement, Institutional Corrections and Probation/Parole. I worked for a year as an Operations Manager for a private security company that specialized in celebrity protection. Due to the nature of the positions I have held, I have had intimate contact with judges, attorneys, doctors, nurses, psychiatrists, forensic psychologists, firemen, military personnel, EMS, the BATF, the FBI, even the CIA - along with celebrities and VIP's. Through professional and personal experiences, I was able to see how all these people and agencies work and think providing a deep education into the inner workings of these entities. I have been trained and mentored by some of the brightest experts in their fields.

I have seen the ugly aftermath of violence and battled alongside my comrades in the middle of it. I have had people try to kill me because I wore a badge and enforced the law. I have been injured more than once in the line of duty. I have investigated some fascinating cases in which the trails I followed led to places I would have never expected.

I have an inside view of the American Dysfunctional Family at its best and worst and have watched them struggle for a piece of the pie. I have appeared in court as both witness and presenter. I have participated in more plea bargains than I can remember. I gave up counting autopsies once I had experienced a dozen of them just as I had given up counting suicides. I also lost track of the number of divorces amongst my colleagues.

I have broken doors down in the middle of the night and watched hardened suspects soil themselves out of fear. I interviewed a guy that was in isolated lockdown at a secure hospital for the criminally insane, and he struck me as being brilliant. I have held dying people in my arms and had to break the news of death to family members. I have protected powerful and wealthy celebrities and VIP's that I can only describe as spoiled brats. From decapitations to creative suicides, from murder to violent sex assaults, I have had a front row seat.

The common theme throughout it all has been dealing with odd, erratic, unstable and violent human behavior coming from people with varying degrees of illness, levels of dysfunction and some who are just plain evil.

I share my career and background with you while I stand in awe of the people, places, positions and training that God has scripted for my life. I never really looked for a particular position. My goal in college was to be a psychologist, but instead I just walked through doors that opened. Here is where those doors led me:

- Former Correctional Institution duties: Juvenile Corrections Agent, Security Team, Research Analyst and Instructor.

- Former Law Enforcement duties: Juvenile Detective, Uniform Patrol Officer, K-9 Officer, Narcotics & Vice, SWAT Team Member, Bomb Squad Member, Arson Investigator, State Emergency Response & Planning Team Member, Lead Investigator, Instructor, and VIP Protection.

- Former Community Corrections duties: Probation/Parole Agent, Research Analyst, Instructor, Fugitive Apprehension, MAVI (Minneapolis Anti-Violence Initiative) Team Member, & JORP (Juvenile Offender Recovery Program) Co-Developer.

- Former Private Security duties: Operations Manager, Use of Force & Executive Safety & Firearms Instructor, Personal Protection Specialist providing protection to celebrities and VIP's, Risk Management, Threat Assessment & Planning.

- Education & Training includes a Bachelor of Science in Human Services and over 5,000 hours of specialized training.

- Certifications include Senior Control Tactics Instructor, Master Handgun Instructor, Lethal Force Training Master Instructor, Certified Personal Protection Specialist, NRA Certified Pistol Instructor, MN DNR Certified Firearms Safety Instructor, Risk Assessment & Threat Management and a Validated Expert in Community Vulnerability Assessments.

- Martial arts practitioner with experience in Karate, Aikido, Silat, Savate & Krav-Maga.

- For over 35 years I have provided consultation and instruction in Behavioral Profiling, Understanding Violence, Self-Defense, Use of Force, Firearms, Explosives, Fire/Arson, Threat Assessment, Verbal Control/De-escalation, Risk & Vulnerability Assessment, Juvenile Issues, Drugs and the Criminal Justice System.

- I have had significant experience in tracking down Fugitives, investigating fraud and conducting background investigations.

In 1997 I formalized the consulting and training I had been conducting for decades as a sole proprietor into Integrated Safety Systems. It was renamed several years later to its current incarnation: Assault Prevention LLC, where I serve as the CEO and Sr. Director of Training & Education.

Assault Prevention helps individuals, groups, and organizations proactively plan for successful mitigation of unexpected violence and emergencies - and as a result, brings about a sense of control to their daily lives. Assault Prevention has educated the public about personal safety, self defense & awareness through assessments, consultation, training & instruction and social media. This includes corporate threat assessment of physical facilities, intellectual property, and key personnel; specialized security and presentation of local, national, and global trend research and analysis.

Assault Prevention has provided consultation, instruction and customized training to 100+ federal, state and local criminal justice agencies, and 50+ private and non-profit organizations. In addition, Assault Prevention provides individual and group instruction to citizen groups and civilians.

Assault Prevention uses a variety of professional networks, resources, people and consultants to provide the services we offer. Our websites are AssaultPrevention.Info and AssaultPrevention.Org

Personal

Friends of mine have joked for years that I am the only guy they know who carries a Bible, a handgun and handcuffs in his briefcase. That is true, but it doesn't make me special. It just makes me different. We all have a unique calling. This one just happens to be mine.

I consider myself a great sinner who has been redeemed by the blood of Christ. I take my next step and my next breath because of God's mercy and grace. He has saved me from many circumstances in which I thought, "Surely, I am going to die."

As a kid, I discovered I had a passion for the underdog, and much to my own amazement, I did things like confront the bullies who picked on other kids. After getting slapped around by bullies more times than I care to remember, I embarked on a personal fitness journey which continues today. I began health training in the form of boxing, martial arts, cardiovascular conditioning and weight lifting. I also began to participate in what would now be referred to as extreme sports. From that point forward, I would lose only one physical confrontation, and it served as a powerful lesson in violence.

I developed a keen interest in violence. This, of course, was directly related to the personal violence I had experienced as a kid. I was just as determined to master violence physically as I was in understanding the psychological, emotional and spiritual aspects of violence.

Ultimately, my deep involvement in police work cost me part of my identity in Christ as I drifted farther from God's word, His fellowship and His principles. All of the experiences I share in this book might sound exciting, but I never viewed myself as exceptional or a hero. I thought I was just doing the right thing. I slowly became an adrenaline junky, taking on more and more risk. My personal life began to unravel. I ended up divorced with my one-year old daughter living in another state.

I was broken. I worked out and practiced my skills during the day, worked hard at night and tried to figure out creative ways to deal with my personal pain in between.

Let me make a few things very clear. I never abandoned my relationship or conversation with God even when I slipped away from His fellowship. I knew Jesus. I tithed. I read the Bible. I prayed. I attended church. I was active in church activities. We had devotions and prayer every night my father was home for dinner. When I would do something I knew was sinful, I usually found myself in bed that night pleading for Jesus not to give up on me or let me go. It was literally a war within me, and I was painfully aware of it. My walk with God has been powerful. My spiritual experiences far outweigh the natural ones.

So What?

Are you facing a personal problem today? Do you think God is not big enough? This book stands as evidence that God deeply cares about people because I should be dead.

Jesus said: "The thief comes only to steal and kill and destroy; I have come that they may have life, and have it to the full." I have rolled around in the dirt with Satan, and I have seen and experienced his destructive power face to face.

Jesus was big enough to provide deliverance for me and he can for you. Evil only understands one thing — an overwhelming amount of power, and that only comes through Jesus Christ. Only He has the perfect solution and plan for whatever you are dealing with, and He will accept you wherever you are and whatever condition you are in. No prerequisites except that you are willing to call on Him.

His grace has carried me through more sin than I want to acknowledge, broken relationships, failed marriages, suicidal thoughts, PTSD, and a list of behaviors and thoughts most people would be embarrassed to speak of. But, this is exactly what God specializes in — restoring the hearts and minds and lives of broken people.

Are you wounded? Are you in pain? Are you in bondage? Does the road look impossible? God is a God of second chances — even third and fourth ones. His love and grace and mercy are far beyond what we can possibly comprehend.

Life here on earth is just the blink of an eye. Take a few seconds and think about that. It can be mind-boggling. What we do here and now will affect how we experience eternity; the only way to experience God's fullness in this life is through His son, Jesus Christ.

The Deal

If this book is in your hands and you are reading this page, it is probably with reason. It is not some random event. There are no accidents or coincidences. It has been arranged by God. Sound crazy?

The proof for this is the fact that you have already formed a strong thought just from those three opening sentences. You may be in full agreement. You may be intrigued and will read on. Or you may be thinking that I am some weirdo religious zealot and put the book down.

God and Satan. Good and evil. Who wins? Who cares?

I am fascinated by what I am about to share with you and offer it as proof that there are spiritual forces at work around us that we do not see, we do not consciously recognize and we often do not acknowledge.

I am a Christian. I am not an evangelist. Evangelism is neither my calling nor my gifting. However, as the years slide by there have been ample opportunities to discuss God, Jesus, the Holy Spirit, spirituality and religion with other people. Most people are open-minded when it comes to discussions about baking, auto repair, shopping, their jobs, courses they attend or a great many other subjects.

When a conversation turns to a subject matter that involves values, most people become a bit more passionate. Discussions about abortion, politics, crime or taxes have a tendency to raise voices and blood pressure.

Discussions about God can be fairly civil because it is politically correct and culturally acceptable to acknowledge God. However, by today's measure, God can be some type of non-specific energy force within you, some cosmic impersonal being who is far away, or a rock. The world at large has watered God down into some type of generic life-force that is non-threatening. Try bringing Jesus into a conversation and see what happens.

I love mankind. I am constantly amazed by human beings. I am a student of human behavior. I love watching people and interacting with them. I have been given this wonderful gift of being able to read people and social situations with a great degree of accuracy. I have had this ability all my life. I can read through people from across the room without personal interaction. I am quite sure my profession honed this skill even further. I have become adept at sensing body language, micro-expressions, gestures and the like – which all serve to tell a story about someone's state of mind. This ability is invaluable when dealing with violent people. In the context of this chapter, I have been conducting several non-scientific experiments for many years, and talking to people about Jesus is one of them.

When I look for opportunities to talk about God in a conversation with someone, I can often find one. I go out of my way to make sure these discussions are non-threatening. I ask a lot of questions in order to understand how other people perceive God. The ensuing discussion usually teeters between neutral and positive, and often I find that their God is far different from mine. That is when I inject Jesus into the conversation. Whereas a discussion about God is usually civil and positive, I find many discussions about Jesus to be negative with hints of hostility. Many people become very uncomfortable as evidenced by tone of voice, pitch of voice, body language and the words they use in these conversations.

General Conclusions

- Many people are okay with God but uncomfortable with Jesus.

- Many people are okay entering into a discussion about any subject, except their personal relationship with Jesus.

- People have varying opinions about any number of things.

- If someone is drawn into a discussion with a subject matter they know little about, they usually will acknowledge they lack the background or training required to intelligently participate in the discussion.

- However, the closer a discussion moves on a continuum from religion to spirituality; from God to Jesus; the greater the degree of negativity expressed in the form of strong, uneducated opinion.

This led me to several questions:

- Why is talking with people about any number of given subjects non-threatening, but talking about Jesus makes people uncomfortable and even angry?

- Why are people so strongly opinionated about Jesus when they have no formal education, training or experience to form a credible opinion about Jesus?

Consistently, the people I am referring to above have not read the Bible or invested any time with God or Jesus developing a relationship. They don't really know anything about the Bible or God or Jesus. To my thinking, this is the equivalent of me walking into the cockpit of a plane and telling the pilots to go relax while I fly the plane – despite the fact that I know nothing about flying planes. Or, trying to discuss a movie or book that you love but I have never seen or read. My attempts to make authoritative statements about them would be ignorant.

Can you provide a rational, logical explanation for these contradictions? There aren't any; which leads me to the conclusion there are other forces at work. The same people who demand open-mindedness from me for their opinions and views will lash out at me when I ask this question. The irony is thick and hypocritical. These people are ignorant, by definition.

Please do not misunderstand. I am very concerned about people. I shed tears wondering if I will see some of them in eternity. I am sickened by the thought of some former friends who openly rejected Jesus and then died never showing any evidence of a change of heart. I desire every man and woman to come to a real relationship with Jesus.

However, I have reached my limit from the politically correct pressure to present a watered down version of the Bible or the principles held in it.

The people I am referring to commonly interpret parts of scripture as they see fit or discard and belittle the parts that do not fit conveniently into their personal positions. They attack the Word of God as something written long ago that is not to be taken literally. That it was just fallible men who wrote it and, "what makes them any more credible then me or you?" They say with all the translations something was bound to have been screwed up. Or, parts of it are just ridiculous. Or that God is cool…but Jesus was just a great religious teacher, like so many other great men that have walked the earth.

Fear

A quick primer on perception: It is most people's reality. Someone's perception may be far removed from reality, but perception is the basis of thoughts, impulses and behavior. Therefore, we act out based on our perceptions. People are not complex. Perception precedes thought. Thought precedes impulse. Impulse precedes action. One type of action is speaking. This is why perception is incredibly important. It is where action begins to form. Perception occurs on a conscious and unconscious level.

Some people when speaking about Jesus seem angry. Anger is okay. It is a natural response to things that move us, touch us and that we are passionate about.

Much anger is actually undergirded by fear. One of the questions I ask myself when anger is being displayed is, "What is this person afraid of?" Law enforcement officers, properly trained, know that if a person is allowed to vent anger, the risk of violence can be reduced tremendously. This is best accomplished by asking leading questions in which the underlying emotional issue that is driving the anger finally comes out. That underlying emotional issue is almost always grounded in fear.

This led me to another question: "What is it about Jesus that these people are afraid of?" Many people who reject Christ have expressed a great deal of fear, whether it be conscious or unconscious, while discussing Him.

There is a healthy type of fear. It causes us to recognize things that can hurt us. There is also fear that comes from Satan. Satan's primary tool for messing with you is thoughts he plants inside your head.

Need Proof?

This, of course, leads us back to part of the focus of this book. If, indeed we are living in the End Times, there is a guarantee that the forces we do not see will be more active than they ever have been.

Take a look at Jesus' life — a historical fact. He performed great miracles; another fact. He said He was the Son of God. Either He was who He said He was or He was a lunatic. There is greater and better historical evidence for the life of Christ and the authenticity of the Bible than many other historical persons or documents we all seem to readily accept. The prophecy it contains has thus far been 100% accurate. It is the most popular book on the planet.

If you need this elaborated upon, please read the books, The Case For Christ by Lee Strobel or Surprised By Faith by Dan Bierle.

God created the world. He created man and woman. He made the rules. You and I do not have the option of arbitrarily changing those rules — at least not without some fairly serious consequences. God said the Bible is His inspired Word. He said He appointed the men who wrote it. He is the author. He said Jesus is His son. He said no one comes to Him except through Jesus. That's what He says. He did not invite us to add to it. He did not encourage us to argue about it.

God said that for every good thing of His, Satan would have a seductive counterfeit. Many who change the scriptures to fit their own meaning have no right to, and frankly, appear to be arrogant in this sense.

If this offends you, please consider that your argument is not with me or others who believe. We care deeply about your spiritual health. Your argument is with the original author – God. Take it up with him. You will eventually — the inevitable standing before God. Man has done much to screw up the word of God, and your perception of God. Do not be afraid to research the authenticity of the Bible. People who study it come away challenged and changed.

Jesus loves and cares about you. It's that simple. If you doubt that, ask God to prove that to you. I exhort you to do so and wonder if you are open-minded enough to enter into that simple task as an experiment. Do it sincerely, and then pay attention to what happens around you.

Your Biggest Challenge on Earth

Romans 3:23-24 "For all have sinned and come short of the glory of God, and are justified freely by his grace through the redemption that came by Christ Jesus."

Romans 6:23 "For the wages of sin is death, but the gift of God is eternal life in Christ Jesus our Lord."

Romans 1:18-20 "The wrath of God is being revealed from heaven against all the godlessness and wickedness of men who suppress the truth by their wickedness, since what may be known about God is plain to them, because God has made it plain to them. For since the creation of the world God's invisible qualities – his eternal power and divine nature – have been clearly seen, being understood from what has been made, so that men are without excuse."

Romans 1:21-23 "For although they knew God, they neither glorified him as God nor gave thanks to him, but their thinking became futile and their foolish hearts were darkened. Although they claim to be wise, they became fools and exchanged the glory of the immortal God for images made to look like mortal man and birds and animals and reptiles."

Romans 1:29-32 "They have become filled with every kind of wickedness, evil, greed and depravity. They are full of envy, murder, strife, deceit and malice. They are gossips, slanderers, God-haters, insolent, arrogant and boastful; they invent ways of doing evil; they disobey their parents; they are senseless, faithless, heartless, ruthless. Although they know God's righteous decree that those who do such things deserve death, they not only continue to do these very things but also approve of those who practice them."

Romans 2:12-14 "All who sin apart from the law will also perish apart from the law, and all those who sin under the law will be judged by the law. For it is not those who hear the law who are righteous in God's sight, but it is those who obey the law who will be declared righteous. Indeed, those who do not have the law, do by nature things required by the law, they are a law for themselves, even though they do not have the law…"

Romans 2:1-3 "You, therefore, have no excuse, you who pass judgement on someone else, for at whatever point you judge the other, you are condemning yourself, because you who pass judgment do the same things. Now we know that God's judgment against those who do such things is based on truth. So when you, a mere man, pass judgment on them and yet do the same things, do you think you will escape God's judgment?"

How To Fix It

John 3:16–17 "For God so loved the world that he gave his one and only Son, that whoever believes in him shall not perish but have eternal life. For God did not send his Son into the world to condemn the world, but to save the world through him. Whoever believes in him is not condemned…."

God made this simple. We are sinners. We are headed toward

eternal damnation. God sent his Son, Jesus, to die for all of us, including you. In Jesus' death the stain of sin is removed giving you access to eternal life and an intimate relationship with Him. This is not some mass corporate deal. God offers you an individual and intimate relationship with Him. It is available to everyone. The choice is yours - because God is a gentle spirit and will never force himself on anyone.

> Romans 10:13 "Everyone who calls on the name of the Lord will be saved."

How do you get saved? Just pray. Tell God you recognize you are a sinner, and that you want to get to know Him. Recognize He sent Jesus to die for your sins. That's it. Pretty simple, huh?

> John 5:24 "I tell you the truth, whoever hears my word and believes him who sent me has eternal life and will not be condemned; he has crossed over from death to life."

Jesus said it. It's a promise.

> Ephesians 4:4 "There is one body and one Spirit – just as you were called to one hope when you were called – one Lord, one faith, one baptism; one God and Father of all, who is over all and through all and in all."

There are not multiple choices. There is one God.

> John 14:6 "I am the way, and the truth, and the life; no one comes to the Father, but through Me."

Jesus said it. Why? Because Jesus was not just another great spiritual man who walked the earth. He was, and is, the Son of God. To believe in God is not enough. To reject Jesus as the Savior completely defeats God's purpose of having a relationship with Him.

Now What?

If you have accepted Jesus as the Lord of your life and your Savior, He is now your King. Begin to look around and see where He has placed you. He has put you into certain situations, relationships and jobs for a reason. It is part of His plan for you.

Give God permission to move you relationally, geographically and career-wise to wherever He wants you to best serve the Kingdom of God.

As a child of the King, you have access now to the following promises.

The Promises

> Hebrews 6:18 "… it is impossible for God to lie…."

God's promises are unchanging and trustworthy because God is unchanging and trustworthy. Two unchangeable things are God's nature and His promises. God embodies all truth; therefore, he cannot lie. Because God is truth, you can be secure in His promises; you don't need to wonder if He will change His plans. There is great power and promise available to you now. God is the Master of the Universe and sits at the control room to the whole thing.

Prayer is our channel of communication to God. It is how we get to know God. Like any other relationship, to get to know someone you need to spend some time with them. Prayer is the conduit to change. It is the way by which we access the power of God.

Here is a sampling of some of the promises you now have access to as a believer.

> Matthew 18:19 "Again, truly I tell you that if two of you on earth agree about anything they ask for, it will be done for them by my Father in heaven."

> Matthew 21:21-22 "Jesus replied, 'Truly I tell you, if you

have faith and do not doubt, not only can you do what was done to the fig tree, but also you can say to this mountain, 'Go, throw yourself into the sea,' and it will be done. If you believe, you will receive whatever you ask for in prayer.'"

Mark 9:23 "'If you can'?' said Jesus. 'Everything is possible for one who believes.'"

Mark 11:21-24 "Peter remembered and said to Jesus, 'Rabbi, look! The fig tree you cursed has withered!' 'Have faith in God,' Jesus answered. 'Truly I tell you, if anyone says to this mountain, 'Go, throw yourself into the sea,' and does not doubt in their heart but believes that what they say will happen, it will be done for them. Therefore I tell you, whatever you ask for in prayer, believe that you have received it, and it will be yours."

John 15:7-8 "If you remain in me and my words remain in you, ask whatever you wish, and it will be done for you. This is to my Father's glory, that you bear much fruit, showing yourselves to be my disciples."

James 1:5 "If any of you lacks wisdom, you should ask God, who gives generously to all without finding fault, and it will be given to you."

1 John 3:21-22 "Dear friends, if our hearts do not condemn us, we have confidence before God and receive from him anything we ask, because we keep his commands and do what pleases him."

1 John 5:14-15 "This is the confidence we have in ap-

> proaching God: that if we ask anything according to his will, he hears us. And if we know that he hears us—whatever we ask—we know that we have what we asked of him."

As Christians we have access to the same power that raised Christ from the dead. But, many Christians barely use what they have access to. We must lay claim to these promises and pray boldly with confidence that God is telling the truth.

> James 1:2-8 "Consider it pure joy, my brothers and sisters, whenever you face trials of many kinds, because you know that the testing of your faith produces perseverance. Let perseverance finish its work so that you may be mature and complete, not lacking anything. If any of you lacks wisdom, you should ask God, who gives generously to all without finding fault, and it will be given to you. But when you ask, you must believe and not doubt, because the one who doubts is like a wave of the sea, blown and tossed by the wind. That person should not expect to receive anything from the Lord. Such a person is double-minded and unstable in all they do."

These verses indicate that when we pray we "must believe and not doubt".

How do we do that? We exercise our faith.

Faith

> Hebrews 11:1 "Now faith is confidence in what we hope for and assurance about what we do not see."

The beginning point of faith is believing in God's character; He *is* who He says. The end point is believing in God's promises; He will *do* what He says. When we believe that God will fulfill His promises even though we don't see those promises materializing yet, we demonstrate true faith.

Hebrews 11 is often referred to as the "Faith Hall of Fame". Read it. There are many examples of faith in action in this chapter of the Bible.

In Exodus, we read the story of the Israelites journey to the Promised Land. After looking at a map of this journey, it looks like they had about 100-150 miles to get from point A to point B. They were given pretty clear direction by God, through Moses, about how to get there. And by any standard that distance can be traveled by foot within a few weeks. However, because the Israelites decided to argue about those directives, due to lack of faith, God let them wander around in the desert for 40 years. The lessons here are pretty clear. If God is telling you to do something, save yourself the wandering through the desert and just get it done. He does honor obedience.

In 1 Kings 17:7-24, a simple act of faith produced a miracle. Faith is the step between promise and assurance. Every miracle begins with an act of obedience. We may not see the solution until we take the first step of faith. And conversely, there are times when despite our prayers, nothing seems to happen. Our response to this also requires the exercise of faith.

In Genesis 25:21, Isaac pleaded with God for children. The Bible encourages us to ask and even plead for our most personal and important requests. God wants to grant our requests, but He wants us to ask Him. This is also part of the deal. You have to ask if you want something. Even then, as Isaac learned, God may decide to withhold His answer for a while in order to deepen our insight into what we really need, broaden our appreciation for His answers, or allow us to mature so we can use His gifts more wisely.

> Romans 8:28 "In all things God works for the good of those who love him."

It takes faith to believe this verse, particularly when horrible things are happening to us or those we love.

A successful, vibrant and victorious life as a Christian is not terribly complex. Prayer is where it begins because it is the foundation of a relationship with God. Prayer changes the world around you. Prayer is the cornerstone of faith. There is great power in prayer.

The Best Recipe in the World

- Study the Bible.
- Embrace the promises in it.
- Pray honestly.
- Listen. Prayer is a conversation, not a one-way street.
- Watch and pay attention to what happens around you.
- Follow the inner prompting and direction of the Holy Spirit.
- Exercise faith.
- Be obedient.
- Sit back and watch the miracles unfold.

The only thing stopping you from living a supernatural and powerful life is the degree of intimacy you are willing to build with God and the degree to which you allow Jesus to work through your life. As the world speeds toward an ordained meeting with eternity, you can stand there and lean against the wall and do nothing; watching Satan distort, destroy, manipulate and deceive those around you. Or, you can pick up the Sword of the Spirit, which is the Word of God, answer the call of Jude and go to war – restraining the influence of Satan and his demons for just a while longer – and fight for the Kingdom of God. When the things of this earth fade away – it will be the only thing left standing.

CPSIA information can be obtained
at www.ICGtesting.com
Printed in the USA
LVOW10s0334130117
520775LV00001B/3/P

9 781937 600419